Social Networks Science: Design, Implementation, Security, and Challenges

T0205597

Nilanjan Dey · Rosalina Babo
Amira S. Ashour · Vishal Bhatnagar
Med Salim Bouhlel
Editors

Social Networks Science: Design, Implementation, Security, and Challenges

From Social Networks Analysis to Social Networks Intelligence

 Springer

Editors
Nilanjan Dey
Department of Information Technology
Techno India College of Technology
Kolkata, West Bengal
India

Rosalina Babo
Department of Information Systems,
  ISCAP
Porto Polytechnic
Porto
Portugal

Amira S. Ashour
Department of Electronics and Electrical
  Communications Engineering,
  Faculty of Engineering
Tanta University
Tanta
Egypt

Vishal Bhatnagar
Department of Computer Science
  and Engineering
Ambedkar Institute of Advanced
  Communication Technologies
  and Research
New Delhi
India

Med Salim Bouhlel
Research Lab Sciences and Technologies
  of Image and Telecommunication
Sfax University
Sfax
Tunisia

ISBN 978-3-030-07924-6   ISBN 978-3-319-90059-9   (eBook)
https://doi.org/10.1007/978-3-319-90059-9

This Springer imprint is published by the registered company Springer Nature Switzerland AG
The registered company address is: Gewerbestrasse 11, 6330 Cham, Switzerland

Preface

Social network analysis is a process of quantitative and qualitative analysis of vast amount of data using different analytical techniques. It measures and maps the flow of relationships and relationship changes between knowledge-possessing entities.

Online social networks are rapidly changing our lives. Their growing pervasiveness and the trust that we develop in online identities provide us with a new platform for security applications. Additionally, the integration of various sensors and mobile devices on social networks has shortened the separation between one's physical and virtual (i.e., Web) presences. We envisage that social networks will serve as the portal between the physical world and the digital world. However, challenges arise when using social networks in security applications; for example, how can one prove to a friend (or Friend) that your Facebook page belongs to you and not a man in the middle? Once you have proved this, how can you use it to create a secure channel between any device belonging to you and one belonging to your friend?

The book is a collection of the eight chapters which are written by eminent professors, researchers, and Industry people from different countries. The chapters were initially peer-reviewed by the editorial board members, reviewers, and industry people who themselves span over many countries. The whole book is divided into three parts, namely Part I Social Network Design and Implementation: An Overview, Part II Social Network Application: An Introduction, and Part III Social Network Security and Challenges.

Chapter 1 by **Md. Lizur Rahman, Md. Golam Sarowar, and Md. Sarwar Kamal** revolves around the sentiment classification. Nowadays social networks generate a huge data from user's view, emotions, thoughts, opinions, suggestions regarding different products, events, places, brands, politics, etc. Those data play an important role in different ways. Technically, in the interval of every 60 s in a social network like Facebook, lots of comments and statuses are updated which are associated with thousands of contexts. However, realization of different ways in which texts are seems to be appeared on Facebook can help us to improve our products. In general, different organizations such as text organization used sentimental analysis for successful classification. They transpired feelings, emotions in different forms like positive, negative, friendly, and unfriendly. To solve this problem, authors have concentrated on different techniques of deep learning. In this paper, authors highlighted few deep learning implementation techniques known as convolutional neural network and recursive neural network with classification of different texts.

Chapter 2 by **Nabanita Das, Surekha Borra, Nilanjan Dey, and Samarjeet Borah** enlightened that movie recommendation systems are a common practice by most of the online stores today. The Web-based movie recommendation systems make predictions about the responses of the users based on their search history or known preferences. Recommendation of items is usually done based on the properties or content of the item or collaboration of the user's ratings, and by using intelligent algorithms that include classification or clustering techniques. Accurate prediction of what the customer may likely to busy or the user my visit is of utmost important, as it benefits both the service providers and customers. This chapter provides the evolution, fundamental concepts, classification, traditional and novel models, requirements, similarity measures, evaluation approaches, issues, challenges, impacts due to social networking, and future of movie recommendation systems.

Chapter 3 by **Sapna Sinha, Vishal Bhatnagar, and Abhay Bansal** analyzed that data available on Twitter can be in form of text, photographs, customer preferences can be identified using Twitter analytics which can help service providers to offer personalized services. If tour operator is able to predict trends, they can easily set optimized price and prepare well in advance to provide unforgettable trip to their customers. Tour operators adopt list pricing policy for deciding price of the tourism product and also there is no set model available for this. The tour operators set the price which helps them to gain high profit, but due to non-availability of any standard formula the decided price varies with the price offered by competitors. Prices are kept high when season is at the peak and more and more tourists are visiting the place or purchasing the tourist products, similarly price is kept low when season is low. In this chapter, authors had proposed pricing model considering different factors that decides rates of the product in the tourism sector. Real-time analytics performed on the data available on the Web portals or social networking sites are used to get the most trending tourist destination, and the tour operators functioning at different destination can set price of their products using the proposed model. Real-time analytics will help tour operators to analyze the demand in coming season.

Chapter 4 by **Arushi Jain and Vishal Bhatnagar** discussed that social media is rapidly providing new standards of interaction between individuals in the recent era. It is known as a computer-intermediated tool that tolerates people to share, or create information, medical notes/reports, ideas, and pictures/videos through virtual communities. The online citizens (netizens) are able to create a colossal network of people to communicate with. Social media such as Facebook, Twitter, YouTube, Instagram, and Tinder have prevalent uses that produce copious amount of data which is beyond the ability of normal software tools to process in the given elapsed time. Apache Hadoop project is the most famous open-sourced frameworks for large-scale computation on the commodity hardware. Hadoop has become kernel for distributed operating system for big data. There are two core components associated with Hadoop—Hadoop Distributed File System (HDFS) and MapReduce. MapReduce distributed the tasks on multiple nodes in the cluster; the developer only have to write code, rest is taken care by MapReduce. The generated data from these social sources is real time and includes information about author's daily activities, feelings, and emotions. The messages often include images, geolocations, and many other annotations. This vast data repository provides researchers with opportunities to study the individuals' behavior/emotions that subject to different conditions. In this chapter, authors found the trending tweets from January 2017 to September 2017 depending upon the eight prominent themes that emerged from the dataset and trending tweets depending upon the geolocation. For this, author divided India depending upon the region, that is North India, West India, South India, East India, Central India, and Northeast India.

Chapter 5 by **C. Sardianos, N. Tsirakis, and I. Varlamis** discussed that it is typical among online social networks' users to share their status, activity, and other information with fellow users, to interact on the information shared by others, and to express their trust or interest for each other. The result is a rich information repository which can be used to improve the user experience and increase their engagement if handled properly. In order to create a personalized user experience in social networks, we need data management solutions that scale well on the huge amounts of information generated on a daily basis. The social information of an online social network can be useful both for improving content personalization and for allowing existing algorithms to scale to huge datasets. All current real-world large-scale recommender systems have invested on scalable distributed database systems for data storage and parallel and distributed algorithms for finding recommendations. This chapter focuses on collaborative filtering algorithms for recommender systems and briefly explains how they work and what their limitations are.

Chapter 6 by **A. L. Chapman, M. Lei, and C. Greenhow** analyzed the design, implementation, benefits, and challenges of using a Facebook application, College Connect, are presented. College Connect was designed to address the persistent educational problem of college access in the USA, part of which stems from students' lack of social capital, the human and information resources available to them in their social networks that can provide needed information, such as how to apply to, enroll in, and pay for college. College Connect, a social networking application which runs on Facebook, the parent platform, was designed to help address this problem by creating a network visualization of each student's Facebook Friends network and showing the student who within the network has college information in their Facebook profile. In this chapter, authors explained the theory and procedures that led to the design of the College Connect application, the process of launching the application, and the benefits and challenges of implementing it with adolescent students preparing for college.

J. G. Tromp, Chung Le Van, Bao Le Nguyen, and Dac-Nhuong Le in Chap. 7 covered the convergence of social media networks and virtual reality systems, labeled as social virtual reality. It reviews the evolution of the World Wide Web from a single-user, static experience into the futuristic 3D multiuser interactive experience. This is followed by a review of bulk data collection in virtual reality, and the ethical risks and threats to privacy that this could create for social virtual reality users. The chapter ends with recommendations to mitigate the ethical risks and threats to privacy, for adult VR users, parents of VR users, psychologists, VR software, and hardware manufacturers.

Chapter 8 by **I. Kožuh and M. Debevc** provided a comprehensive insight into the use of social media among the deaf and hard of hearing, along with the benefits and challenges in use. Existing recommendations toward overcoming the challenges are reviewed, and approaches for design of social media and its efficient use are proposed. The findings may serve social media developers, educators, social inclusion advisors, and policy makers on how to apply social media as an inclusive tool for participation in society.

Kolkata, India   Nilanjan Dey
Porto, Portugal   Rosalina Babo
Tanta, Egypt   Amira S. Ashour
New Delhi, India   Vishal Bhatnagar
Sfax, Tunisia   Med Salim Bouhlel

Contents

About the Editors

Nilanjan Dey is an Assistant Professor at the Department of Information Technology, Techno India College of Technology, Kolkata, WB, India. He holds an honorary position of Visiting Scientist at Global Biomedical Technologies Inc., CA, USA, Research Scientist of Laboratory of Applied Mathematical Modeling in Human Physiology, Territorial Organization of Scientific and Engineering Unions, Bulgaria, and Associate Researcher of Laboratoire RIADI, University of Manouba, Tunisia. His research topics are medical imaging, soft computing, data mining, machine learning, rough set, computer-aided diagnosis, and atherosclerosis. He has 20 books and 300 international conferences and journal papers. He is the editor in chief of *International Journal of Ambient Computing and Intelligence* (IGI Global), USA; *International Journal of Rough Sets and Data Analysis* (IGI Global), USA; the *International Journal of Synthetic Emotions (IJSE)*, IGI Global, USA; and *International Journal of Natural Computing Research* (IGI Global), USA, Series Editor of Advances in Geospatial Technologies (AGT) Book Series, (IGI Global), USA; Executive Editor of *International Journal of Image Mining (IJIM)*, Inderscience, and Associated Editor of *IEEE Access Journal* and the *International Journal of Service Science, Management, Engineering and Technology*, IGI Global. He is a life member of IE, UACEE, ISOC.

Rosalina Babo is a Coordinator Professor at the School of Accounting and Administration of Porto/Polytechnic of Porto (ISCAP/IPP), Portugal. Since the year 2000, she is the head of the Information Systems Department and was a member of the university scientific board for 12 years (2000–2012). Rosalina Babo was one of the founders (2006) of CEISE/STI research center and its director until the year 2011. Having several published papers in international conferences and books, her main areas of research are e-learning, usability, e-commerce, and social networks.

Amira S. Ashour is currently an Assistant Professor and Head of Department-EEC, Faculty of Engineering, Tanta University, Egypt. She has been the Vice Chair of Computer Engineering Department, Computers and Information Technology College, Taif University, KSA, for one year from 2015. She has been the Vice

Chair of CS department, CIT college, Taif University, KSA, for five years. Her research interests are smart antenna, direction of arrival estimation, targets tracking, image processing, medical imaging, machine learning, signal/image/video processing, image analysis, computer vision, and optimization. She has 6 books and about 70 published journal papers. She is an editor in chief of the *International Journal of Synthetic Emotions (IJSE)*, IGI Global, USA. She is an Associate Editor for the *IJRSDA*, IGI Global, USA, as well as the *IJACI*, IGI Global, USA. She is an editorial board member of the *International Journal of Image Mining (IJIM)*, Inderscience.

Vishal Bhatnagar holds B.Tech., M.Tech., and Ph.D. in the engineering field. He has more than 18 years of teaching experience in various technical institutions. He is currently working as a Professor in Computer Science in Engineering Department, Ambedkar Institute of Advanced Communication Technologies and Research (Government of Delhi), GGSIPU, Delhi, India. His research interests include database, advance database, data warehouse, data mining, social network analysis, and big data analytics. He has to his credit more than 110 research papers in various international/national journals and conferences. He is also member of many international journals as editorial board, editor or reviewer board member. He has been guiding the postgraduate and Ph.D. students in the field of data science from 2010.

Med Salim Bouhlel was born in Sfax (Tunisia) in December 1955. He is a full professor at Sfax University, Tunisia. He is the Head of the Research Group: Sciences and Technologies of Image and Communication since 2003.

He was the Director of the Higher Institute of Electronics and Communications of Sfax—TUNISIA (ISECS) 2008–2011. He received the golden medal with the special appreciation of the jury in 1999 on the occasion of the first International Meeting of Invention, Innovation and Technology (Dubai, UAE). He was the Vice President and Founder Member of the Tunisian Association of the Specialists in Electronics and the Tunisian Association of the Experts in Imagery. He is the President and Founder of the Tunisian Association on Human–Machine Interaction since 2013. He is the editor in chief of the *International Journal "Human-Machine Interaction"* and a dozen of special issues of international journals. He is the chairman of many international conferences and member of the program committee of numerous international conferences. His research interests are image processing, telecommunication, and human–machine interaction in which he has obtained more than 20 patents so far. More than 400 articles were published in international journals, conferences, and books. Moreover, he has been the principal investigator and the project manager for several research projects dealing with several topics concerned with his research interests mentioned above.

Part I
Social Network Design and Implementation: An Overview

Chapter 1
Teenagers Sentiment Analysis from Social Network Data

Lizur Rahman, Golam Sarowar and Sarwar Kamal

Abstract Now a day's social networks generate a huge data from user view, emotions, thoughts, opinions, suggestions regarding different products, events, places, brands, politics etc. Those data plays an important role in different ways. Technically, in the interval of every 60 s in a social network like Facebook, lots of comments and statuses are updated which are associated with thousands of contexts. However, realization of different ways in which texts are seems to be appeared on Facebook can help us to improve our products. In general, different organizations such as text organization used sentimental analysis for successful classification. They transpired feelings, emotions in different form like positive, negative, friendly, unfriendly etc. To solve this problem we have concentrated on different techniques of deep learning. In this paper we highlight about few deep learning implementation techniques known as Convolutional Neural Network and Recursive Neural Network with classification of different texts.

Keywords Facebook · Sentimental analysis · Deep learning · Convolutional neural network · Convolutional hidden layer · Max pooling · Softmax layer Recurrent neural tensor network

1.1 Introduction

Sentiment classification is one of the most important tasks in social network analysis in current circumstance sentiment analysis for various social networking sites seems

L. Rahman · G. Sarowar · S. Kamal (✉)
Department of Computer Science and Engineering, East West University,
Dhaka, Bangladesh
e-mail: skamal@ewubd.edu

L. Rahman
e-mail: Lizur.sky@gmail.com

G. Sarowar
e-mail: sojolewu6@gmail.com

to be a very potential research equipment. The main reason behind this includes online user's free authorization and assessment to their account whenever they want. Various recent surveys demonstrate that companies collect huge amount of data through the web to extend their customers satisfaction analysis. Setters can also watch terrorist's activity through collecting data from web to extend sentimental analysis and are getting aware and taking steps about their baleful events. The authors used sentimental analysis to find the imaginative sentiment automatically from uses reviews [1]. Sentiment analysis is a natural language processing problem where text is understood and the underlying intent is predicted. Few authors have already published lots of contributions associated with sentimental analysis. Most of the contributions have been accomplished targeting to twitter, product reviews, political party, tweet updates, brands of products [2]. These system expresses a positive or a negative opinion(e.g., blog post, product review, etc.) about a given entity(e.g., product, policy, person etc.). Before imposing appropriate mechanism over data they collect raw data from twitter or facebook and apply their implemented methods on the data they gathered. Since, twitter has a restriction of using 140 characters of total length while posting something in twitter [2], thus users supposed to get narrow scope to express their thoughts, expressions, emotions.

In general, recent years highly keep in touch with available social networks and collaborative technologies. Thousands of research associated with social media has been conducted already. However, various study demonstrate that this social media and collaborative technology can negotiate with traditional way of learning into a collaborative one [3]. Meanwhile, social media seems to be effective in health care technology areas also. For the time being health care is becoming sharing and cooperative which makes realizing about the necessity of social media technologies. Moreover, for present time online based social networking sites are providing the platform for the people to express their opinions, thoughts, emotions, short messages etc. within a second of click. With the help of social networks nowadays it's easier to be interconnected. This phenomenon results with effective outcome. However, with the increasing effectiveness of social networks and collaborative technologies the data passing through various platforms associated with these appeared to be a great evolution. Enormous posts, comments, emotions, reactions etc. are need to be manipulated with the shortest possible time. Despite all of this present circumstances of various social networks negotiate with lots of real life conditions among which advertisement of various products and prospects are comparatively most significant. Thus, social networks play an important role in this era providing multimedia enriched data, aggregated feedback and personal information sharing. Among all the social networks Facebook is considered most popular one by connecting every stages of people together within a single shade. According to Wikipedia Currently Facebook is dealing with approximately 2 billion people, twitter with 319 million users, 375 million users. However, the researchers are mainly concerns with determining exact sentiment, emotions, and reactions filtering lots of multimedia based data. Thus, this study is concerned with this issue.

In this paper, in most cases we have concentrated on Facebook as our targeted website. From the perspective of virtual world status is creating an updated feature

Fig. 1.1 Graphical representation of tweets rate of growth [55]

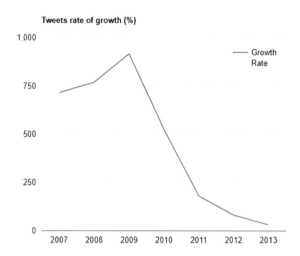

of regular activity, thoughts, emotions etc. From users side. Facebook has a total number of 5000 characters for updating every status which has a big difference from Twitter [4]. Therefore, the main advantage is people transpired emotions clearly which is desirable. Total Facebook users are enormous and so it is much easier to collect samples. Analyzing these samples we can get identify user's motion of interest which would be good enough. Realization of different ways in which texts are seems to be appeared on Facebook can help us to improve our products.

According to June 2017, a survey [5] on Facebook statistics shows Every 60 s on Facebook: 510,000 comments are posted, 293,000 statuses are updated. Understanding the various ways texts are used on Facebook can help us to improve our products. In general, whenever a user expresses his views, it becomes important for the community to correctly identify the requirements of user to make him stay longer. By the analysis of product reviews given by the customers, an organization can decide about the future circumstance on any particular product. Thus, it becomes mandatory for the organizer to analyze the comments given in social media to extract any essential information from huge volume of data. However, the annual tweet growth rate for twitter from 2006 to 2013 [6] is followed by Fig. 1.1.

In general, sentiment analysis or opinion mining is a most hotly debated topic nowadays. This is basically the computational illustration of people's comments, attributes, comments, posts, and tweets on any specific issue. Those issues can demonstrate both individuals as well as events and topics. However, both the topic sentiment analysis and opinion mining refers to interchangeable circumstances of some issues. Despite of this some of the researchers in this field who have conducted various contributions have estimated that both of the term SA (sentiment analysis) and OM (opinion mining) indicates different motion rather than indication same dimension. According to their derivation, sentiment analysis is such kind of machine learning approach which works with opinion mining whereas sentiment analysis refers to the sentiment explicated on various issues for this context in various tweets. Therefore, according to sentiment analysis this specific topic illustrate opinions regarding a topic or event then identifying the sentiment expressed by the users and determining their polarity. Basically, sentiment analysis overall process is the combination of three kinds defined as document-level, sentence-level, and aspect-level [7]. Initially, the given sentence will be evaluated whether it is a subjective or objective sentence. Thereafter, SA will determine which sentiment is depicted by the sentence given. Since current world is stepping towards the evolution of higher dimensional, complex and complicated data, it will be main obstacle for the previous methods to cope with new dimension of data. Moreover, various social network associated data like those information produced from twitter, Facebook, Google etc. are increasing in an exponential manner and for which it demands strong fundamental machine learning approaches to be in action to manipulate with better accuracy and efficiency [8]. Realizing the worth of this issue we have concentrated on convolutional neural network as well as Recursive tensor neural network for sentiment analysis and text mining. Our derived approaches represents better performance for conducting this task. However, for this study we only highlight on English data classification or analysis. Our future contribution may include all the available language data analysis. However, collected data can be noise full, irreverent which are considered to be the main obstacle for the context of accurate analysis and efficient classification of sentiment provided by the users un some specific events, topics etc. therefore, various mapping algorithms like self-organization map, Ordinary Least Squares Regression (OLSR), Linear Regression., Logistic Regression., Stepwise Regression., Multivariate Adaptive Regression Splines (MARS), Locally Estimated Scatter plot Smoothing (LOESS) those algorithms are highly appreciated. Thus, our future contribution will include mapping based machine implementation of mapping based machine learning algorithms for sentiment detection and opinion mining.

1.2   Literature Review

Many authors applied and contributed different methods for performing sentimental analysis. Alongside, lots of researchers have used deep learning, machine learning, vector machine etc. In literature, lots of outperformers' methods have been exposed through various researchers in paragraph and sentence level. In [9], the contributors have drawn their attention towards minimum cut in text graphs to achieve the main partition of the words from the whole text. Moreover, though the use of machine learning methods they have performed sentiment analysis on the selected texts only. In [10], the authors have embedded convolutional neural networks to train handwritten digits. The researchers of this work have been able to take their performance to the highest level though demonstration of 99.6% accuracy. In [11] authors have used different techniques to reduce over fitting and they have improved the performance to a top level up to 99.67%. They have emphasized on 10,000 MNIST test images (seen except training session) and the system defined by them determine 9,967 correctly. From rest 33 images many of those are tough even for a human being to differentiate. They used an ensemble of networks and build a model to improve entire performance. In [12], the contributors mentioned support vector machine mechanism for better classification from various data source collected from specific social networks. In [3], initially the authors have classified texts into neutral and polar first then have determined whether the text is expressed as positive or negative sentiment. In [13], the authors have depicted distant learning approach to differentiate sentiment analysis data. They have emphasized on twitter's every tweet's concluding emotions. If concluding emotions are in positive emoticons like ":)", ":-)" are considered as positive and if rest emotions are appeared like ":(", ":-(" then that will be considered as negative. They build models using different classifiers and report that Support Vector Machines (SVM) outperforms other classifiers comparatively. They also have employed different models in terms of feature space and they report that Unigram model outperforms all other models. Moreover, according to the contribution mentioned in [14] overall sentiment has been taken in account rather than concentrating on topic based analysis which is fruitful when overall input datasets are noise free or irreverent free. But from the perspective of big data analysis or noise full data this contribution can be detected as slower prediction mechanism. In this respect of view our contributed approach works better even after the presence of noise or irreverent data. Another contribution regarding sentiment analysis [15] indicate the use of corpus for sentiment analysis as well as decision or opinion mining. This contributions reveals that their proposed approach represents higher accuracy along with efficiency for twitter data analysis. Initially for this they have drawn their attention towards prediction of positive, negative and neutral sentiments for every document they have in English language. The authors also demonstrate that their future work will be conducted on all the language available currently. Since our contribution highlights on various neural network based algorithm to train the datasets, thus overall accuracy as well as efficiency outperforms its alternatives. Additionally, the work [16] has explored lots of work associated with sentiment analysis in recent time. Details discussion of various works create a new way to know gist content in a while.

More research on sentiment analysis along with big data has been also conducted by thousands of researchers. Among them the contribution [17] deals with vast amount of sentiment rich data or texts through status updates, reactions, comments, likes, tweets etc. the authors of this paper have highlighted into analysis of sentiment for electronic devices including mobiles, Tabs, laptops etc. to be user friendly than before. They have demonstrated that through the use of sentiment analysis in specific domain the effect of domain information can be extracted easily. Along with analyzing vast amount of data the authors have also implemented a new feature defined as vector classifier for determination of more accuracy. According to the contribution of [18], the authors in this study mostly concentrated on feature selection, negation dealing and emotion handling. For the purpose of increasing performance of machine learning algorithms this study negotiates with huge numbers of text datasets like tweets or movie reviews and evaluates the performance of machine learning algorithms. Thus, evaluation of public opinion as well as sentiment analysis has been taken into account in this study for enhancement of available machine learning algorithms in this field. Intuitively, the study [19] refers to illustration or details demonstration of those datasets which are increasing in an exponential manner including contents on the Web like twitter, amazon, Facebook etc. since these types of large volume of data can create a great harm for the efficiency as well as accuracy and sensitivity of machine leaning algorithms. From the perspective of contribution [20] lots of papers regarding sentiment analysis have been explored in details for probable acquisition of whole knowledge at a time from one paper. Moreover, nowadays Facebook, twitter, amazon and other social websites support the feature of using various slang, Gif images, emotions, reactions, comments which are mainly responsible for production of higher dimensional large volume of datasets. This study also concentrates on this issue and demonstrates the machine learning ways through which we can resolve these types of problems. Since nowadays the datasets are increasing in an exponential manner for which the classification task is becoming slower data by day. Avoiding this situation various mapping based machine learning approaches can be most helpful for classification, feature detection as well as to resolve inefficient sentiment analysis problems. In this respect [21–27] these study have proposed various mapping less as well as mapping based algorithms which are capable of classifying the data in a complex as well as complicated situation. However, another studies mentioned in [28–37] highlights various automated machine learning system for manipulation of imbalance, large volume of data and also to extract gist information from data gathered from Facebook, tweeter data. Details performance evaluation also demonstrates outperformances of those algorithms implemented and proposed in those contributions. Moreover, [38–48] contributions highlight developing various artificial intelligence algorithms which are capable of conducting various classification as well as alignment task with higher accuracy and efficiency compared to other alternatives in literature.

1.3 Deep Learning Algorithms (CNN) Used in Sentiment Analysis

Basically, deep learning refers to combination of various algorithms. Such as Convolutional Neural Network (CNN) extended version of neural network (NN), Recursive Neural Tensor Network (RNTN) extended version of Recursive NN basically concerned with the use of specific sparse tree for every input data, Recurrent Neural Network (RNN) etc. those are very popular. Basically NN are very efficient for text generation, image classification, pattern classification, vector representation, classification of sentence etc. [49]. Deep learning networks can be used for its automatic learning capability and we can training for supervised as well as unsupervised both [50]. Due to supervised and unsupervised learning techniques deep learning is very useful. Many researchers used deep learning for handle sentiment analysis. Authors used data from rottentomatoes.com and make the representation of movie review by using Recursive Tensor Neural Network (RNTN) [51].

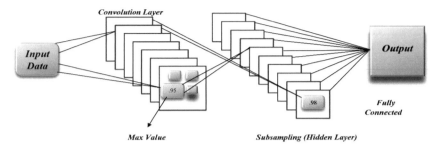

Fig. 1.2   Overall infrastructure of convolutional neural network

1.3.1   CNN (Convolutional Neural Network)

In general, convolutional neural network is the extended version of previously revealed neural network. This new version of neural network includes one of the amazing features defined as multiple perceptron. From the perspective of artificial neural network this term multiple perceptron focuses on lesser preprocessing which was not included in the previous neural network. Therefore, for this extraordinary feature of convolutional neural network this mechanism performs better compared to all the previous neural nets. Moreover, this specific capability which convolutional neural nets owns inside itself makes the way easier by processing the input data initially just to avoid redundant or irreverent data. Basically, this evolutionary algorithm got concentrated on after successful interpretation of a well-known research work explored by LeCun and Bottou [52]. This work illustrates CNN as inspired by biological knowledge as well as mathematical theorem along with co-operation of computer science. Therefore, for this study the convolutional neural network is being focused for its extraordinary ability of dimensionality reduction along with pre-processing strategy built in inside it. The basic infrastructure of convolutional neural network is illustrated in Fig. 1.2.

Mathematical derivation of convolutional neural network illustrates a straightforward way of representing an overall process of machine learning algorithm. In usual cases, the input matrix size of convolutional neural network covers the input image or datasets successfully. However, the back-propagation paradigm is one of the glamorous thing to be attracted by convolutional neural network. The general back propagation algorithm for convolutional neural network is demonstrated as follows:

Back Propagation Algorithm for CNN

Start Procedure

Input v_i : initially the input should be v_1 .

For each iteration i=1 to limit need to compute,

$$p^i_{x,y} = w^i * \sigma(p^{i-1}_{x,y}) + b^i_{x,y} ....(1.1) \text{ As well as } a^i_{x,y} = \sigma(p^i_{x,y}).......(1.2).$$

Computing output error,

$$E^L = \nabla_a C \Theta \sigma'(A^L)................................(1.3).$$

Back propagate the error through,

$$\partial^i_{x,y} = \partial^{i+1} * ROT180(w^{i+1}_{x,y})\sigma'(A^i_{x,y})..................(1.4).$$

Output is given by the gradient function,

$$\frac{\partial C}{\partial w^i_{a,b}} = \partial^i_{a,b} * \sigma(ROT180(A^{i-1}_{a,b}))............................(1.5)$$

End Procedure.

Thus, discussion conducted above represents the successful illustration of convolutional neural network algorithm for the purpose of sentiment analysis. Here initial phage depicts input datasets in a compacted matrix. Subsequently, computation of $p^i_{x,y}$ for each and every iteration becomes mandatory on the initial input datasets compacted within a matrix. Meanwhile, estimated output error need to be concentrated on for successfully implementation of back-propagation algorithm. If error seems to be appeared then using back-propagation mechanism we need to propagate the error and need to be minimized the error as much as possible. Now, gradient function is usually used for achieving desired output from the overall CNN approach.

Basically, the input matrix of convolutional neural network covers overall input data. Besides, internal calculation is simpler to define and easy to implement. For interpretation of CNN if we have $N x N$ input matrix and if we consider a $K x K$ filter ω then overall outcome matrix will be $(N - K + 1) \times (N - K + 1)$. Thus, outcome of 1st layer $\left(O^l_{ij} \right)$ same time input of 2nd layer $\left(O^l_{ij} \right)$ can be defined as follows,

$$O^l_{ij} = \sum_{a=0}^{K-1} \sum_{b=0}^{K-1} \omega_{ab} y^{l-1}_{(i+a)(j+b)} \tag{1.6}$$

However, outcome of convolutional neural layer is depicted using following equation in practical,

$$C^l_{ij} = \sigma(O^l_{ij}) \tag{1.7}$$

Meanwhile, error calculation rate $\left(\frac{\partial E}{\partial C^l_{ij}} \right)$ which is defined as partial derivative of error rate (E) with respect to the outcome of previous calculation layer is mandatory to summarize to determine all the output of each neuron lies on any layer. Therefore, the equation is,

$$\frac{\partial E}{\partial \omega_{ab}} = \sum_{i=0}^{N-K} \sum_{j=0}^{N-K} \frac{\partial E}{\partial O_{ij}^l} \frac{\partial O_{ij}^l}{\partial \omega_{ab}} = \sum_{i=0}^{N-K} \sum_{j=0}^{N-K} \frac{\partial E}{\partial O_{ij}^l} C_{(i+a)(j+b)}^{l-1} \tag{1.8}$$

For further proceedings what we need to do is to compute the gradient. Computation of gradient can be demonstrated as,

$$\frac{\partial E}{\partial O_{ij}^l} = \frac{\partial E}{\partial C_{ij}^l} \sigma'(O_{ij}^l) \tag{1.9}$$

Above all, for achieving final result following mathematical chain rule can be adjusted,

$$\frac{\partial E}{\partial C_{ij}^{l-1}} = \sum_{a=0}^{K-1} \sum_{b=0}^{K-1} \frac{\partial E}{\partial O_{(i-a)(j-b)}^l} \frac{\partial O_{(i-a)(j-b)}^l}{\partial C_{ij}^{l-a}} = \sum_{a=0}^{K-1} \sum_{b=0}^{K-1} \frac{\partial E}{\partial O_{(i-a)(j-b)}^l} \omega_{ab} \tag{1.10}$$

Thus, above discussion bears the realization that Convolutional neural network (CNN) follows a specific infrastructure which particularly has been marked as better classifier. This mechanism is quite faster compared to other alternatives along with faster training facility and also allows us to train deeply by forming lots of network layers internally. Here for this context, we have explored some powerful techniques including convolutions, pooling, dropout technique (to reduce unnecessary data) etc. we have also used some integrating ideas such as softmax, back propagation, regularization etc. CNN is a combinational feature of three basic ideas- local receptive fields, shared weights and biases and pooling.

In usual cases, whenever a data is inserted into CNN it will be sent into different layers (first layer is considered input layer, last layer is considered output layer and in between first and last is hidden layers) subsequently and finally will produce sentimental results (e.g., positive, negative, neutral, etc.). However, every layer contains lots of neurons. For clarification we have considered that input layer contains 28*28 square of neuron and whose value corresponds to the 28*28 pixel. Basically, each and every neuron of any layer is fully connected to the neurons of their neighbor layer. However, in every local receptive field all the hidden neurons are not connected under manual supervision, rather each neuron will be connected to a small region of the input neurons. Graphical representation of local receptive field is as follows Fig. 1.3,

Same matrix is taken into account while considering bias, then the same weights and bias for each of the 24*24 hidden neurons will be applied to execute overall process. For the j, k hidden neurons, output is-

$$C(b + \sum_{i=0}^{4} \sum_{m=0}^{4} w_{l,m} a_{j+l, k+m}); \delta = neural\ activation\ function,$$
$$b = shared\ value\ for\ bias, w_{l,m} = 5*5\ array\ of\ shared\ weights \tag{1.11}$$

Very often Eq. 1.11 is defined as convolution. Shared weights and biases greatly reduce total parameters involving in the convolutional network.

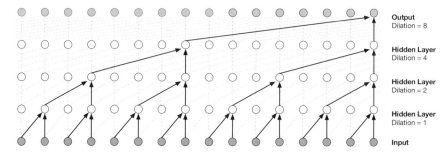

Fig. 1.3 Basic infrastructure of Local receptive field

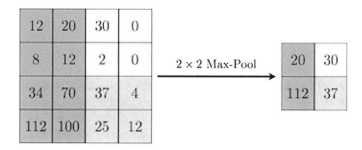

Fig. 1.4 Generalized form after applying max pooling

Pooling mechanism is usually used immediately after convolutional layers. The pooling mechanism usually filters the immediate output from the convolutional neural layer and also preprocess the resultant data. Each unit of a pooling layer mainly summarize approximately 2*2(say) neurons from whatever we get from the previous layer. A common procedure for pooling can be characterized as max pooling (Fig. 1.4).

After pooling Softmax layer will be in action automatically to remove the problem of learning slowdown. This is basically used for faster as well as efficient learning process. We use softmax to create a new type of connection in the final layer. Because the connection between a hidden layer to next hidden layer is not fully connected. If we do not change the connection as fully connected, output of any neuron could be missed from last hidden layer.

$$\sum_j a_j^L = \frac{\sum_j e^{z_j^L}}{\sum_k e^{z_k^L}} = 1 \tag{1.12}$$

where, a_j^L = output activation for j neuron of L layer.

And z_j^L = corresponding weighted input for j neuron of L layer.

This equation shows us output of activations for j'th neuron of L'th layer are positive, because of positive exponential function and output range in between 0

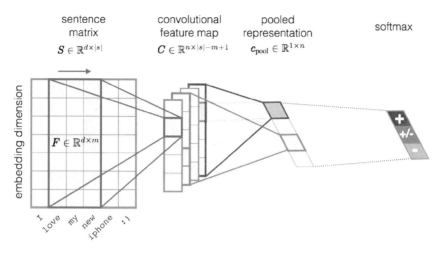

Fig. 1.5 Overall basic infrastructure of this contribution

to 1(positive, negative, neutral). Thus, all the functions are combined together and accomplished a convolutional neural network (CNN). This can be performed well in both supervised and unsupervised learning. However, for sentiment analysis a system has been proposed for twitter [53]. For this purpose they used convolutional neural network with initialize the weight. While they avoiding requirement for new features they find train accurately is critical (Fig. 1.5).

We will input a text into CNN and it will show the sentiment rate of positive, negative and neutral by using sentimental algorithms, build up by CNN (Table 1.1).

1.3.2   Recursive Neural Tensor Network (RNTN)

In general, Recursive neural tensor networks (RNTNs) are some kinds of neural nets which are exceptionally useful for all kinds of language processing including natural language. They have specific tree structures corresponding to a neural net at each node. Basically, Recursive neural networks can be significant for the purpose of boundary segmentation, differentiation between positive and negative word groups etc. for sequential classification word vectors are usually referred as features and served as basic infrastructure, after which all the findings are compacted within various sub groups and phases for final sentiment determination purpose. For this contribution Recursive Neural tensor network performs better because of branching factor it uses. However, RNTN (Recursive tensor Network) usually deals with some specific structures or sparse tree for hierarchical processing of overall steps structured in a tree. This specific algorithm seems to be working better while time is not being concentrated on. This is basically a recursive chain process which follows one process after another. Sentiment analysis is also possible through the use of convolutional

Table 1.1 Findings of sentiment analysis using CNN

Input:	Output

{
  "sentence": "I love my new phone "
}
	[
	  {
	    "negative": 0,
	    "neutral": 0.417,
	    "positive": 0.583,
	    "sentence": "I love my new phone "
	  }
	]

{
  "Sentence": "Although I'm well in math but I don't Like math... "
}
	[
	  {
	    "negative": 0.238,
	    "neutral": 0.624,
	    "positive": 0.138,
	    "Sentence": "Although I'm well in math but I don't Like math... "
	  }
	]

{
  "Sentence": "First half is interesting, but last half is boring :("
}
	[
	  {
	    "negative": 0.426,
	    "neutral": 0.574,
	    "positive": 0,
	    "Sentence": "First half is interesting, but last half is boring :("
	  }
	]

neural network but the main obstacle of using CNN in this circumstance is it never follows any concept of sparse tree for further proceedings whereas RNTN (Recursive tensor Network) is concerned with the use of specific sparse tree for every input data. In addition, the basic infrastructure in this work compute compositional vector representation of every phrase in each node of a binary sparse tree constructed while taking input. Further steps are followed by computation of parent vector in a bottom up fashion corresponding to the input sparse binary tree.

Thus, the above Fig. 1.6 mentioned here represents the structured illustration of input for recursive neural network. From the illustration we get informed that hierarchical analyzing technique has been the main mechanism for this specific circumstance. For this contribution this method contributes to analyze the data collected from one of the famous social media which is Facebook. Thousands of comments along with various emotions, reactions, observations have been depicted here in details. While working with bottom up fashion this algorithm basically labels all the words through vector analysis using the following formula,

$$y^a = soft \max(W_s a) \qquad (1.13)$$

For illustration of this equation we can conclude that W_s is the sentiment classification matrix applying the overall proposed approach on which we will acquire our desired output. Moreover, a is one of the vector through which every word has been labeled.

Fig. 1.6 Basic infrastructure of a hierarchical sparse tree

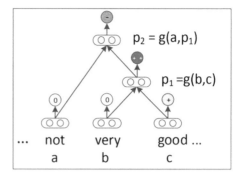

However computing parent vector is mandatory for recursive neural tensor network. Therefore, the computation of target vectors can be defined through the formula mentioned below,

$$t_1 = f\left(W\begin{bmatrix} b \\ c \end{bmatrix}\right) \ \& \ t_2 = f\left(W\begin{bmatrix} a \\ t_1 \end{bmatrix}\right) \tag{1.14}$$

Here, f is considered as one of the element from standard nonlinearity function. Also w is the main parameter to learn whereas bias has been omitted for simplicity purpose. However, the bias can be added to the overall vectors through the addition of an extra column especially for the bias. One of the main problem for almost all the neural nets are seems to be appeared when the parameters become large and inhabited as indivisible. For those circumstance recursive neural tensor network outperforms most. Though the use of single layered vector form if we want to define overall output the then that should be taken place as the following,

$$O_i = \begin{bmatrix} b \\ c \end{bmatrix}^T V^i \begin{bmatrix} b \\ c \end{bmatrix} \tag{1.15}$$

For the context of Eq. 1.15 the V^i is the tensor form of the multiple bilinear form. O_i (Output) is the ith output tensor term which is the desired expectation of our proposed system. For recursive neural tensor network to achieve any concluding point the parent vectors usually defined as $P_1 \& P_2$ must be defined and calculated. For this contribution the parent vectors have been calculated through the use of following formulation,

$$P_i = f\left(\begin{bmatrix} b \\ c \end{bmatrix}^T V^i \begin{bmatrix} a \\ P_i \end{bmatrix} + W\begin{bmatrix} a \\ P_i \end{bmatrix}\right) \tag{1.16}$$

Here, ith number if parents definition has been calculated through Eq. 1.16. Intuitively, one special case for the RNTN algorithm is when i = 0 the infrastructure can

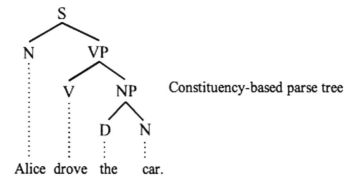

Fig. 1.7 Graphical representation of constituency based parse tree

directly relate to the input datasets which results in efficient and faster calculation to the way of output.

For organizing sentences, recursive neural nets work as parsers, which after parsing groups all the negative as well as positive words within particular groups for further calculation. Some sub groups and phases are also created in this stage of recursive neural nets. The sub phases includes Noun phases (NU), Verb phases (VP) etc. further steps depend on various machine learning algorithms to classify exact sentiment. By parsing the sentences, they can be successfully structured as tress which is ordinarily known as parse trees (Fig. 1.7).

In [54], authors propose a Recursive Neural Tensor Network (RNTN). The contributors of this work draw their main concentration towards tensor-based composition function for sentiment analysis. And record that RNTN perform better than other methods of Deep Learning.

So we can use the idea of RNTN to analyze the sentiment. RNTN use 5 sentiment classes, very negative to very positive $(--, -, 0, +, ++)$, at every node of a parse tree and capturing the negation and its scope in given sentence.

In Fig. 1.8 we can see that RNTN cannot detect any emotion sign "☹". And this is like supervised learning so 'boring' get the very negative sign. Despite of these, RNTN is quite good for text and its accuracy rate also good.

1.3.3 Detection of Positive, Negative and Neutral Sentiment

A simplest technique called 'Keyword Spotting' used in sentimental algorithms. After input the data it is scanned for detecting the positive and negative words like 'love', 'happy', 'good', 'bad', 'sad', 'terrible' and 'great' etc. This approach is called 'Bag of Words' (BOW). This contains information of sentiment along with sentiment scores. Like the word 'bad' is negative and the word 'love' is positive. Some list of words in BOW given below in the Table 1.2:

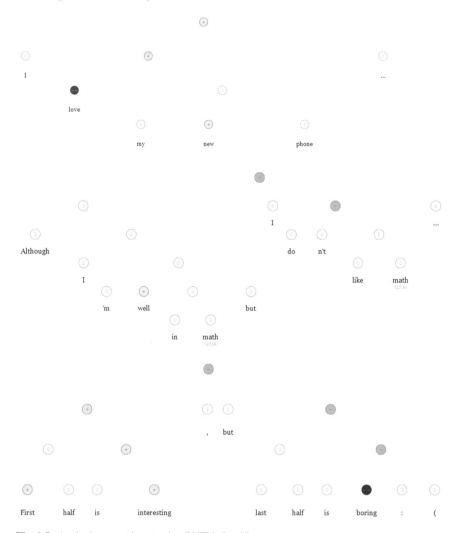

Fig. 1.8 Analyzing a sentiment using RNTN algorithm

Then use negation detection measures to differentiate between 'happy' and 'not happy'. Thus we can go for a phrase 'not happy' is negative sentimental. Based on those words, algorithm shows the sentiment rate of positive, negative and neutral. Thus we do not use NLP, sarcasm problem might arise. For example, "Wow, thanks for show your reality", may be a negative sentence rather than positive one. To solve it, we have to do Natural Language Processing. In our future work we will do this.

Table 1.2 List of positive negative word from BOW

Positive words	Negative words
Happy	Bad
Good	Sad
Honest	Cheating
Pleasant	Annoying
Interesting	Hate
Wonderful	Sorrow
Love	Evil
Like	Dishonest
Gorgeous	Impure
Fantastic	Unhappy
Beautiful	Ugly

1.3.4 RNTN Compared to CNN

By applying recursively same set of weights RNTN created. RNTN is successful for tree structures, learning sequence in NLP. Sentiment analysis is possible through the use of convolutional neural network but the main obstacle of using CNN in this circumstance is it never follow any concept of sparse tree for further proceedings where as RNTN (Recursive Neural Tensor Network) is concerned with the use of specific sparse tree for every input data. For example, this is a movie review "First half is interesting, but last half is boring☹". The sentences have both positive and negative sentiment. Thus RNTN create a tree structure where RNTN make two part of this sentence based on some logical terms [56], one is positive part (First half is interesting,) another is negative part (but last half is boring☹). But in CNN it will show an overall rate of positive, negative and neutral based on words (positive, negative).

1.3.5 Comparison of Different Sentimental Analysis Techniques

In research area, sentiment analysis played an important rule. Many researchers discussed about different methods of sentiment analysis. Many researches are still going on to find out the efficient and alternatives approach for sentiment analysis. There are many methods of sentiment analysis such as- Machine Learning Approach, Rule Based Approach, Lexicon Based Approach, and others. Table 1.3. Shows three main techniques used for sentiment analysis. Every technique has some strength and limitation of its own.

Table 1.3 Comparison between different techniques of sentimental analysis

Techniques	Classification	Advantages	Disadvantages
Machine learning	• Supervised learning • Unsupervised learning	• No need dictionary • Show high rate accuracy on classification	• In most of the time classifier does not perform properly on training data.
Rule based	• Supervised learning • Unsupervised learning	• For review data accuracy is 91% • For text data accuracy is 86% • Sentiment analysis of text shows better result than word data	• Accuracy of data depends on defining rules.
Lexicon based	• Unsupervised learning	• Not need to labeled data • Not required any learning approach	• Strong linguistic sources is needed, but not obtainable every time

In our paper we used machine learning approach which is for both supervised and unsupervised learning. CNN works as unsupervised and RNTN works as a supervised.

1.4 Discussion

Before start working in this paper, we collected thousand of raw status from Facebook. We collected data from students aged 16 to 22. Since we did not use any tools, we collected data in simple way. We told all students to add one common account (created for our research purpose) to their Friendliest. Then we access the data from the common account. This was the primary process of our data collection which was only for learn 'how to collect data directly?' But this process is time consuming.

Then we started to use "Facebook Graph API" tools for collecting data. This tool can extract data from specific Facebook group given by the user. User will only mention the Facebook group, a time range (start date, end date), and number of posts. The Tool will provide the data based on that information. Since we did not use Natural Language Processing (NLP), system cannot convert others language to one common language. For that reason we keep only English language status and discard others status. We did the selection process by ourselves.

1.5   Challenges and Recommendations

We faced a lot of challenges for this paper. Finding open datasets and other privacy issues are main challenges for us. Sarcasm is also one of the major challenges for us. If sarcasm which is positive will be classified as positive and same for negative is the problem. Another challenge for us is to detect Neutral sentiment. That is 'How can we detect whether the sentence sentiment is neutral? On the other side sentiment analysis itself faces some technical challenges. Implicit sentiment, spam, context dependency are the general challenges. Those are the big challenges for us.

If we want to solve sarcasm problem, we have to use Natural Language Processing (NLP). Detect a neutral sentiment we use a special technique "Rate of Sentiment". It defines the rate of positive, negative, neutral sentiment. If we want to find only one answer, then we will compare the sentiment rate of each others.

1.6   Conclusion

Since sentiment analysis refers to accurately identify, study and quantify subjective information, thus SA becomes mandatory for nowadays for the social network sites to survey responses, healthcare materials, online media etc. However, Sentiment analysis has been perused to find the sentiment of any meaningful sentence. Necessity of sentimental analysis is increasing day by day. Because by analyzing the hidden information we can find the actual information and try to improve many things. Due to the automatic learning capability of deep learning techniques, we can used it for implementing sentiment analysis. Different studies conducted on deep learning depict that's why deep learning techniques are very successful in sentimental analysis. Therefore, in this contribution, we have implemented the sentiment analysis for text using Deep Learning such as CNN and RNTN. We have proposed different example of text and classify against CNN and RNTN. We just consider the text and do not consider any emotions sign and all the text is in English. Thus, our future contribution associated with this work will propose new machine learning approaches which will be capable of classifying approximately all the available languages. However, various mapping based procedures will be considered for the purpose of pre-processing and avoiding irrevent or houseful data.

References

1. Luo, F., Li, C., Cao, Z. (2016). Affective-feature-based sentiment analysis using SVM classifier. In *2016 IEEE 20th International Conference on Computer Supported Cooperative Work in Design*, pp. 276281.
2. Agarwal, A., Xie, B., Vovsha, I., Rambow, O., & Passonneau, R. (2011). Sentiment analysis of Twitter data. In *LSM '11 Proceedings of the Workshop on Languages in Social Media,*

Association for Computational Linguistics (pp. 30–38).

3. Wilson, T., Wiebe, J., & Hoffman, P. (2005). Recognizing contextual polarity in phrase level sentiment analysis. In *Proceedings of the conference on Human Language Technology and Empirical Methods in Natural Language Processing* (pp. 347–354).

4. Inside Facebook. http://www.insidefacebook.com/2011/09/21/5000-character-limit-floating-navigation-bar/.

5. Mueller, J., & Stumme, G. (2017). Predicting rising follower counts on Twitter using profile information. In *Proceedings of the 2017 ACM on Web Science Conference (WebSci '17)* (pp. 121–130). New York, NY, USA: ACM. https://doi.org/10.1145/3091478.3091490.

6. Karwa, V., Slavković, A. B., & Krivitsky, P. (2014). Differentially private exponential random graphs. In J. Domingo-Ferrer (Eds.), *Privacy in statistical databases. PSD 2014.* Lecture Notes in Computer Science (Vol. 8744). Cham: Springer.

7. Farra, N., Challita, E., Abou Assi, R., & Hajj, H. (2010). Sentence-level and document-level sentiment mining for Arabic texts. In *Proceedings of the 2010 IEEE International Conference on Data Mining Workshops (ICDMW '10)* (pp. 1114–1119). Washington, DC, USA: IEEE Computer Society. http://dx.doi.org/10.1109/ICDMW.2010.9510-K Annual Report. SEC Filings. Facebook. January 28, 2017. Retrieved February 3, 2017.

8. Goller, C., & Kuchler, A. (1996). Learning task-dependent distributed representations by backpropagation through structure. *Neural Networks.* IEEE. https://doi.org/10.1109/icnn.1996.548916.

9. Pang, B., & Lee, L. (2004). A sentimental education: sentiment analysis using subjectivity summarization based on minimum cuts. In *ACL '04 Proceedings of the 42nd Annual Meeting on Association for Computational Linguistics* (pp. 271–278).

10. Simard, P. Y., Steinkraus, D., & Platt, J. (2003). *Best practices for convolutional neural networks applied to visual document analysis.*

11. Ciresan, D. C., Meier, U., Gambardella, L. M., & Schmidhuber, J. (2010). Deep, big, simple neural nets excel on handwritten digit recognition.

12. Mullen, T., & Collier, N. (2004). Sentiment analysis using support vector machines with diverse information sources. In *Proceedings of Conference on Empirical Methods in Natural Language Processing* (pp. 412–418).

13. Go, A., Bhayani, R., & Huang, L. (2009). *Twitter sentiment classification using distant supervision.* Stanford: Technical report.

14. Pang, B., Lee, L., & Vaithyanathan, S. (2002). Thumbs up? sentiment classification using machine learning techniques. In *Proceedings of the ACL-02 Conference on Empirical Methods in Natural Language Processing (EMNLP '02)* (vol. 10, pp. 79–86). Stroudsburg, PA, USA: Association for Computational Linguistics. https://doi.org/10.3115/1118693.1118704.

15. Pak, A., & Paroubek, P. (2010). Twitter as a corpus for sentiment analysis and opinion mining. In *Proceedings of the Seventh conference on International Language Resources and Evaluation (LREC'10), Valletta, Malta.* European Language Resources Association (ELRA).

16. Medhat, W., Hassan, A., Korashy, H. (2014). Sentiment analysis algorithms and applications: A survey. *Ain Shams Engineering Journal, 5*(4), 1093–1113. ISSN 2090-4479, https://doi.org/10.1016/j.asej.2014.04.011. Retrieved from http://www.sciencedirect.com/science/article/pii/S2090447914000550.

17. Neethu, M. S., & Rajasree, R. (2013). Sentiment analysis in twitter using machine learning techniques. In *2013 Fourth International Conference on Computing, Communications and Networking Technologies (ICCCNT), Tiruchengode, 2013* (pp. 1–5). https://doi.org/10.1109/icccnt.2013.6726818.

18. Wang, Z., Tong, V. J. C., & Chin, H. C. (2014). Enhancing machine-learning methods for sentiment classification of web data. In A. Jaafar, et al. (Eds.), *Information retrieval technology. AIRS 2014.* Lecture Notes in Computer Science (Vol. 8870). Cham: Springer.

19. Gautam, G., & Yadav, D. (2014). Sentiment analysis of twitter data using machine learning approaches and semantic analysis. In *2014 Seventh International Conference on Contemporary Computing (IC3), Noida, 2014* (pp. 437–442). https://doi.org/10.1109/ic3.2014.6897213.

20. Gupta, M. N., Vishwakarma, K., Rawat, G., Badhani, P. (2017). Study of Twitter sentiment analysis using machine learning algorithms on Python. *International Journal of Computer Applications, 165*(9), 0975–8887.
21. Kamal, M. S., Sarowar, M. G., Dey, N., et al. (2017). *International Journal of Machine Learning and Cybernetics.* https://doi.org/10.1007/s13042-017-0710-8.
22. Farhana Nimmy, Sonia, Kamal, Sarwar, Iqbal Hossain, Muhammad, Dey, Nilanjan, Amira Ashour, S., & Shi, Fuqian. (2017). Neural Skyline filtering for imbalance features classification. *International Journal of Computational Intelligence and Applications, 16,* 03.
23. Kamal, M. S., Chowdhury, L., Ibrahim Khan, M., Ashour, A. S., Tavares, J. M. R. S., & Dey, N. (2017). Hidden Markov Model and Chapman Kolmogrov for Protein Structures Prediction from Images. *Computational Biology and Chemistry, 68*, 231–244. Elsevier.
24. Kamal, M. S., Ashour, A. S., & Dey, N. (2017). Large scale medical data mining for accurate diagnosis: A blueprint. In S. U. Khan, A. Y. Zomaya, & A. Abbas (Eds.), *Handbook of large-scale distributed computing in smart healthcare.* Springer.
25. Kamal, M. S., Parvin, S., Ashour, A. S., Shi, F., & Dey, N. (2017). De-Bruijn graph with MapReduce framework towards metagenomic data classification. *International Journal of Information Technology, 9*, 59–75. Springer. http://link.springer.com/article/10.1007/s41870-017-0005-z.
26. Kamal, M. S., Dey, N., Ashour, A. S., Ripon, S. H., Balas, V. E., & Kaysar, M. S. (2017). FbMapping: An automated system for monitoring Facebook data. *Neural Network World, 27,* 27–57.
27. Kamal, M. S., Nimmy, S. F., & Parvin, S. (2016). Performance evaluation comparison for detecting DNA structural break through big data analysis. *Computer System Science & Engineering, 31,* 275–289.
28. Kamal, S., Dey, N., Nimmy, S. F., Ripon, S. H., Yousuf Ali, N., Ashour, A. S., et al. (2016). Evolutionary framework for coding area selection from cancer data. *Neural Computing and Applications,* Springer, 1–23. https://doi.org/10.1007/s00521-016-2513-3.
29. Chowdhury, L., Ibrahim Khan, M., Deb, K., & Kamal, S. (2016). MetaG: A graph-based Metagenomic gene analysis for big DNA data. *Network Modeling Health Informatics and Bioinformatics, 5,* 27. https://doi.org/10.1007/s13721-016-0132-7. Springer.
30. Kamal, M. S., Ripon, S. H., Dey, N., Ashour, A. S., & Santhi, V. (2016). A MapReduce approach to diminish imbalance parameters for big deoxyribonucleic acid dataset. *Computer Methods and Programs in Biomedicine, 131*, 191–206. Elsevier [SCI Index].
31. Kamal, M. S., & Nimmy, S. F. (2016). StrucBreak: A computational framework for structural break detection in DNA. *Interdisciplinary sciences: Computational life* (Vol. 9, pp. 1–16). Springer.
32. Kamal, S., & Arefin, M. S. (2016). Impact analysis of Facebook in family bonding. *Social Network Analysis and Mining* (Vol. 6, No. 1). Springer.
33. Kamal, M. S., Ibrahim Khan, M., Deb, K., Chowdhury, L., & Dey, N. (2016). An optimized graph based metagenomic gene classification approach: Metagenomic gene analysis. In N. Dey, & A. Ashour (Eds.), *Classification and clustering in biomedical signal processing* (pp. 290–314). Advances in Bioinformatics and Biomedical Engineering (ABBE) Book Series.
34. Ripon, S., Kamal, M. S., Hossain, S., & Dey, N. (2016). Theoretical analysis of different classifiers under reduction rough data set: A brief proposal. *International Journal of Rough Sets and Data Analysis (IJRSDA), 5*(1).
35. Farhana Nimmy, S., & Kamal, M. S. (2015). Next generation sequencing under De-Novo genome assembly. *International Journal of Biomathematics, 8*(5), 1–29.
36. Hossain, M. S., Zander, P.-O., Kamal, M. S., Chowdhury, L. (2015). Belief-rule-based expert systems for evaluation of E-government: A case study. *Expert System, 31*(4).
37. Ibrahim Khan, M., Kamal, M. S., & Chowdhury, Linkon. (2015). MSuPDA: A memory efficient algorithm for sequence alignment. *Interdisciplinary Sciences: Computational Life Sciences, 7*(1), 1–10. Springer.
38. Kamal, M. S., Xu, S., Farhana Nimmy, S., & Ibrahim Khan, M. (2015). DGPPIsAS: A dynamic global PPIs alignment system. *IJCSNS International Journal of Computer Science and Network Security, 15*(2), 29–37.

39. Kamal, M. S., & Ibrahim Khan, M. (2014). Performance evaluation of Warshall algorithm and dynamic programming for markov chain in local sequence alignment. *Interdisciplinary Sciences: Computational Life Sciences, 7*(1), 78–81. Springer.
40. Kamal, Sarwar, & Ibrahim Khan, Mohammad. (2014). Chapman-Kolmogorov equations for Global PPIs with Discriminant-EM. *International Journal of Biomathematics, 7*(4), 1–2.
41. Kamal, M. S., & Ibrahim Khan, M. (2014). Memory optimization for global protein network alignment using pushdown automata and de Bruijn graph based Bloom filter. *Journal of Software, 9*(10).
42. Kamal, M. S., & Ibrahim Khan, M. (2014). An integrated algorithm for local sequence alignment. *Network Modeling Analysis in Health Informatics and Bioinformatics, 3*(1), 68.
43. Ibrahim Khan, M., & Kamal, M. S. (2013). Sequencing ontology alignment for DNA annotation and damage identification. *European Journal of Scientific Research, 103*(3), 441–450. ISSN: 1450-216X/1450-202X.
44. Kamal, Sarwar, & Farhana Nimmy, Sonia. (2013). New algorithm to inspect adenoids. *International Journal of Computer Applications, 43,* 6–13.
45. Kamal, M. S., Farhana Nimmy, S., & Chowdhury, L. (2012). Vagueness anlaysis towards adenoids inspections. *International Journal of Physical and Social Sciences, 2*(6), 475–495. http://www.ijmra.us. ISSN: 2249-5894.
46. Kamal, M. S., Parvin, S., Saleem, K., Al-Hamadi, H., & Gawanmeh, A. (2017). Efficient low cost supervisory system for Internet of Things enabled smart home. In *Proceedings of the ICC2017: WT04-5th IEEE International Workshop on Smart Communication Protocols and Algorithms (SCPA 2017), Paris, France.*
47. Kamal, M. S., Farhana Nimmy, S., Hossain, M. I., Dey, N., Ashour, A. S., Sathi, V. (2016). ExSep: An exon separation process using neural skyline filter. In *International Conference on Electrical, Electronics, and Optimization Techniques (ICEEOT).*
48. Moustafa, M. N., & Chowdhury, L., & Kamal, M. S. (2012). Student dropout prediction for intelligent system from tertiary level in developing country. *IEEE Digital Library.*
49. Zhang, Y., Er, M. J., Wang, N., Pratama, M., & Venkatesan, R. (2016). *Sentiment classification using comprehensive attention recurrent models* (pp. 15621569).
50. Vateekul, P., & Koomsubha, T. (2016). A study of sentiment analysis using deep learning techniques on Thai Twitter Data.
51. Socher, R., & Lin, C. (2011). Parsing natural scenes and natural language with recursive neural networks. In *Proceedings* (pp. 129136).
52. LeCun, Y., et al. (1998). Gradient-based learning applied to document recognition. In *Proceedings of the IEEE 86.11,* 2278–2324.
53. Severyn, A., & Moschitti, A. (2015). Twitter sentiment analysis with deep convolutional neural networks. In: Proceedings of the 38th International ACM SIGIR Confernce on Research and Development in Information Retrieval- SIGIR 15, pp. 959962.
54. Socher, R., Perelygin, A., Wu, J. Y., Chuang, J., Manning, C. D., Ng, A. Y., et al. (2017). *Recursive deep models for semantic compositionality over a sentiment Treebank.* Stanford University, Stanford, CA 94305, USA.
55. http://www.internetlivestats.com/twitter-statistics/.
56. Li, C., Xu, B., Wu, G., He, S., Tian, G., & Hao, H. (2014). Recursive deep learning for sentiment analysis over social data. *Proceedings 2014 IEEE/WIC/ACM International Joint Conference on Web Intelligence, Intelligent Agent Technology—Work. WI IAT 2014,* (vol. 2, pp. 13881429).

Chapter 2
Social Networking in Web Based Movie Recommendation System

Nabanita Das, Surekha Borra, Nilanjan Dey and Samarjeet Borah

Abstract Movie Recommendations Systems are a common practice by most of the online stores today. The web based movie recommendation systems makes predictions about the responses of the users based on their search history or known preferences. Recommendation of items is usually done based on the properties or content of the item or collaboration of the user's ratings, and by using intelligent algorithms that include classification or clustering techniques. Accurate prediction of what the customer may likely to busy or the user my visit is of utmost important, as it benefits both the service providers and customers. This chapter provides the evolution, fundamental concepts, classification, traditional and novel models, requirements, similarity measures, evaluation approaches, issues, challenges, impacts due to social networking, and future of movie recommendation systems.

Keywords Recommendation systems · Content based filtering
Collaborative based filtering · Deep learning · Social networks · Web

2.1 Introduction

With the rapid growth in the Internet and related technologies, online movie stores are gaining lot of interest. The online movie stores display movies without biasing towards the popularity and sales figures. Further there is no shelf space limitation as

N. Das
Bengal Institute of Technology, Kolkata, India
e-mail: nabanita.das2008@gmail.com

S. Borra (✉)
K. S. Institute of Technology, Bangalore, India
e-mail: borrasurekha@gmail.com

N. Dey
Techno India College of Technology, Kolkata, India
e-mail: neelanjandey@gmail.com

S. Borah
Sikkim Manipal Institute of Technology, Majitar, Sikkim, India
e-mail: samarjeet.b@smit.smu.edu.in

© Springer International Publishing AG, part of Springer Nature 2018
N. Dey et al. (eds.), *Social Networks Science: Design, Implementation,
Security, and Challenges*, https://doi.org/10.1007/978-3-319-90059-9_2

opposed to physical movie stores. Recommendation systems are a kind of personalized services that recommends products or services to the users based on their needs, and find its applications in almost every domain. Displaying a sequence of items in order of their usefulness to the user is called Recommendation. The first commercial collaborative recommender systems based on user ratings was developed by Goldberg et al. [1] in mid 1990s. Later developed are content based filtering system, where the recommendation is based on the user's history of actions or purchases [2]. The recommendation systems has evolved from traditional Web, progressed through social Web, and progressing towards the Internet of Things (IoT).

The basic elements of any recommender system are: user and item. While the inputs of recommender system are database of users and items, the outputs are the recommendations [3]. Recommender Systems first acquire user information either directly by asking the user for inputs or the users past history such as books read, songs heard, and movies watched or downloaded etc., The information can even be acquired explicitly by user ratings for the books, songs, videos, movies, applications etc.

Recommendation systems make use of information from a variety and vast sources, in providing suggestions and making predictions. The algorithms inside the recommender system perform intelligent filtering of databases. The Content based algorithms works out majorly on the user database, performs filtering by making use of users priorities, interests and favourites, which are filled and updated by the user. The performance of these algorithms reduces if the user data is not available in advance. The collaborative filtering algorithms on the other hand filters the databases based on the user ratings or indirectly the user preferences. These algorithms are the most widely used, as they make decisions based on the user ratings which indirectly reflect the user's personal experiences, and partly his/her neighbours experiences. Social filtering [4–7] approaches filters the database based on the social data such as friends, trust, followed, followers, credibility, reputation, taxonomies and social tagging and user's recommendations to groups. While the information available and posted by the users in social websites such as timeline posts, friends, communities, groups, tweets, likes, friends are very commonly used features, some more advanced recommendation systems takes decisions based on the signals acquired by the Internet of things in real-time such as health signals. While some recommendation systems are based on the user gender, age, nationality etc., which is demographic information, some more recommendation systems are based on the physical locations of the users.

There also exists hybrid algorithms which integrates users interests as well as the users reviews (both text and ratings) to performs better. Hybrid techniques integrate several techniques and several sources of information such as implicit and explicit data, social data, demographic data, knowledge-based data, sensors data, user content, user collaborative data etc., to gain the advantages of all.

The traditional product recommendation principles or technologies which are often employed to suggest news articles, blogs, sites, and images are extended to recommend even the movies/videos from among millions of movies available online.

The advantages of Movie Recommendation Systems are:

- Cuts down the costs and time incurred in choosing and finding the movies online.

- Performs automatic decision
- Speeds decision making
- Allows users to search beyond the requirements in difficult areas.
- Generates profits and improves e-commerce quality
- Assists new users in making decisions choices.
- Resolves the issues related to Big Data in E-Commerce by filtering the data.

The general requirements of any recommendation system are: accuracy, stability, dispersity, novelty, non-intrusiveness, and flexibility. The system should also be capable of handling sparsity, cold-starts, limited content, overspecializations, real-time customization etc. The performance of Movie Recommendation systems depends mostly on the available databases and the filtering technique. These recommendations are mostly based on the training sets, theory of statistics such as priori and posterior probabilities relating to the prior purchases, tastes and ratings of the same or similar customers.

This chapter focuses on Movie Recommendation techniques and their challenges. Section 2.2 gives the background. Section 2.3 briefs the content based filtering approaches for movie recommendation. Section 2.4 briefs the collaborative based filtering approaches and Sect. 2.5 discusses about Hybrid approaches for movie recommendation. Section 2.6 presents the deep learning based approaches. Section 2.7 discusses about social network based movie recommendation systems. Section 2.8 gives various evaluation measures used in the recommender systems. Section 2.9 gives the future directions and challenges. Finally, Sect. 2.10 concludes the chapter.

2.2   Background

Movie Recommendation systems filter large and dynamic databases, suggests movies, provide personalized services or content for the users based on their profiles, history, interests and preferences as shown in Fig. 2.1. Movie Recommendation systems suggest the users, their likely interested movies to watch or buy.

The procedure for Movie Recommendation [8] involves several steps: The first step involves database collection which includes users and items (movies) information. The users' information may include user's content, users resources, search

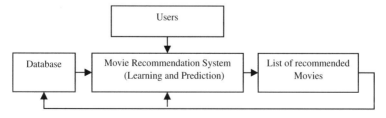

Fig. 2.1 Movie recommendation system

history, users attribute etc. More the user information available, more accurately the system predicts. A recommendation system or model then makes use of the information in database or from user's feedback. Explicit inputs are also collected by the system prompts and interfaces. The type of data collected can be user's interests and ratings to items. While the explicit inputs are reliable, the system demands user's efforts. Further, the accuracy greatly depends on the quantity of the ratings, users experiences in interfacing with the system, user's willingness to rate etc.

The explicit inputs provide high quality recommendations, as it is transparent and does not require preferences extraction. Implicit inputs include user's behaviour and preferences such as user history of navigation, purchases, clicked links and tabs, time durations etc. Implicit input collection does not require users effort as the system itself extracts the users preferences. Further the implicit inputs give unbiased results and are free from self ratings. While it is proved that the implicit inputs are more objective, they are less accurate when compared to the explicit input based systems. There are recommendation systems that consider hybrid inputs which are of implicit and also explicit in nature, in order to improve the accuracy by reducing the user effort. The accuracy of the system mostly is based on the design of the system and construction of user profiles, which are obtained from personal and associated information such as interaction, search abilities, interests, learning capabilities, preferences etc. The recommendation system then uses a learning algorithm that extracts and exploits the features from the collected database, and predicts the movies which are preferable to the user. The filtering techniques are broadly classified into three types: (a) Collaborative filtering technique (b) Content-based filtering technique (c) Hybrid filtering technique. These are discussed in the following sections.

2.3   Content Based Filtering Technique

This recommender [9–11] system makes use of the user provided data (implicitly or explicitly) such as user browsing history, clicks, and his ratings for making movie suggestions. More the user inputs, more efficient and accurate the recommendation system is. This approach is based on creating a profile for each purchased/viewed movie. The profile may include characteristics/features/properties of a movie such as artists in the movie, directors, producers, year, tags, or category of movie such as (romance, comic, fiction etc.), which is often denoted by genre in Internet Movie Database (IMDB), and the highest probable words (TF.IDF score) that explain the movie. The similarity of movies depends on the measurements of distances between their features.

The Content-based Filtering approach considers the items which the user interacted already, and analyzes and provides similar movie recommendations. Content, in movie recommendation are the features or attributes or characteristics that are used to describe the movie. The content based movie recommendation system assumes that the users have preferences in buying/watching a movie, and based on the user profile, it suggests movies that have close features similarity. The features can be as simple as movie released year, the actors or creators of the movie, genres, etc.

Most of the models for recommendation systems are based on the sparse utility matrix representation, whose entries indicate preferences (ratings) relating the entities such as items and users. The objective is then to predict the unfilled entries of the matrix based on the properties of the item or to identify the most likely occurring entries so as to suggest the same to the users. The complexity of this approach lies in building the utility matrix and extracting inferences from it, as it relies on the user behaviour in providing likes, dislikes and ratings which are often not sufficiently available. Each row of this matrix can be treated as a feature vector for calculation of distances.

2.3.1 Topic Similarity Models

In general, Movie similarity includes the computation of their feature vectors/matrix and checking how close they are using distance metrics or similarity score or movie plots. The feature vector construction involves keywords extraction, stop words removal, lemmatization, initial weights computation, modification of weights, feature reduction and similarity computation.

In topic similarity models, keywords denote the movie titles and generes that represent the contents and people related to the movie. The keyword should be chosen discriminately. After discarding the stop words which are usually less discriminative the other words are denoted with lemmas. Later weights are computed based on the frequency of occurrence of keywords in the movie. Techniques such as tf-idf technique can be used in finding the weights. The vector size is often minimized to reduce the processing time by removing the redundancy. Modification of weights is often required to deal with problems due to changes/removal of some keywords at a later stage without recomputing. Topic models are used for this purpose. Topics, which are often less than the number of keywords, are constructed based on a linear weighted combination of set of keywords. Two main Topic Models other than basic weighting techniques (such as tf-idf and log) are Latent Semantic Allocation (LSA) and Latent Dirichlet Allocation (LDA). The LSA is better than that of LDA. The Latent Dirichlet Allocation (LDA) represents ambiguous words in a variety of linguistic tasks and performs better than LSA.

2.3.2 Simple Content Based Filtering

The basic content-based filtering approaches rely on genres only. The more advanced systems depend on various attributes and associated weights. Commonly used algorithm for this purpose is Term Frequency Inverse Document Frequency algorithm (TFIDF), where the prediction and hence recommendation of a movie is determined based on two parameters: Inverse Document Frequency (IDF) and Term Frequency (TF) as follows:

- Inverse Document Frequency (IDF) is the inverse of the movie Term Frequency in the database. Since the probability of occurrence of some words is more frequent than the others, calculating TF alone is not efficient. In such cases, the calculation of TF-IDF scores which include some weights to the frequency of occurrence of words is better as it provides the relative importance of the words.
- Term Frequency (TF) gives the probability of occurrence of words in the movie. Ex: The word "in" occurs more frequently than Love in the movie title "Shakespeare in Love".

The similarity of movies is predicted by creating a Vector Space Model, where in each movie is represented by a set of n attributes (Movie Feature vectors). Attribute are the characteristics of the movie such as the words in the movie titles or tag lines. The similarity/likeliness of any two feature vectors can be calculated using the cosine angle between those two vectors, as the cosine value increases with decreasing angle.

Given the database of Movies, with titles and tag lines, a search for a particular "Movie", creates a word frequency table with columns as the words related to the title, and rows as the movies in the database as in Table 2.1.

In the Table 2.1, N represents the total movies available in database, and FNm represents frequency of occurrence of word m in the Movie N.

For each movie, Calculate the word frequency weights using the formula:

$$WTF = 1 + \log_{10} TF \tag{2.1}$$

Each row of this table represents a vector for the Movie n. A sample inverse document frequency table is shown in Table 2.2.

The Word1 appears in F1 movies out of N movies. IMF is the logarithmic inverse TF.

$$WIDF = \log_{10} \frac{N}{N1} \tag{2.2}$$

where N1 is the number of movies with word1.

Table 2.1 Creation of term frequency table

Movie title	Word1	Word2	Wordm
Movie1	F111	F12	F1m
Movie2	F21	F22	F2m
MovieN	FN1		FNm

Table 2.2 Inverse document frequency table

Movie title	Word1	Word2	Wordm
	F1	F2	Fm

The normalization of vectors is done by calculating the Vector Magnitudes, which is the square root of sum of the squared values of each weight (row element) in the vector. Normalization includes dividing each weight in TF table with the corresponding vector magnitude. This is done to make all the vector lengths equal to 1. Once the vectors are equalized, the similarity between different vectors is calculated by measuring the angle between them as in Table 2.3. The rows of this table are arranged in decreasing order of cosine values. Higher the value, smaller the angle between vectors, and more similar those vectors are.

To frame the vector representation of user profiles, a set of user profile vectors (User Feature Vectors) are calculated based on the users past history of clicks and watches of those movies. In a movie features matrix, the rows remain are movies, the columns can be the genres reflecting the category of the movie such as Documentary, Animation, Children, Comedy, Romance, Adventure, Crime, Drama, Thriller, Science-Fiction etc. Construction of a user profile matrix is based on the user ratings and preferences as in Table 2.4. The element Rnm is the rating given by the user to Movie n and the Genere m.

Binarizing the above matrix gives Table 2.5, where the total attributes for each row indicates the user taste of the movie to each genre.

The normalization here is performed by dividing the rating occurrence (1/0) with sqrt of number of attributes in each movie. The dot product/sum product of each attribute column with the total number of attributes column fills the user profile

Table 2.3 Angle between movies

Movie vectors	Angle
Cos(Movie1 Movie2)	
Cos(Movie1 Movie3)	
Cos(Movie1 MovieN)	
Cos(Movie2 Movie1)	
Cos(Movie2 Movie3)	
…	

Table 2.4 Movie recommendation based on TF-IDF score of user ratings

Movie title	Genre1	Genre2	Genrem
Movie1	R11	R12	R1m
Movie2			
MovieN			

Table 2.5 Binarized matrix

Movie title	Genre1	Genre2	Genre m	Total attributes
Movie1	0	1	1	2
Movie2				
MovieN				

matrix. The values in this matrix indicate the user likeness to each movie. The higher the value, the higher is the likeness. Having the Movie Vectors and the user profile vectors, the task is to predict the users' likeness to the movies which he has not rated earlier. The TF and IDF vectors are calculated for the Movie Vectors. The Movie Vectors and the IDF vector is dot producted to obtain weights vector which is further dot producted with user profile vector to predict the user's likeness to the movies.

These algorithms are domain-dependent and are the most successful where documents like web pages, publications and news are recommended, relying on the features extracted from the contents of the past items which the user evaluated. Items that are Mostly Positive rated are recommended to the user. In order to generate meaningful recommendations, CBF uses different types of models such as Vector Space Model or Probabilistic models such as Naive Bayes Classifier, Decision Trees or Neural Networks to model the relationship between different documents within a corpus. All techniques make recommendations by learning the underlying model with either statistical analysis or machine learning techniques. CBF technique is not dependent on the profile of other users since they do not influence recommendation. The major disadvantage is the requirement of depth knowledge and description of the features of the items in the profile.

Content based filtering techniques have the ability to recommend new items even if there are no ratings provided by the users. In a short span of time it has the capability to adjust its recommendations with user profile change. This kind of systems manages the identical items according to their intrinsic features without sharing profile, and this ensures privacy for users. The drawbacks of this technique includes its dependency on items' metadata which require rich description of items and very well organized user profile before recommendation can be made to users. This phenomenon is called limited content analysis. It depends on the availability of descriptive data. Content overspecialization is another serious problem of this content based technique.

Strengths:

- Simple
- Requires less user data

Weaknesses:

- Efficiency decreases if the user data has biased distribution.
- Inadequate usage of inter-dependencies calculations and complex behaviours.

2.4 Collaborative Filtering Technique

Most of the web based movie recommendation systems are based on the clustering techniques or the collaborative filtering techniques [12]. These techniques consider the movies which the user had already seen and the corresponding ratings/feedbacks as inputs and recommend other movies which have similar ratings. Collaborative filtering can be divided into two approaches: model based filtering and memory based filtering. Memory-based systems recommends dynamically the movies to active users based on the neighbours. The major limitations are data sparsity, memory bottleneck issues and computation complexity. The memory based collaborative filtering technique can be further grouped into either item or user based on the type of neighbourhood region. The studies indicated that the item-based methods are fast and accurate.

Model-based collaborative technique is an offline technique that solves the issues related to scalability and data sparsity, by building a model that includes the database of users rating patterns. The drawback of Model-based collaborative filtering is that they are slow. Yet another offline technique that deals with the issues of scalability are clustering based techniques, which partition movies with similar distance into several clusters. A widely used precise and reliable algorithm for this purpose is the k-nearest neighbour (kNN) algorithm. More advanced, fast and quality clustering is achieved with bio-inspired algorithms. Web based movie recommendation systems assigns a cluster to the online user based on calculation of weights. Hybrid approaches that combine both KNN and bio-inspired algorithms are also available. Cuckoo search algorithm [13] is employed in improving the reliability and accuracy in recommending personalized movies.

Advantages of memory based Collaborative Filtering Approach (CF):

- Easy to implement.
- Addition of new data is very simple and also gradually incremented.
- Content of items is not recommended
- There is no scalability issue and also very correlated items

Limitations of memory based Collaborative Filtering Approach (CF): (CF):

- Sparsity and scalability issues with rating matrices and new and rising items and users

Advantages of model based (CF):

- Sparsity and scalability problem is very carefully handled.
- Prediction performance is improved.

Limitations of model based (CF):

- Model building is very much costly.
- The performance is affected by scalability issues and feature selection and reduction techniques

Collaborative filtering (CF) evaluates items based on other people's opinion. Two categories: recommendations and predictions define the functionality of collaborative filtering. CF collects and establishes profiles followed by determining the relationships amongst the data based on the similarity models. Profile data categorization includes user preferences, user behaviour patterns and item properties. User needs ratings to design a recommender system which will suggest a particular item or a product. Collaborative filtering is one of the most efficient way of movie recommendation system (MRS) based on nearest-neighbour mechanism.

The advantages of CF algorithms are:

- Content analysis is not mandatory
- Focuses on the clustering algorithms
- Generates user and item profiles
- Characteristics of Collaborative Filters

The drawbacks of CF algorithms are:

- Dealing with a Sparse and large range of items in collaborative filtering based Recommendation systems is a difficult task as it increases the user-item matrix size.
- With the available resources, it is difficult to meet the demands of rising users and items.
- Often, the system recommends the same old recommended items in different categories.
- The Blacksheep/Graysheep who are either unpredictable or against to the recommender systems cannot gain benefit of the system.
- False recommendations are possible.
- Privacy of users on the other hand limits the performance of system as many people will not be willing to share their habits, preferences, taste, and views in public forums.

The performance of the Collaborative Filtering algorithms is affected by limited availability of ratings of user or items. The challenging tasks are: selection of threshold for comparison of ratings in the process of predictions and dealing with the rarely rated items remains same.

2.5 Hybrid Filtering

The results of different recommenders to generate a recommendation list or prediction are often combined linearly in a weighted fashion [14]. These techniques are given equal weights at first, but weights can be adjusted as predictions are confirmed or otherwise. The benefit of a weighted hybrid filtering technique is that all the recommender system's strengths are utilized during the recommendation process in a straightforward way.

- **Switching hybridization**

The recommendation system swaps the ratings in a heuristic way. The benefit of this strategy is that the system is sensitive to the strengths and weaknesses of its constituent recommenders. The main disadvantage with switching hybrids is that it usually introduces more complexity to recommendation process because the switching criterion, which normally increases the number of parameters to the recommendation system, has to be determined.

- **Cascade hybridization**

In this approach the item preference order includes a process that iteratively refines based on the knowledge.

- **Mixed hybridization**

In Mixed hybrids, each item has multiple recommendations associated with it from different recommendation techniques. The individual performances do not always affect the general performance of a local region.

- **Feature-combination**

The features produced after comparing specific recommendation technique are fed to another recommendation technique.

- **Feature-augmentation**

These techniques accumulate the ratings and other information produced by the previous recommender and it also requires additional functionality from the recommender systems.

- **Meta-level**

Sparsity problem of collaborative filtering techniques is resolved by meta–level technique.

2.6 Deep Learning Based Movie Recommendation Systems

The traditional Movie Recommendation Systems are based on nearest neighbours algorithm, simple matrix factorization (MF), factorization machine (FM), probabilistic matrix factorization (PMF) etc.

Recently, deep learning methods based movie recommendation [15] is gaining due to its innovative capabilities of complex problem solving skills and due to its effective extraction, modelling and analysis of complex users and items profiles, demands and corresponding interactions. Other factors that motivated the usage of deep learning for movie recommendation are as follows:

- Most of the movies watched on top movie sites [Ex: Netflix and You tube] are based on recommendations by the system.
- Deep learning based approaches proved their efficiency in providing recommendations at a fast rate and high quality.
- There are enhanced applications and enormous growth in researches and publications in deep learning methods
- It allows multiple abstractions and representations of data

This section briefs the state of the art of current movie recommendation systems based on deep learning assuming that the readers are aware of the basic terminology.

The objective of deep learning based movie recommendation systems may be to:

- Predict missing user ratings for the items
- Provide a ranked list of recommended movies
- Classification of items based on the category

Deep Learning Techniques performs a variety of learning tasks as a part of machine learning. The widely used deep learning approaches are Generative Adversarial Network (GAN), Neural Autoregressive Distribution Estimation (NADE), Restricted Boltzmann Machine (RBM), Convolutional Neural Network (CNN), Autoencoder (AE), Recurrent Neural Network (RNN), Multilayer Perceptron (MLP), Deep Semantic Similarity Model (DSSM). While some movie recommendation systems may make use of more than one of the deep learning approaches to gain more benefits, some systems can integrate both traditional and deep learning techniques.

The number of users and their relations keep changing in social networks. While movie recommendation systems based on Back propagation algorithms and Bayesian Networks (BN) performs poorly with such dynamic networks and real time data, systems based on fuzzy Logic proved their effectiveness in making use of floating data of social networks such as Instagram, Orkut2, Twitter, Friendster1, MySpace3 Facebook etc. A set of movie related keywords or strings are searched and the corresponding likes, reactions, interactions and comments are analyzed using fuzzy logic.

2.7 Social Network Based Movie Recommender Systems

These days with the rapid use of social networks, movie recommendation systems which are based on the identities, tastes, hobbies, everyday interests and changing social network profiles are gaining usage and importance because of the accuracy that they provide. Such social data mining based recommendation systems are more powerful as they are based on word-of-mouth. The general procedure followed in the movie recommendations based on the analysis of social activities and blogs are: collecting, creating and normalizing user profiles composing of their passions, interests, acquaintances and friends, languages; and to classify and cluster the profiles using intelligent techniques like Machine Learning.

The emerging trend is the development of movie recommendation systems based on Mobile platform based social networks and GPS locations, as they provide unique distinctive data in real time along with location contexts. Apart from traditional content or collaborative filtering methods, social network based recommendation systems are developed using trust based approaches where users' implicit and/or explicit trust relations are combined with Collaborative filtering techniques for effective prefiltering and enhancement of accuracy. Trust values depends on co-rated items and can form relationship based models or reputation based models. Movie Recommendation using social networks design based web technology makes use of users' interaction, centrality concepts, cohesive groups, and subgroups.

In the movie industry, a movie recommendation is a manner of advertisement or promotion. It is not only the film makers who rely mainly on social networks for the promotion and feedback about their movie, the movie recommender systems too are relying on the reviews and YouTube comments as they are user-generated data that contains people's opinions.

Out of various approaches and a lot of existing research of movie recommendation systems in which social networks and blogs are involved, the clustering based method proposed by Tithrottanak You et al. uses the facebook likes and user genere interests to resolves the "cold-start problem". Systems based on Latent Semantic Model (LSM) and The Internet Movie Database (IMDb), and Social Networks is presented by Kodzo Wegba et al. [16]. There are also movie recommendation systems that deals with vote stuffing, based on neuro-fuzzy decision trees (NFDT) [17]. Some systems [18] use movie reviews and YouTube comments for movie recommendation. These systems provide better accuracy as they are based on aspect-based approaches.

There also exist two methods, which are based on "TDF-IDF" and "Genre Score". The "TDF-IDF" is designed to extract genre specific keywords and the "Genre Score" indicates a degree of correlation between a movie and genres. To resolve the sparsity problems of Social-aware Movie Recommendation systems (SMRs) [19], hetero-geneous systems are developed which apart from social relationships, movie-poster images. Hybrid systems [20] which are based on various contextual information are also developed and named as MyMovieHistory.

2.8   Evaluation Metrics of Movie Recommendation Systems

The success of any E-business predominantly depends upon the recommendation systems that they employ in filtering the wide variety of their products and suggesting the most likely interested items to the customer.

The performance of recommendation systems is limited by the users search pref-erences, size of training set, users' exposure to the recommendation system. There are several evaluation parameters that are commonly used for evaluation of performance of any movie recommender system. The common classification of performance mea-sures are based on standard metrics, user evaluations and commercial approach. These are further divided into three categories such as Predictive Accuracy param-eters, Classification Accuracy parameters, and Rank Accuracy parameters [21, 22]. The predictive accuracy parameters measures how movie recommender system pre-dicts actual rating of the movie. The classification accuracy parameters measure the frequency with which a movie recommender system makes a right/wrong decision with regard to rating of the movie. The rank accuracy parameters measure the cor-rectness of the ordering of movies performed by the movie recommendation system.

The accuracy evaluation parameters are Root Mean Square Error (RMSE), Mean Absolute Error (MAE), Normalized MAE (NMAE), Movie Similarity Calculation, recall, precision, F-measure, Swet's measure, Receiver Operating Characteristic (ROC) Curve, Predication-Rating Correlation, Kendall's Tau, and Half-life Utility Measure. These evaluation parameters are further classified in two classes such as statistical and decision-support accuracy parameters [23]. The statistical accuracy parameters compare the prediction ratings of the movie with true user ratings of movie in test data set. Examples include MAE, RMSE, and Movie Similarity Calculation. The decision-support accuracy parameters are measured based on prediction rate of movie recommender system. Examples include parameters such as precision and recall.

The definitions of evaluation parameters used for movie recommender system are given below:

- **Mean Absolute Error (MAE) and Related Parameters** [13, 24]

The Mean Absolute Error (MAE) is mostly used parameter for evaluation of performance of any movie recommender system. MAE is a measure of deviation of recommendation from user's rating value. It is calculated as follows [25]:

$$MAE = \frac{\sum |PR_{x,y} - TR_{x,y}|}{N} \qquad (2.3)$$

where, N is total movies of database, PR is predicted rating for user x on movie y, and TR is the true rating. The lesser the MAE, the more accurate a movie recommendation system is.

- **Root Mean Square Error (RMSE)**

It is given by Cotter in 2000 [26] and is given by:

$$RMSE = \sqrt{\frac{1}{N} \sum_{x,y} (PR_{x,y} - TR_{x,y})^2} \qquad (2.4)$$

The lower the value of RMSE, better the recommendation accuracy is.

- **Normalized MAE (NMAE)**

It measures accuracy of the system for available rating range for movie data set. Let R_{max} and R_{min} is the maximum and minimum ratings of movie. Then, NMAE is calculated as follows:

$$NMAE = \frac{1}{N} \frac{\sum |PR_{x,y} - TR_{x,y}|}{R_{max} - R_{min}} \qquad (2.5)$$

These parameters results in actual prediction measurement of system, easy to calculate and are used to find accuracy of recommender system for different types of movie data set. The limitations of these parameters is that the output results of these parameters are more specific which may sometimes measure wrong accuracy of the system and hence cannot be used for recommender system with lower rating values.

- **Movie Similarity Calculation** [26–29]

Two movies are similar if they are referenced by similar contents. Similarity in movie recommender systems can be done by referring to various features such as release date, movie stories, and user rating. The generally used movie similarity measures are Euclidean Distance, Cosine Similarity, and Pearson Correlation (PC) Coefficient.

Euclidean Distance

Considering critics rating C to any movie data set and users rating U to a similar data set, the Euclidean distance between movie data set is calculated as follows:

$$D(C, U) = \sqrt{(C_1 - U_1)^2 + (C_2 - U_2)^2 + \ldots + (C_N - U_N)^2}$$

$$= \sqrt{\sum_{i=1}^{N} (C_N - U_N)^2} \tag{2.6}$$

where N is total movies in data set, the D being Euclidean distance.

The similarity between movie data set using this distance is measured as follows:

$$Sim(C, U) = \frac{1}{1 + D(C, U)} \tag{2.7}$$

If the distance between ratings is 0, then corresponding similarity between movies is 1. If the distance is ∞, then the corresponding similarity between movies is 0.

Cosine Similarity

The cosine similarity of movie recommender system is calculated as cosine angle of two movie ratings vector. The behaviour of the cosine is such that it tends towards $+1$ as angle between rating values decreases, and it tends towards -1 as angle between rating values increases. This concept is used to find similarity of the movie. If cosine angle of movie ratings is close to $+1$, it suggests a close similarity between movies where as those close to -1 can mean there is no similarity between movies. Suppose if M denotes all movies in the data set, $M_{C,U}$ is the set of ratings by critic C and user U, $\vec{C}$ and $\vec{U}$ be the two vectors representing ratings of critic C and rating of user U. The cosine similarity between movie rating vectors is given by:

$$Sim(C, U) = \frac{\vec{C} \cdot \vec{U}}{\left\| \vec{C} \right\| \times \left\| \vec{U} \right\|} = \frac{\sum\limits_{m \in M_{C,U}} R_{C,m} \cdot R_{U,m}}{\sqrt{\sum\limits_{m \in M_{C,U}} R_{C,m}^2} \sqrt{\sum\limits_{m \in MC,U} R_{U,m}^2}} \tag{2.8}$$

where, Sim is similarity of movie rating, $R_{C,m}$ is rating of critic C on movie m in M data set, and $R_{U,m}$ is the rating of user U on any movie m in the M data set.

Pearson Correlation (PC) Coefficient

Correlation indicates linear relationship between two vectors. A correlation coefficient is a number that measures the relationship strength of vectors. The Pearson correlation has a range of -1 to $+1$. The interpretation of this value is similar to cosine. Let two ratings C and U have covariance COV, the PC coefficient of rating is calculated as follows:

$$PC(C, U) = \frac{COV(C, U)}{\sigma_C \times \sigma_U} \qquad (2.9)$$

where, σ_C is standard deviation of critic rating and σ_U is standard deviation of user rating.

PC is the most commonly used coefficient measurement of movie ratings in movie recommender systems. PC coefficient in a movie recommender system is calculated as follows:

$$Sim(C, U) = \frac{\sum_{m \in M_{C,U}} (R_{C,m} - \bar{R}_C)(R_{U,m} - \bar{R}_U)}{\sqrt{\sum_{m \in M_{C,U}} (R_{C,m} - \bar{R}_C)^2} \times \sqrt{\sum_{m \in M_{C,U}} (R_{U,m} - \bar{R}_U)^2}} \qquad (2.10)$$

where, $\bar{R}_C$ and $\bar{R}_U$ is mean rating of the critic and user on all movies $m \in M_{C,U}$.

- **Classification Accuracy Parameters [30–32]**

These parameters are used for evaluation of decision ability of movie recommender systems, which uses user-movie pairs such as Recommend/Not recommend. The parameters: Precision, Recall, F-Measure, ROC curve and Swet's measure are used for this purpose.

Precision and Recall

For evaluation of precision and recall, movie recommendation is set into two classes: relevant and not relevant, which can be denoted with a binary value. Each movie can be either relevant or not relevant to the user. Based on these values, the matrix in Table 2.6 is built.

Precision is the ratio of selected relevant movie to total movies. It indicates the frequency of relevance of selected movie and is given as follows:

$$Pr = \frac{MR}{REC} \qquad (2.11)$$

Recall is the ratio of selected relevant movies to total such movies. It denotes the frequency that a relevant movie will be chosen using equation:

Table 2.6 Relevance matrix

	Recommended	Not recommended	Total value
Relevant	MR	MNR	$R = MR + MNR$
Not relevant	MNRR	MNRNR	$NR = MNRR + MNRNR$
Total	$REC = MR + MNRR$	$NREC = MNR + MNRNR$	$M = R + NR$

$$\text{Re} = \frac{MR}{R} \tag{2.12}$$

F-Measure

Precision and Recall measures the different accuracy values of the movie recommender system. The single quantity for accuracy measure, F-measure based on precision values and recall values is given as follows:

$$F = \frac{2 \cdot \text{Pr} \cdot \text{Re}}{\text{Pr} + \text{Re}} \tag{2.13}$$

ROC Curve and Swet's Measure

This curve measures the ability of a movie recommender system to recommend a relevant movie for user from non relevant movie data set. This curve is plotted as follows:

- Rank all movies rating recommendation score.
- For each movie rating cut-off point:

    – Calculate Recall, and Fallout as follows

$$Fallout = \frac{MNRR}{REC} \tag{2.14}$$

- Plot curve between Recall (y axis) and Fallout (x axis).

The Swet's measure is defined as the area under the ROC curve. The advantage of these parameters is that they measure the actual performance of a movie recommender system, the drawback being requirement of actual knowledge of rating values and large data sets.

- **Rank Accuracy Parameters**

These parameters evaluate movie recommender system with high accuracy. The high ranked recommendations system is used for relevant movie rating of critic and user. The parameters: Prediction-Rating Correlation, Kendall's Tau, and Half-life utility measure are often used for rank accuracy evaluation of the system.

Prediction-Rating Correlation

If a variance of one movie rating can be explained by the variance of another movie rating, then these two movie ratings are said to correlate. Let $m_1 \dots m_N \in \{1 \dots N\}$ be movies in movie data set, $r_1 \dots r_N \in \{1 \dots N\}$ be their true ranks, the movie recommender system predicts the ranks $p_1 \dots p_N \in \{1 \dots N\}$. Let $\bar{r}$ is the mean of true rank and $\bar{p}$ is mean of predicted rank. The prediction-rating correlation ρ is calculated as follows:

$$\rho = \frac{\sum_{x=1}^{N} (r_x - \bar{r}_x) \cdot (p_x - \bar{p}_x)}{N \cdot stdev(r) \cdot stdev(p)} \tag{2.15}$$

Kendall's Tau

Considering $m_1 \ldots m_N \in \{1 \ldots N\}$ be movies in movie data set and let $r_1 \ldots r_N \in \{1 \ldots N\}$ be their true rank. Let movie recommender system predicts the ranks $p_1 \ldots p_N \in \{1 \ldots N\}$. Let A be the number of correctly predicted rankings of movies and B be the number of incorrectly predicted ranking of movies. Let TA be number of movies in the true rank ordering, and TB be number of movies in the predicted rank ordering. Kendall's Tau is calculated as follows:

$$Tau = \frac{A - B}{\sqrt{(A + B + TA)(A + B + TB)}} \qquad (2.16)$$

Half-life Utility Measure

This measure assumes that the user is predicted with long recommendation movie list, but only seen few movies of them. The measure finds the difference between the users rating of a movie and true rating of a movie. The user can see a specific movie on the movie data set and the estimation is an exponential decay function parameter. Let $R\,(U,\,m_j)$ be user U rating of movie m_j, which is the jth movie on the recommendation movie list. Let γ be the half-life decay parameter and r be true rating of movie. The expected utility of movie m_j is calculated as follows:

$$R = \sum_j \frac{\max(R(U,\,m_j) - r, 0)}{2^{\frac{j-1}{\gamma-1}}} \qquad (2.17)$$

The half-life is the rank of the movie on the movie data set, such that there is a 50% chance that the user will view that movie.

Most all the performance metrics used for evaluation for MRS can also be used in evaluation of the social networks.

The Average Mean Absolute Error (MAE) can be defined as:

$$Avg.MAE = \left\{ \sum_{x=1}^{N} \left(\sum_{y=1}^{n} \left| PR_{x,y} - TR_{x,y} \right| \Big/ n \right) \right\} \Big/ N \qquad (2.18)$$

where N is the number of users in the dataset T, n is the number of items in the dataset T, $PR_{x,y}$ is the predicted ratings of user x for the item y, and $TR_{x,y}$ is the actual ratings of user x for the item y.

Other performance metrics for the evaluation of the social networks in the MRS are density, size, network centrality, degree centrality, factions and clique membership. The details of these metrics are given below.

Density gives a measure of relationship of users, whether it is restrictive or strong. With m size network, the ties can be up to (m*(m – 1)). It is rare to have full density social networks.

Size usually helps in finding other parameters and indicates the total users present in social network, and is useful in order to calculate other measures.

Degree Centrality measures the total relations (ties) of a user. They can be in-degree or out-degree depending on whether the ties are sent or received. There are many other centralities which can be measured depending on various sources, such as flow centrality, betweenness centrality closeness centrality, and network centrality.

Cliques and Factions Cliques are closely tied subsets of network which are usually formed based on the race, gender, age, race etc. The clique gives a count of users with ties among themselves (i.e. in terms of graphs, a maximal complete subgraph). Less restrictive cliques are called Factions and are the subsets of various groups where users are more likely to be tied to each other. Cliques and Factions are substructures that help in predicting how a network as a whole is likely to behave.

2.9   Future Research Directions and Open Issues

This section presents some insights [33, 34] of the future evolution of Movie recommendation systems (MRS).

- Users and Items can be much more deeply understood by the MRS, may be by employing data that is extracted from users circumstances, situations in a comprehensive manner
- MRS may intensively use social media and Internet of things with different models
- MRS may consider temporal data with users profiles.
- MRS may integrate unstructured multimedia data [textual, audio, visual, features] for recommendations.
- Automation of feature selection may be possible, which can eventually reduce the time and complexity.
- More effective hybrid and composite models can be developed to improve the salient features.
- More Session-based recommender systems can be developed to deal with issues related to temporal dynamics.
- MRS based on evolution of items as well as users, and their corresponding co-evolution with respect to time can be considered.
- Cross Domain Recommendation systems that can focus on multiple domains can be developed using knowledge transformation techniques.
- Multi-Task Learning methods can be integrated with multiple domains as a solution to data sparsity problems.

2.10   Conclusions

This chapter gives an overview of the Movie Recommendation Systems, its classification, vulnerabilities, and recommendations for future development. Performance measures related to the real time implementation of recommender systems through various algorithms is also featured. An integration of movie recommendation mechanisms with deep learning techniques which effectively deal with noisy and lengthy inputs is introduced. However, more efficient methods to deal with real time incremental and dynamic data can be developed. Resolving trade-off between scalability and complexity and other parameters can be focused. Novel Evaluation Metrics and similarity measures can be developed. Development of systems that can improve the privacy and trustworthiness of user profiles and interests will certainly satisfy and attract the users of recommendation systems.

References

1. Goldberg, D., Nichols, D., Oki, B. M., & Terry, D. (1992). Using collaborative filtering to weave an information tapestry. *Communications of the ACM, 35*(12), 61–70.
2. Bobadilla, J., Ortega, F., Hernando, A., & Gutiérrez, A. (2013). Recommender systems survey. *Knowledge-based systems, 46,* 109–132.
3. Sharma, M., & Mann, S. (2013). A survey of recommender systems: approaches and limitations. *International Journal of Innovations in Engineering and Technology, 2*(2), 8–14.
4. Amato, F., Moscato, V., Picariello, A., & Piccialli, F. (2017). SOS: A multimedia recommender system for online social networks. In *Future generation computer systems*.
5. Ioanăs, E., & Stoica, I. (2014). Social media and its impact on consumers behavior. *International Journal of Economic Practices and Theories, 4*(2), 295–303.
6. Yang, X., Steck, H., Guo, Y., & Liu, Y. (2012). On top-k recommendation using social networks. In *Proceedings of the Sixth ACM Conference on Recommender Systems* (pp. 67–74). ACM.
7. Zhou, L. (2009). Trust based recommendation system with social network analysis. In *International Conference on Information Engineering and Computer Science*, 2009. ICIECS 2009. (pp. 1–4). IEEE.
8. Adomavicius, G., & Tuzhilin, A. (2005). Toward the next generation of recommender systems: A survey of the state-of-the-art and possible extensions. *IEEE Transactions on Knowledge and Data Engineering, 17*(6), 734–749.
9. Basu, C., Hirsh, H., & Cohen, W. (1998). Recommendation as classification: Using social and content-based information in recommendation. In *AAAI/IAAI* (pp. 714–720).
10. Arora, G., Kumar, A., Devre, G. S., & Ghumare, A. (2014). Movie recommendation system based on users' similarity. *International Journal of Computer Science and Mobile Computing, 3*(4), 765–770.
11. https://rpubs.com/jeknov/movieRec.
12. Suganeshwari, G., & Ibrahim, S. S. (2016). A survey on collaborative filtering based recommendation system. In *Proceedings of the 3rd International Symposium on Big Data and Cloud Computing Challenges (ISBCC–16')* (pp. 503–518). Springer International Publishing.
13. Katarya, R., & Verma, O. P. (2017). An effective collaborative movie recommender system with cuckoo search. *Egyptian Informatics Journal, 18*(2), 105–112.
14. Kim, K. J., & Ahn, H. (2012). Hybrid recommender systems using social network analysis. In *Proceedings of World Academy of Science, Engineering and Technology (No. 64)*.
15. Zhang, S., Yao, L., & Sun, A. (2017). Deep learning based recommender system: A survey and new perspectives. arXiv preprint arXiv:1707.07435.
16. Wegba, K., Lu, A., Li, Y., & Wang, W. (2017). Interactive movie recommendation through latent semantic analysis and storytelling. arXiv preprint arXiv:1701.00199.
17. Bhatt, R. B. (2009). Neuro-fuzzy decision trees for content popularity model and multi-genre movie recommendation system over social network. In *TENCON 2009–2009 IEEE Region 10 Conference* (pp. 1-6). IEEE.

18. Han, Y., & Kim, Y. (2017). An extracting method of movie genre similarity using aspect-based approach in social media. *ACM SIGAPP Applied Computing Review, 17*(2), 36–45.
19. Zhao, Z., Yang, Q., Lu, H., Weninger, T., Cai, D., He, X., & Zhuang, Y. (2017). Social-aware movie recommendation via multimodal network learning. *IEEE Transactions on Multimedia.*
20. Pham, X. H., Jung, J. J., & Park, S. B. (2014). Exploiting social contexts for movie recommendation. *Malaysian Journal of Computer Science, 27*(1), 68–79.
21. Herlocker, J. L., Konstan, J. A., Terveen, L. G., & Riedl, J. T. (2004). Evaluating collaborative filtering recommender systems. *ACM Transactions on Information Systems (TOIS), 22*(1), 5–53.
22. Pal, G., Acharjee, S., Rudrapaul, D., Ashour, A. S., & Dey, N. (2015). Video segmentation using minimum ratio similarity measurement. *International journal of image mining, 1*(1), 87–110.
23. Kirmemis, O., & Birturk, A. (2008). A content-based user model generation and optimization approach for movie recommendation. In *Workshop on ITWP.*
24. Isinkaye, F. O., Folajimi, Y. O., & Ojokoh, B. A. (2015). Recommendation systems: Principles, methods and evaluation. *Egyptian Informatics Journal, 16*(3), 261–273.
25. Miranda, T., Claypool, M., Gokhale, A., Mir, T., Murnikov, P., Netes, D., & Sartin, M. (1999). Combining content-based and collaborative filters in an online newspaper. In *Proceedings of ACM SIGIR Workshop on Recommender Systems.*
26. Cotter, P. and Smyth, B., 2000. PTV: Intelligent personalized TV guides. In *Proceedings of 12th Conference on Innovative Applications of Artificial Intelligence* (pp. 957–964).
27. Shimodaira, H. (2014). Similarity and recommender systems. School of Informatics, The University of Eidenburgh, 21.
28. Lee, G. Y., & Tseng, W. P. (2015). An enhanced memory-based collaborative filtering approach for context-aware recommendation. In *Proceedings of the World Congress on Engineering* (Vol. 1).
29. Bergamaschi, S., Po, L., & Sorrentino, S. (2014). Comparing topic models for a movie recommendation system. In *WEBIST (2)* (pp. 172–183).
30. Su, X., & Khoshgoftaar, T. M. (2009). A survey of collaborative filtering techniques. *Advances in Artificial Intelligence, 2009,* 4.
31. Wang, Z., Yu, X., Feng, N., & Wang, Z. (2014). An improved collaborative movie recommendation system using computational intelligence. *Journal of Visual Languages & Computing, 25*(6), 667–675.
32. Hameed, M. A., Al Jadaan, O., & Ramachandram, S. (2012). Collaborative filtering based recommendation system: A survey. *International Journal on Computer Science and Engineering, 4*(5), 859.
33. Singh, A., Sharma, A., Dey, N., & Ashour, A. S. (2015). Web Recommendation Techniques–Status. *Issues and Challenges, 5*(2), 57–65.
34. Singh, A., Sharma, A., & Dey, N. (2015). Semantics and Agents Oriented Web Personalization: State of the Art. *International Journal of Service Science, Management, Engineering, and Technology (IJSSMET), 6*(2), 35–49.

Chapter 3
Sifting Through Hashtags on Twitter for Enterprising Tourism and Hospitality Using Big Data Environment

Sapna Sinha, Vishal Bhatnagar and Abhay Bansal

Abstract Big Data and its importance in inferencing a value out of it is not hidden from anyone. Social networking sites like Twitter proved to be abundant source of information. Like any other sector tourism data can also be extracted out from tweets posted by people all around. Data available on twitter can be in form of text, photographs, Customer preferences can be identified using twitter analytics which can help service providers to offer personalized services. If tour operator are able to predict trends they can easily set optimized price and prepare well in advance to provide unforgettable trip to their customers. Tour operators adopt list pricing policy for deciding price of the tourism product and also there is no set model available for this. The tour operators set the price which helps them to gain high profit, but due to non- availability of any standard formula the decided price varies with the price offered by competitors. Prices are kept high when season is at the peak and more and more tourists are visiting the place or purchasing the tourist products, similarly price is kept low when season is low. In this chapter authors have proposed pricing model considering different factors that decides rates of the product in the tourism sector. Real time analytics performed on the data available on the web portals or social networking sites are used to get the most trending tourist destination and the tour operators functioning at different destination can set price of their products using the proposed model. Real time analytics will help tour operators to analyze the demand in coming season.

Keywords Tourism · Pricing model · Big data analytics · MapReduce · Hadoop

S. Sinha (✉)
Amity University, Noida, India
e-mail: ssinha4@amity.edu

V. Bhatnagar
Ambedkar Institute of Advanced Communication Technologies and Research, New Delhi, India
e-mail: vishalbhatnagar@yahoo.com

A. Bansal
Amity School of Information Technology, Noida, India
e-mail: abansal1@amity.edu

© Springer International Publishing AG, part of Springer Nature 2018
N. Dey et al. (eds.), *Social Networks Science: Design, Implementation, Security, and Challenges*, https://doi.org/10.1007/978-3-319-90059-9_3

3.1 Introduction

Big Data is being used by service sector to identify the customer preferences and to offer personalized services to them. Big data not only deals with Volume of data, it also deals with Variety, Veracity, Value and Velocity, and in the center lays Complexity. Tourism data is available and can be extracted from various heterogeneous sources like tradition databases managed by tour operators, enterprise data warehouses and social networking sites. Tourism data is available in abundance but in scattered form. Tourism data has all the characteristics of big data (Fig. 3.1).

Tourism data is available and can be extracted from various heterogeneous sources like tradition databases managed by tour operators, enterprise data warehouses and social networking sites. Tourism data is available in abundance but in scattered form, therefore tools and technologies that can collaborate together to get the integrated view of data is needed. Sinha et al. [1] has proposed the framework for consolidating data from heterogeneous sources for effective data analytics using big data analytics (Fig. 3.2).

Besides other available data sources social networking is playing very important role in real time analytics for gaining competitive edge over competitors. Social networking sites like twitter, has proved a goldmine of data and used by many researchers for gaining the answer of their questions. Twitter data can be extracted using API provided by twitter for the developers based on keywords like twitter hastags like: #travelgram, #vacation, #visiting, #instatravel, #instago, #trip, #holiday, #travelling, #tourism, #tourist, #instatraveling, #mytravelgram, #travelingram, #travelgoals, #travel, #traveling, #travelingproblems, #travelingstress.etc. and from those most trending places can be identified. This information can be used the government or service providers for preplanning and setting effective price for their products.

Fig. 3.1 Characteristics of big data (Sinha et al. [1])

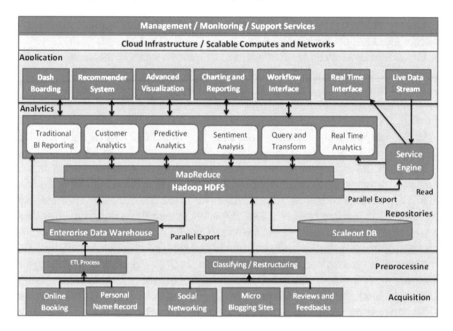

Fig. 3.2 Framework of tAdvisor (Sinha et al. [1])

Setting a right price for the tourism product is one of the challenging job. Right price of tourism products can lead to generation of huge profit whereas if product is priced wrongly then there is a chance that customers may drift away to new vendor.

Tourism sector depends on many factors like: Season, climate, infrastructure, facilities, services, political condition, tourist destinations and environment. Change of any one factor has impact on overall business. There are many pricing model available, but there is no specific pricing model available for tourism domain that keeps factors mentioned above into consideration.

Factors that are considered before setting a price are: position of the product and services in the market, target customers and cost. Position of product and services in the market helps to decide price that can be offered, if there are competitors in the market price should be kept around the price offered by the competitors. Information about the target customer helps to keep the base price of the product that is in reach of the target customers. Cost of the product or services can be used in addition to profit margin for deciding net price. The different types of existing pricing models are:

Cost Plus Pricing: It is a cost-based pricing method, in this total cost, labor cost is added with profit margin. This method has assured profit returns but ignores competitions.

Value-Based Pricing: It is a strategy for setting different price for different customers which they are willing to pay.

Hourly Pricing: It takes time and expense into consideration while setting a price, charges are set as per hourly bases.

Portfolio-Based Pricing: It identifies the tourism mix for the customers with different income group and then price is set for the identified tourism mix.

Tiered and Volume Pricing: In tiered pricing, prices are charged as per unit within the range and in volume pricing, price is charged for all units within the range (Fusebill [2]).

In this chapter, authors has proposed pricing model that can be used by stake holders to set price of the tourism product. MapReduce is used for implementation of proposed algorithm due to its compatibility to work on large scale data or big data. The chapter is divided into different sections to make is more organized. In Sect. 3.2, authors have presented literature survey, Sect. 3.3, discusses different players involved in tourism business, Sect. 3.4 contains description of factors involved in pricing, Sect. 3.5 consist of mathematical model considering all the factors of pricing. In Sect. 3.6 discusses about demand and supply in tourism sector, Sect. 3.7 discusses tour type and accommodation details. In Sect. 3.8 mark up percentage is discussed, Sect. 3.9 discusses about proposed algorithm using MapReduce programming framework. MapReduce is used for the implementation of algorithm because it can easily works on Hadoop, cost effective because Hadoop is freely available, hardware part can be accommodated using cloud environment, it uses HDFS which uses authentications, and Sect. 3.10 includes results and discussion, followed by Sect. 3.11 on conclusion and future work.

3.2 Literature Survey

Big data has started gaining its importance in tourism sector due to its increased impact inside the organization and within whole domain. In tourism sector big data analytics can be used to develop more customer centric applications (Song H., 3). In [4] author studied the perception of both domestic and international student towards the hotel industry.

Sinha et al. [1] has identified different challenges in the tourism sector, like the complexity of the available data in different silos, lack of standard platform for big data analytics and technological alignment. The authors have also proposed framework for big data analytics which will in-tegrate data from multiple sources and allow tourism industry to compre-hend customer preference and to develop strong bond with the customers by providing right service at right time.

The aim of any business is to gain revenue, which is directly related to the price set for the product. The revenue is directly related price and volume tradeoff. If the price set is too high, customers will not purchase that product but it also reflects the desirability of customer for the particular product [5]. Setting appropriate price maximizes the profit earned, where price relies on market demand, cost and competitions [6]. Kim et al. [7] proposed the mathematical model for optimal booking of patients to increase the profit to run the healthcare setup. In [8] authors have studied the difference between activity based and volume based pricing, according to their study volume based costing system has flaws.

According to study conducted [9] the sector is using haphazard pricing strategies, there is no set pricing model used by tourism sector. The small business operators identify the floor price of the product and change it according to customer and price charged by their competitors. Avlonitis et al. [10] conducted the survey and found that list pricing- policy adopted by the majority of the surveyed companies. Companies are using customer's information for cash discount and competition based information for deciding trade discounts.

The key factor for getting success in the tourism sector is setting appropriate price of the product. The set price should be homogeneous, unambiguous and reasonable (Kotler et al. [11]). Pricing in Tourism is elastic in nature and there are many determinants that decides price of tourism product.

According to (Kotler et al. [11]) availability of alternate options, prices within budget of customer, travel category falls in necessity or luxury, duration of visit and change in rates is permanent or temporary. Kotler et al. [11] also discusses about life cycle of the tourism product, like other products tourism product life cycle consists of phases namely: Discovery, Launch, Stagnation and Decline. Discover is first phase of tourism product lifecycle, in this phase new destinations are explored. Second phase is the Launch, in this phase tourists start visiting the new explored destination. In third phase Stagnation, explored destination reach to maturity level and quality of services falls below due to peak exploitation of destination environment and resources.

In fourth phase is basically the dead phase in which profit falls to minimum level and service providers start withdrawing their business from that destination. There are different pricing strategies used while deciding price of tourism product, Premium pricing, Penetration Pricing, Economy Pricing and Price Skimming are the strategies (Kotler et al. [11]). Premium Pricing is charged for the luxury and when service provider has competitive edge over other competitors. Penetration Pricing are the initial price charged by service provider at the time of entering into the market and after getting stable in the market price is increased. Economy Pricing is very low price or minimum price. Price skimming is the high price charged by service provider, seeing which other competitors enter into the market and price falls due to increase supply.

This chapter discusses the need of pricing model which takes the entire factor into consideration, for this many research papers, literature available on internet and blogs were referred.

3.3   Players of Tourism Business

There are different players involved in functioning or running tourism business are:

Retail Travel Agents

Retail travel agents are also known as travel agents. The job of travel agents is to sell the product of tour operators to the customers. They work in association with tour operators and works for bringing the business for them. Retail agents, works in retails space and sells packages through their retail outlets. The source of earning of retail travel agents are the commissions from tour operators. Usually they get 10% of the retails price as a commission.

Domestic and Overseas Wholesalers

Domestic and overseas wholesaler's works through distribution networks of retail travel agents and online agents on behalf of tour operator. In return they also get commission for the business generated through them. Often they work as intermediary between tour operators and retail agents. 20% of the retails price is offered to them as a commission by tour operators.

Inbound Tourism Operators

Inbound tourism operators (ITOs) design and coordinate all travel arrangements on behalf of overseas agents and wholesalers. They negotiate price costs and other components of the tour like transportation and accommodations of the tourists. They also get commission for the business generated through them. Usually 25–30% of retail rate is offered to them as a commission by tour operators.

Tour Operators or Suppliers

Tour Operators are the actual supplier of the tourism product. They offer commissions to other players of the business for generating business for them. They set net rate and retail rate of the products offered by them. A tour operator appoints retail travel agents or wholesalers for selling their product on their behalf. All strategic decisions are taken by tour operators to run their business.

Domestic Customers takes services from tour operators or retail travel agents. The retail travel agents are connected to tour operators and wholesale agents, wholesalers also has tour operators network for generating business for them. Overseas Customers take services from tour operators, wholesaler travel agents or retail travel agents. Where wholesaler travel agents has network of tour operators and inbound tour operators and retail travel agents also has network of inbound tour operators and wholesaler agents which has tour operators network. Besides all above mentioned distribution channels both domestic and overseas customers can directly purchase product from internet.

Figures 3.3 and 3.4 shows the interconnection between different players for domestic and overseas customers.

Fig. 3.3 Players involved in business for domestic customers

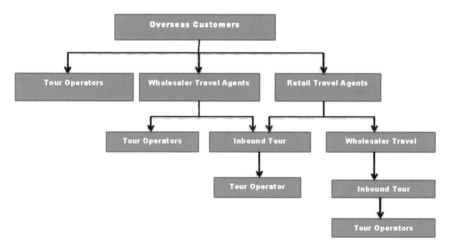

Fig. 3.4 Players involved in business for overseas customers

3.4 Key Factors of Pricing

Price is also known as Rate in tourism industry. There are two types of rates, namely net rate and retail rate. Net rate is the gross rate of shelf rate which includes operating cost and profit margin. It is the minimum rate of the product that can be offered to customer. Retail rate includes net rate plus commissions to be given to different players.

$$\text{Net Rate} = \text{Operating Cost} + \text{Profit}$$

$$\text{Retail Rate} = \text{Net Rate} + \text{Commissions}$$

Operating Costs

Operating costs is the expenses incurred for running the business like cost of employee, infrastructure, network, advertisement, promotion, stationary, electricity etc. operating costs can be categorized into fixed cost and variable cost.

Fixed Cost

Fixed cost remains static that means it doesn't change with change of input or output. Fixed cost includes cost of building, rent, insurance, registrations, licenses and cost of infrastructure.

Variable Cost

Variable cost changes with the change of input or output. It includes cost of salary, electricity, maintenance, stationaries, linen, marketing and promotions etc.

Profit Margins

Profit margins are the extra percentage of operating cost that is earned by any business. It is usually decided by the supplier after seeing the products offered by competitors and in which their product fits in.

Distribution Costs

Distribution costs are the cost incurred in paying commission to retail travel agents, domestic and overseas wholesaler travel agents and inbound tourism operators.

Other Factors

Competition

The price offered by competitors plays very important role in setting price. One can't set price too high or too low than the price offered by competitors. If the price is too high, customer will go to their competitor and if it is too low than it will be very difficult to get even the operating cost of the business.

Demand

Tourism business is also based on demand and supply theory. If demand is very high, tour operator has limited products to offer, than high price will paid by real desirable customers only. Profit can be earned which will compensate to the less profit during low demand period.

Target Markets

Target market means, customers to whom business is targeting. It can be domestic or overseas customers. Overseas customers generally go for package deals where as domestic customers are interested in retails products. Profit margin increases if customers are from overseas.

Seasonality

Season also decides flow of customers. Tour operator can charge good rate when season is in peak and can offer discount when season is off.

Type of Tourism

There are different types of tourism, like business trips, recreational trips or educational trips. Different types of products can be offered depending of the type of tourism. Like if person is going for the business trip, to and fro ticket can be offered in subsidized rate. Similarly for educational trips, products with transport facilities and accommodations can be offered.

3.5   Dynamic Pricing Model for Merchandising Tourism and Hospitality

In the proposed model authors have considered all the factors that affect pricing of the tourism product. The proposed pricing model are as follows:

3.5.1   Seasonality (S)

Natural (N): There are many natural factors affects the tourism industry. People like to visit hill stations or cool places in summers and similarly to hot places in winters. The effect of natural factors can easily observed when people do not get accommodation due to overcrowded tourist destination. Hotels charge in haphazard manner from their customers and quality of services also degrades. The natural factors considered are:

Temperature = T * x1
Hours of Sunshine = HOS * x2
Latitude and Altitude = L&A * x3
Climate, Rain/Snowfall = C * x4
Snow Depth = SD * x5

$$N = \frac{T * x_1 + HOS * x_2 + L\&A * x_3 + C * x_4 + SD * x_5}{T + HOS + L\&A + C + SD}$$

Institutional (I): Purpose of visit also has impact on pricing charged by tourism sector, like if person visits for Business purpose frequently they prefer to stay in same hotels which economical and provides good service. There may be other purpose too, like: school holidays, religious place visit and calendar effects. All these factors are considered in the proposed model.

School Holidays = SH * x6
Religious Holidays = RH * x7
Calendar Effects = CE * x8
Business Seasons = BS * x9

$$I = \frac{SH * x_6 + RH * x_7 + CE * x_8 + BS * x_9}{SH + RH + CE + BS}.$$

Thus the following factor can be calculated,
$x_n \to 0$ to 1 $[n = 1$ to 39] and all others are constant

$$F1 = \frac{a * N + b * I}{a + b}. \tag{3.1}$$

3.5.2 Business Operating Costs (BOC)

Fixed Cost Items (FCI)

FCI is the cost of items which do not change and remain same throughout the year. The items included in this category is:

Salaries = S * x10
Office Lease = OL* x11
Interest and repayment on startup cost borrowing = I&R * x12
Trade association membership fees = TAM * x13
Banking Services = BS * x14
Professional Indemnity Insurance = PII * x15
Web Hosting = WH * x16

$$FCI = \frac{S * x_{10} + OL * x_{11} + I\&R * x_{12} + TAM * x_{13} + BS * x_{14} + PII * x_{15} + WH * x_{16}}{S + OL + I\&R + TAM + BS + PII + WH}$$

Variable Cost Items (VCI)

VCI is the cost of the items which changes due to external factors like increase in taxes due to government policy, amount spent on marketing etc.

Sales & Marketing = SM * x17
Marketing Campaign = MC * x18
Cost of Sales = COS * x19
Gas Bills = G * x20
Electricity Bills = E * x21
Cleaning, maintenance, repairs = CMR * x22

$$VCI = \frac{SM * x_{17} + MC * x_{18} + COS * x_{19} + G * x_{20} + E * x_{21} + CMR * x_{22}}{SM + MC + COS + G + E + CMR}$$

$$F2 = \frac{c*FCI + d*VCI}{c + d} \tag{3.2}$$

3.5.3 Competition (Comp)

Market Entry (ME)
New Entrants = NE * x23
Professionalism = P * x24

$$ME = \frac{NE * x_{23} + P * x_{24}}{NE + P}$$

Product Competition (PC)
Climate = CL* x25
Safety = SAF * x26
Reputation = REP * x27
Accessibility = ACC * x28
Price = PR * x29
Value for Money = VFM * x30
Attraction/Activities = AA * x31

$$PC = \frac{CL * x_{25} + SAF * x_{26} + REP * x_{27} + ACC * x_{28} + PR * x_{29} + VFM * x_{30} + AA * x_{31}}{CL + SAF + REP + ACC + PR + VFM + AA}$$

Company Competition
Degree of Rivalry = DOR

$$F3 = \frac{e*ME + f*PC + g*DOR}{e + f + g}. \tag{3.3}$$

3.6 Demand and Supply in Tourism

Like any other sector, this sector also works on demand and supply theory. If demand is high and supply is low, prices can be kept high so that only eligible customer can buy it. Similarly if demand is low prices are kept low.

DEMAND

Individual (Education, awareness, paid holiday, family influence) = IND * x32
Economic (Cost of travel, cost of product, competitive price, exchange rate) = ECO * x33

Fig. 3.5 Relationship between marketing and promotion

Geographic (Seasonality, Location and distance, attraction available) = GEO * x34

Destination (safety and security, quality of product, technology and development) = DES * x35

Political (Visas formalities, health checkups, currency, transport facilities) = POL * x36

$$DEM = \frac{IND * x_{32} + ECO * x_{33} + GEO * x_{34} + DES * x_{35} + POL * x_{36}}{IND + ECO + GEO + DES + POL}$$

SUPPLY

Infrastructure (telecommunication, accommodation) = INF * x37

Superstructure (Facilities constructed primarily to support visitation and visitor activities) = SUP * x38

Attraction (Theme parks, museums, buildings, ski-slopes) = ATT ** x39

$$SUP = \frac{INF * x_{37} + SUP * x_{38} + ATT * x_{39}}{INF + SUP + ATT}$$

Cumulative factor (Fig. 3.5)

$$F4 = \frac{h*DEM + i*SUP}{h + i}. \tag{3.4}$$

3.7   Tour Type and Accommodation Details

Tourism Type

Tourism itself is a very broad term. There are various different types of tourisms. Each in its own significant way attracts a lot of tourists.

3.7.1 Recreational

It consists of various tourist offers which persuade people to visit an area. These offers cover a wide range of interests. There are a lot of other crowd pullers such as medicinal offerings, spiritual leaders and recreational parks such as Disneyland etc.

3.7.2 Sports

Sporting events greatly promote tourism to a country. There are a huge number of sports fans all over the world and thus significant tournaments and events attract tens of thousands of tourists. The world cups of various sports such as football, cricket, hockey; tennis grand slams and tours; sporting events such as the Olympic, commonwealth, asian, Pan-American games; all are very famous sporting events and bring with them a large number of tourists to their host cities.

3.7.3 Business Trips

Business trips also has significant share in the tourism in the country. By creating favorable policies for organizations to invest in a country, huge revenues are generated because of increase in job opportunities for local population as well as influx of people from the organizations to the country. People on business trip are very rich and therefore are able to spend a lot of money during their stay in the country.

Thus the factor considering tour type and can be calculated as, $yn \rightarrow 0$ to 1 [$n = 1$ to 16] and all others are constant

Recreation = REC * y1
Sports = SPO * y2
Business trip = BUS * y3

$$TT = \frac{REC*y_1 + SPO*y_2 + BUS*y_3}{REC + SPO + BUS}$$

Accommodation details can also be considered for price estimation. It consists of

Room type = RT * y4
Stay Length = ST * y5
Number of persons = NOP * y6

$$AD = \frac{RT*y_4 + ST*y_5 + NOP*y_6}{RT + ST + NOP}$$

The cumulative factor considering tour type and accommodation details can be calculated as

$$F5 = \frac{j*TT + k*AD}{j + k}. \tag{3.5}$$

3.8 Mark up Percentage

Markup percentage is the commission amount received from adjunct services used by the customer of any service provider like, if tourist purchases gift from the gift sow of the hotel, hotel gets certain percentage of the profit made by gift shop as a markup percentage.

Transport = 0.01 * TRA * y7
Camping Grounds = 0.01 * CG * y8
Gift Shops = 0.01 * GS * y9
Guest house operation = 0.01 * GHO * y10
Hotel Operation = 0.01 * HO * y11
Restaurant Operation = 0.01 * RO * y12
Travel Agency Service = 0.01 * TAS * y13

$$F6 = \frac{0.01*TRA*y_7+0.01*CG*y_8+0.01*GS*y_9+0.01*GHO*y_{10}+0.01*HO*y_{11}+0.01*RO*y_{12}+0.01*TAS*y_{13}}{0.01*TRA+0.01*CG+0.01*GS+0.01*GHO+0.01*HO+0.01*RO+0.01*TAS} \tag{3.6}$$

Commission

Commission is paid to travel agent, distributors and inbound tour operators for the business brought by them.

Travel Agents = 0.01 * TA * y14
Travel Wholesales = 0.01 * TW * y15
Inbound Tour Operator = 0.01 * ITO * y16

$$F7 = \frac{0.01 * TA*y_{14} + 0.01 * TW*y_{15} + 0.01 * ITO*y_{16}}{0.01 * TA + 0.01 * TW + 0.01 * ITO} \tag{3.7}$$

The process of estimation can prove to be too heavy for the conventional data handling techniques to cope with as the data sets are really formidable. The problem can be however solved using big data analytics. Map Reduce programming has been used by the authors to quickly and efficiently calculate their estimates. Hadoop Cluster Mode: Pseudo-Distributed Hadoop cluster mode is used that is Hadoop daemons run on the local machine.

The pseudo code for the same is as follows:

3.9   Algorithm of Proposed Model

Mapper Algorithm:

N = number of hotel
A[N] = Pricing Index of hotels
x[i][] = factors of ith hotel
y[i][] = factors of ith hotel
A [i] = Pricing index of ith hotel
for i = 1 to n {

$$N = \frac{T * x_1 + HOS * x_2 + L\&A * x_3 + C * x_4 + SD * x_5}{T + HOS + L\&A + C + SD}$$

$$I = \frac{SH * x_6 + RH * x_7 + CE * x_8 + BS * x_9}{SH + RH + CE + BS}$$

$$F_1 = \frac{a * N + b * I}{a + b}$$

$$FCI = \frac{S*x[i][10]+OL*x[i][11]+I\&R*x[i][12]+TAM*x[i][13]+BS*x[i][14]+PII*x[i][15]+WH*x[i][16]}{S+OL+I\&R+TAM+BS+PII+WH}$$

$$VCI = \frac{SM*x[i][17]+MC*x[i][18]+COS*x[i][19]+G*x[i][20]+E*x[i][21]+CMR*x[i][22]}{SM+MC+COS+G+E+CMR}$$

$$F_2 = \frac{c * FCI + d * VCI}{c + d}$$

$$ME = \frac{NE * x[i][23] + P * x[i][24]}{NE + P}$$

$$PC = \frac{CL*x[i][25]+SAF*x[i][26]+REP*x[i][27]+ACC*x[i][28]+PR*x[i][29]+VFM*x[i][30]+AA*x[i][31]}{CL+SAF+REP+ACC+PR+VFM+AA}$$

$$F_3 = \frac{e * ME + f * PC + g * DOR}{e + f + g}$$

$$DEM = \frac{IND * x_{32} + ECO * x_{33} + GEO * x_{34} + DES * x_{35} + POL * x_{36}}{IND + ECO + GEO + DES + POL}$$

$$\mathrm{SUP} = \frac{INF * x_{37} + SUP * x_{38} + ATT * x_{39}}{INF + SUP + ATT}$$

$$\mathrm{F_4} \frac{h * DEM + i * SUP}{h + i}$$

$$\mathrm{TT} = \frac{REC * y[i][1] + SPO * y[i][2] + BUS * y[i][3]}{REC + SPO + BUS}$$

$$\mathrm{AD} = \frac{RT * y[i][4] + ST * y[i][5] + NOP * y[i][6]}{RT + ST + NOP}$$

$$\mathrm{F_5} = \frac{j * TT + k * AD}{j + k}$$

$$\mathrm{F_6} = \frac{0.01*TRA*y[i][7]+0.01*CG*y[i][8]+0.01*GS*y[i][9]+0.01*GHO*y[i][10]+0.01*HO*y[i][11]+0.01*RO*y[i][11]+0.01*TAS*y[i][12]}{0.01*TRA+0.01*CG+0.01*GS+0.01*GHO+0.01*HO+0.01*RO+0.01*TAS}$$

$$\mathrm{F_7} = \frac{0.01 * TA * y[i][14] + 0.01 * TW * y[i][15] + 0.01 * ITO * y[i][16]}{0.01 * \mathrm{TA} + 0.01 * \mathrm{TW} + 0.01 * \mathrm{ITO}}$$

Reducer Algorithm

{
Net Rate $= \mathrm{F_2} + \mathrm{F_3} + \mathrm{F_5} + \mathrm{F_6}$
Retail Rate $=$ Net Rate $+ \mathrm{F_7}$
return (Net Rate, Retail Rate)
}.

3.10   Results and Discussions

In (Sinha et al. [12]) MapReduce program is implemented on 150000 tweets extracted from twitter, after cleaning tweets are categorized into different labels of issues raised by the tourism (Table 3.1).

(Sinha et al. [12]) used tweets to identify trending top 25 tourist destination, this information can help service providers, government and tour operators for prior planning. Deciding the optimal price for the services the proposed mathematical model was implemented on data of hotels, Net Rate and Retail Rate of each hotel was calculated. Figure 3.6 shows the format of the data considered for the result calculation:

Table 3.1 The four major groups and the significant words in each group (Sinha et al. [12])

Group	Significant words
Political	Government management, Corruption free environment, political stability, safety, security
Social	Urbanization, Technological progress, human development index, tourist taxis, local language, health issues, global standardization, heavy rush, sanitary condition
Tourist attraction	Hotel, catering, leisure, sports, level of comfort, architecture, culture, transport connectivity, natural and cultural value, art, literature, music, theater
Infrastructure	Road, lightening, parking, gardens

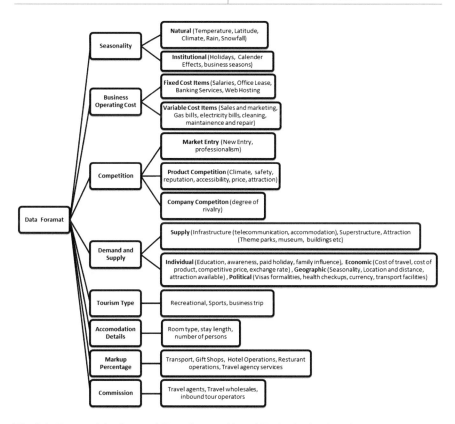

Fig. 3.6 Format of the data used [Data Source: Akamai Technologies, Banglore]

The data was implemented on the proposed model and net rate and retail rate of hotels were calculated. Figure 3.7 shows the graphical representation of net rate

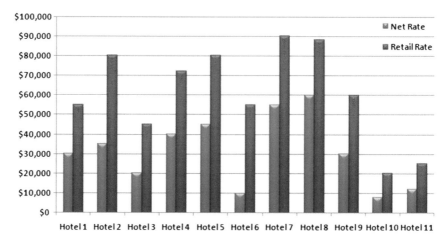

Fig. 3.7 Graphical presentation of net rate and retail rate of each hotel

Table 3.2 Numerical presentation of net rate and retail rate of each hotel

Hotels	Net rate	Retail rate
1	$30,000	$55,000
2	$35,000	$80,000
3	$20,000	$45,000
4	$40,000	$72,000
5	$45,000	$80,000
6	$10,000	$55,000
7	$55,000	$90,000
8	$50,000	$88,000
9	$30,000	$60,000
10	$8,000	$20,000
11	$12,000	$25,000

and retail rate of the 11 hotels. These calculated rate changes when the parameters considered changes (Table 3.2).

The value of the different factors are assumed while calculating Net Rate and Retail Rate, only the actual value of the factors can help to compare the actual and calculated rates. The main challenge is the frequent change in the value of the factors can lead to inconsistent rate schedule. It is also suggested not to keep too many schedules, best is to keep quarterly rate schedule decided well in advance.

3.11 Conclusion and Future Work

In this chapter, authors have proposed a dynamic pricing model pricing model for merchandising tourism and hospitality that can be used by stake holders to set price of the tourism product. The aim of any business is to gain revenue, which is directly related to the price set for the product. The revenue is directly related price and volume tradeoff. If the price set is too high, customers will not purchase that product but it also reflects the desirability of customer for the particular product. Setting appropriate price maximizes the profit earned, where price relies on market demand, cost and competitions. The results demonstrate the estimation of net rate and retail rate of 11 hotels which can be used to take strategic decision to maximize the profit earned.

If any of the factor changes, new retail and net rate can be calculated depending on season, demand/supply, tour type, accommodation, purchases, services availed.

There is some interesting work left for the future and can include:

- This analysis can be further carried out on Fully Distributed Cluster mode that is Hadoop daemons run on a cluster of machines.
- Inclusion of new parameters that will add new dimension to the work which can be continued for further enhancement in the already existing algorithm
- Setting standard value for the factors will help in authenticating results.

References

1. Sinha, S., Bhatnagar, V., & Bansal, A. (2017). A framework for effective data analytics for tourism sector: Big data approach. *International Journal of Grid and High Performance Computing (IJGHPC), 9*(4).
2. Fusebill, (2016). *Recurring billing models – difference between tiered versus volume pricing.* http://blog.fusebill.com/2013/10/28/tiered-vs-volume-pricing-do-you-know-the-difference.
3. Song, H., & Liu, H. (2017). Predicting tourist demand using big data. In *Analytics in smart tourism design* (pp. 13–29). Berlin: Springer Internation-al Publishing.
4. Akaegbu, J. B. (2013). An exploratory study of customers' perception of pricing of hotel service offerings in Calabar metropolis, Cross River State, Nigeria. *International Journal of Business and Social Science, 4*(11).
5. Skinner, R. C. (1970). The Determination of Selling Prices. *The Journal of Industrial Economics, 18*(3), 201–217.
6. Claret, J., & Phadke, P. D. (1995). Pricing - A challenge to management accounting. *Financial Management, 73*(9), 20–21.
7. Kim, S., & Giachetti, R. E. (2006). A stochastic mathematical appointment overbooking model for healthcare providers to improve profits. *IEEE Transactions on systems, man, and cybernetics-Part A: Systems and humans, 36*(6), 1211–1219.
8. Briers, M., Luckett, P., & Chow, C. (1997). Data fixation and the use of traditional versus activity based costing systems. *Abacus, 33*(1), 49–68.
9. Tosun, C., & Jenkins, C. L. (1998). The evolution of tourism planning in third-world countries: A critique. *Progress in Tourism and Hospitality Research, 4*(2), 101.
10. Avlonitis, G. J., & Indounas, K. A. (2006). Pricing practices of service organizations. *The Journal of Services Marketing, 20*(5), 346–356.

11. Kotler, P., & Armstrong G. (1999). Chapter 11 pricing products: Pricing strategies PRINCI-PLES OF MARKETING 11-1 Upper Saddle River: Prentice Hall.
12. Sinha, S., Bhatnagar, V., & Bansal, A. (2016). Multi-label Naïve Bayes classifier for identification of top destination and issues to accost by tourism sector. *Journal of Global Information Management*, *26*(3), Article 5.

Chapter 4
Hashtag# Perspicacity of India Region Using Scalable Big Data Infrastructure Using Hadoop Environment

Arushi Jain and Vishal Bhatnagar

Abstract Social media is rapidly providing new standards of interaction between individuals in the recent era. It is known as a computer-intermediated tool that tolerates people to share, or create information, medical notes/reports, ideas, and pictures/videos through virtual communities. The online citizens (netizens) are able to create a colossal network of people to communicate with. Social media such as Facebook, Twitter, Youtube, Instagram and Tinder have prevalent uses that produce copious amount of data which is beyond the ability of normal software tools to process in the given elapsed time. Apache Hadoop project is the most famous open sourced frameworks for large scale computation on the commodity hardware. Hadoop has become kernel for distributed operating system for big data. There are two core components associated with Hadoop–Hadoop Distributed File System (HDFS) and MapReduce. MapReduce distributed the tasks on multiple nodes in the cluster, the developer only have to write code rest is taken care by MapReduce. The generated data from these social sources is real time and **includes information about author's daily activities, feelings and** emotions. The messages often include images, geo-locations and many other annotations. This vast data repository provides researchers with opportunities to study the individuals' behavior/emotions that subject to different conditions. In this chapter we will find the trending tweets from January 2017 to September 2017 depending upon the eight prominent themes that emerged from the data set and trending tweets depending upon the geolocation. For this we divide India depending upon the region that is North India, West India, South India, East India, Central India, Northeast India

Keywords Big data · Hadoop · Twitter · MapReduce · Hadoop distributed file system · Tweets · Hashtag#

A. Jain (✉) · V. Bhatnagar
Department of Computer Science and Engineering, Ambedkar Institute of Advanced
Communication Technologies and Research, Geeta Colony, New Delhi 110031, India
e-mail: arushijain1391@gmail.com

V. Bhatnagar
e-mail: vishalbhatnagar@yahoo.com

4.1 Introduction

Social media is rapidly providing new standards of interaction between individuals in the recent era. It is known as a computer-intermediated tool that tolerates people to share, or create information, medical notes/reports, ideas, and pictures/videos through virtual communities. The online citizens (netizens) are able to create a colossal network of people to communicate with. Social media such as Facebook, Twitter, Youtube, Instagram and Tinder have prevalent uses that produce copious amount of data daily. The generated data from these social sources is real time and includes information about author's daily activities, feelings and emotions. The messages often include images, geo-locations and many other annotations [5]. This vast data repository provides researchers with opportunities to study the individuals' behaviour/emotions that subject to different conditions. The generated data from portals such as Twitter is in an unregulated environment hence provides huge amount of inherent knowledge and a fresh perspective about human feelings and activities. Traditionally, such kind of researches was done by the means of surveys, interviews, feedback forms and brain storming sessions. These methods cannot be replicated and the test space is also limited, which considered the main drawback. Alternatively, social media mining can assist the automation of the whole process as well as significantly increase the people diaspora being observed. Recently, Twitter mining becomes prominence for researchers and agencies using the data and its analysis with respect to their individual domains. Big Data is the term used for the data which is beyond the ability of normal software tools to process the given elapsed time. The big data is characterised by 5 V's: Volume, Velocity, Veracity, Varity and Value. Traditionally computation was done on single processor but later on distributed environment has evolved which allowed to distribute computing task on multiple processors. With the technological and growth in communication technology, humans are generating data in large volume. Gadgets are becoming smart day by day, inbuilt sensors are generating data at very fast pace. Organizations and researchers are using this data set to extract knowledge out of it to gain competitive advantages over the competitors. Volume of big data can easily understood with the figures provided by facebook that 600 TB of data is generated daily and data warehouse of facebook has experienced 3 times growth in the volume of the data stored, 300 h video is uploaded to You Tube every minute and on Instagram user uploads approx. 21600 photos every day. In total social media, IoT and other sources of data are generating approximately 2.5 Exabyte of data. Due to low cost storage technologies, powerful multicore processors, high speed networks has big data analytics possible and efficient. Many cloud service providers have started providing Hadoop as a Platform, Data as a Service, analytics as a Service, HBase, Big Query and Prediction API.

Seeing the importance of Big Data Analytics after prediction made on the bases of twitter data in US presidential election, Big Data Analytics suddenly got the importance worldwide, also French Presidential election and Manchester attack prediction too proved the importance of Big Data Analytics. Government of different countries have started funding projects on Big Data Analytics. Big data can be categorized into: Structured Data, Unstructured Data and Semi Structured Data

Structured Data:

Structured data has well defined structure and can be organized pre-defined format. Databases are the example of structured data. Structured Data requirement of ACID properties (Atomicity, Consistency, Isolation and Durability)

Unstructured Data:

Unstructured data do not have any format or structure. Text, docs, video are the example of unstructured Data. Unstructured data has a requirement of BASE property (Basically Available, Soft, and Eventual consistency)

Semi Structured Data:

Semi Structured Data does not contain any formal format like structured data, but it follows certain semantics, tags or marker. JSON and XML are the example of semi structured Data.

Semi Structured Data

```
<?xml version="1.0" encoding="UTF-8"?>
-<note>
<to> Engineer</to>
<from> Manager</from>
<heading> Reminder</heading>
<body> Don't forget to follow deadline!</body>
</note>
```

Apache Hadoop project was the result of Google MapReduce and Google File System paper is a standout amongst the most famous flexible, open sourced frameworks for large scale computation on the commodity hardware. There are to core components associated with Hadoop–HDFS(Hadoop Distributed File System) and MapReduce. There are other projects like Pig, Hive, Hbase, Flume, Oozie and Sqoop etc. based around Hadoop platform are all together referred as "Hadoop Ecosystem" The hadoop distributed file system (HDFS) stores data on the commodity hardware cluster. Hadoop uses two types of nodes for storing the data. NameNode is used to store metadata of the data and DataNode stores the actual data which is replicated three times on the clusters. For reading a data from HDFS firstly NameNode is referred and then information about the blocks used to store the data is fetched. MapReduce distributed the tasks on multiple nodes in the cluster, it works as a unix pipeline. It takes care of automatic parallelism and distribution of task, it also take care of automatic re-execution of task on failure. It also handles all the housekeeping task from developer, the developer only have to write code rest is taken care by MapReduce. Hadoop has become kernal for distributed operating system for big data. The component of hadoop ecosystem, ZooKeeper maintains status information, configuration information and location information as coordination data across the nodes for reliable messaging. HBASE is another open source project of Hadoop Ecosystem, it is inspired from Google Big Table supports Non-relational, distributed database developed in Java. HBASE has Master Server which assigns regions to region servers and monitors the health of region servers, which handles client read/write requests. Flume—Data Integration Framework is a distributed data collection service. It can help user in collection, integrating and moving huge volume of data and has fault tolerant features and recovery mechanism. It support all available data formats. Sqoop provides easy import/export of parallel databases. Sqoop is suit of tools that connect Hadoop and database systems for deep analysis. It also export MapReduce results to end-users, it also have ability to import data from SQL databases to Hive data warehouse. Tedious user-side code can be generated automatically and act as interface between SQL and Hadoop.

Pig and Hive are the analytical languages part of the Hadoop Ecosystem. Hive is the SQL like interface to Hadoop. It allows to query data warehouse using SQL queries for the users not compatible or comfortable in writing code in Java. Pig Latin is a high level scripting language supported by Hadoop. It processes data one step at a time, very easy to understand and debug. Oozie—Job Workflow and Scheduling is a web application for workflow scheduler for Hadoop. Oozie cascades jobs and allows to restart from the failure. Hue is a web console for Hadoop, it is platform custom application. Mahout is a machine learning tool having inbuilt distributed and scalable machine learning algorithms for building intelligent applications. It has inbuilt functions for data mining operations.

4.2 Related Work and Motivation

Twitter mining becomes prominence for researchers and agencies using the data and its analysis with respect to their individual domains [37]. For example, healthcare sector uses twitter feed to analyze the outbreak of influenza and other communicable diseases for better handling. Moreover, the analysis of political campaigns on social media to judge the mood of the mob is also prevalent. The tone of hashtags being used can shed some light upon whether government policies are being well received attributing the hashtag to either positive, negative or neutral [18]. The Twitter data comes along with annotations such as geo-locations, emoticons, images and the other tags to signify the author's mood. All these factors lead to better analysis of the data set, which ultimately lead to precise results.

Sentiment analysis, linguistic analysis, network analysis, content analysis and many other simplistic models are considered popular methods for social media data analysis. In [6] location of the tweet user is estimated by analysing the content of the tweet posted by users in discussion based on the same topic. The probabilistic estimation is used and probable cities are identified and accuracy is calculated. Cheng [10] proposed probabilistic framework for predicting location of user which is purely content based in absence of geospatial data, no IP address, private login information is needed. The proposed method identifies words in tweets having strong geographical relevance. In their work, lattice based neighbourhood smoothing model for refinement of result. Davis [11] proposed the concept of relationship between following-follower to trap the location of location less tweets. Gelernter [14] proposed the approach of geo-parsing the microtext for determining the location of the user. The problem with approach was that it can only predict the location of the user having proper noun in the text. Hecht [19] has used location information provided by user in their profile, which is not the effective method because most of the time information provided by the user is not accurate. Mahmud [30] has proposed algorithm which can easily infer the home location of user, the algorithm can easily find city, state and geographic region of the user using the content of tweet and behaviour of user while tweeting. The proposed algorithm uses statistical and heuristic classifiers for location prediction.

Zhang [40] has used supervised machine learning to weigh fields of metadata associated with twitter message and used feature of world gazetteer. This method works efficiently when geolocation is enabled on the devices used to tweet. Khanwalkar [26] has presented the approach that uses frequency of user for tweeting to collate multilingual tweets into a documents and location-entity clustering.

Chen H. et al. in their special issue for business intelligence research [8] suggested the current progress focusing on the present research areas in the fields of big data analytics suggesting the big impact on the industries from big data. The MIS Quarterly Special Issue is intended to serve as the platform for the Information systems in the fields of BI&A using the emerging Big Data and Prediction analytics presenting the "best of best" research with high research quality displaying the real world problems.

Auley and Leskovec in their research on Hidden Factors and Hidden topics benefited in providing the database to carry out the analysis and prove the results. Also their research publication "Understanding Rating Dimensions with the Review text" benefitted in understanding the review text from the amazon review database taken under consideration for recommending the products in reference to the customer reviews and satisfaction feedback by them. The authors have successfully combined the latent rating dimensions that are usually tough to interpret with the latent review topics for the purpose of latent-factor recommender systems using learning by topic models like LDA. Furthermore their approach is more accurate in predicting the product ratings through the review text by the feedback by the customers. Further highlighted different algorithms used in predictive analytics impressively presented in their Oracle White Paper (2010), "Predictive Analytics: Bringing Tools To the Data". Focusing on predictive analytics and proposing the better classification approach for predictive analytics. It efficiently describes the predictive models, descriptive models and the Decision models. However, different functionality i.e. Classification, Regression, Anomaly Detection, Attribute Importance, Association Rules, Clustering and Feature Extraction are described for different algorithms they use and their applicability. These have been very helpful in applying the application area in the dissertation work.

Aggarwal C. et al. have focused on association rules, clustering and market basket analysis in their publication, "Finding Localized Associations in Market Basket Data" have propounded in discovering localized associations in data segments using clustering. They are more concerned about the customer patterns instead of their aggregate behaviour and have proved that localized associations are more efficient in case of customer patterns for calculating the market basket data. The clustered item set and the aggregate item set are compared to find important correlations in data. Their algorithm is able to find a significant percentage of item sets beyond a random partition of the transactions. The applicability for their research takes into account the target marketing applications.

Another application of predictive analytics is being proposed by Ravi V., Kurniawan et al. in their research publication "Soft Computing system for Bank Performance Prediction"(2007). As the title suggests, they covered the efficient bank performance prediction application through an ensemble system with contributing models as- multi-layered feed forward network trained by back propagation (MLFF-BP), Radial Basis Neural Network (RBNN), Probalistic Neural Network (PNN), fuzzy rule based classifier. An independent production set is used to validate the results and a tenfold-cross-validation is performed on the training set. The ensemble is proved to be more efficient in Ph.D. thesis submitted in Florida State University, "Predicting poor bank profitability: a comparison of neural network, discriminant analysis and professional human judgement".

"An ensemble for Neural Networks for weather forecasting", by Maqsood I. et al. describes the ensembles constituting the Artificial Neural Networks(ANN) and the learning algorithms for efficient weather forecasting. The performance of the proposed model compared with MLPN, ERNN, RBFM, HFM predictive models and the regression techniques. The temperature, wind speed and relative humidity are used as the variables considered to train the training set and for the seasons spring, winter, summer and fall, a 24-h ahead weather forecast is predicted. Hence, the performance and the reliability of the 7 models are evaluated to prove that RBFN is slightly more accurate than HFM for weather forecasting. The research gives a very significant insight of various soft computing techniques in real life applications that helped in understanding the objective of the dissertation work.

The soft computing techniques in the medical application were is studied and proposed by Pratap A. et al. in their research publication entitled "Soft Computing Models for Predictive Grading of Childhood Autism—A Comparative Study" (2014). The article propounded by them covers the performance of soft computing models for assigning grades in identifying childhood autism facilitating the predictive analytics using soft computing techniques in medical applications. The results displays that acceptable prediction accuracy is achieved using the soft computing techniques in autism grading that faces primarily the challenges of uncertainty and imprecision.

Acampora G and Cosma Georgina in their research publication entitled "A Hybrid Computational Intelligence Approach for Efficiently Evaluating the Customer Sentiments in E-Commerce Reviews", 2014 is taken as one of the base papers for this dissertation. It has been very helpful in understanding the customer sentiments for imparting computing intelligence and hence, performing business intelligence through predictive analytics. The authors propounds a very innovative framework for analyzing the customer's textual reviews efficiently to extract their sentiments, compute the corresponding numerical ratings for the products in order to benefit the companies to accordingly plan their future activities and business endeavors.

Daoudi, M. et al. in their research on MapReduce and Big data successfully propounded parallel differential evolution clustering algorithm. It has been very helpful in designing the algorithm for this dissertation. The paper entitles "Parallel Differential Evolution Algorithm based on MapReduce", 2014 successfully implemented the differential evolution clustering algorithm using MapReduce in order to deal efficiently optimize the results for Big data [16]. Gene expression analysis is performed by the authors such the algorithm implemented on 3 levels consists of the DE operations at each level. It is observed to provide accurate and stable results in comparison with K-means and the PSO MapReduce.

Karwa S. and Chatterjee N. in their research "Discrete Differential Evolution for Text Summarization", 2014, majorly helped in designing the objective function for the dissertation such the optimized review text analysis can be done. The research by the authors proposes a modified version of DE and propounds Discrete DE for the text summarization applications. It has been observed a 95.5% improvement in time with discrete DE in comparison to the conventional DE methods.

Abuobieda A. et al. propounded in their research publication entitled "Differential Evolution Cluster-based Text Summarization Methods", the differential evolution to optimize the data clustering and perform efficient text summaries.

Coletta L.F.S. et al. in their research on twitter text sentiment analysis facilitated the dissertation work with the data preparation of the amazon review dataset through their publication entitled "Combining Classification and Clustering for Tweet Sentiment analysis", 2014. The authors performed sentiment analysis on tweets categorizing them as positive or negative using traditional classifiers Naïve Bayes, Maximum Entropy and SVM. The resulting classifier propounded is observed to be competitive with the best results found in the literature.

4.2.1 Problem Formulation and Research Methodology

The following Fig. 4.1. describes the research methodology adopted.

To fetch the data from twitter we used apache flume, apache flume is used to inject unstructured data into HDFS. It has a flexible structure and reliable for the services like aggregating, moving and storing unstructured data. We store the data in HDFS which is in JSON format by default. Further to read the all the fields, we used map-reduce, JSON SerDe (Serializer/Deserializer) to read JSON data. In this, we are storing data in hdfs from twitter by using apache flume, reading the data and after map-reduce, storing the result again in hdfs.

Twitter is a micro blogging website used by people all over the world to broadcast or receive messages. 140 character long messages are known as tweet, which is used to analyze the different patterns, finding trends and prediction. Twitter is used worldwide for finding interesting people, as unlike other social networking sites, twitter does not require agreement from other side to get connected. It is also great platform form breaking news, because it has been observed that news outbreak is faster on tweeter than any other mode of communications.

The internal format or structure of tweet is the major source of information which reveals lots of hidden information. The information associated with each tweet is as follows:

Fig. 4.1 Research methodology

1.   Id : it is a unique identifier for each tweet
          "id": 831569219296882008,
2.   Actor: it is user who has tweeted,   it contains metadata about user.
      "actor"
{
objectType": "person"
"id":
"link" :
"displayName":
"postedTime":
"image":
"summary":
"links":
"friendsCount":
"followersCount":
"listedCount":
"statusesCount":
"twitterTimeZone":
"verified":
"utcoffset":
"preferredUsername":
"languages":
"location":
"favoiritesCount":
}
3.   Verb : defines type of action by user like, "post", "share" or "delete"
      "verb": "post"
4.   Generator : defines utility used to post the tweet. There are two subfield "displayName" and "link" which defines source application used to generate tweet.
    "generator":
{
   "displayName": "Twitter for Android",
   "link":"http:VVtwitter.comVdownloadVandroid"
}

5. Provider: defines provider of the activity. "service", "displayName" and "link" subfield specifies objectType, name of the provider and link to the website of the provider:

"provider":
{
  "obectType": "service",
  "displayName": "Twitter",
  "link": "http:\/\/www.twitter.com"
}
6. inReply To: provides link to tweet in which reference tweet has been done.
"inReplyTo":
{
  "link"; "http:\/\/twitter,com\/statuses\/3243435354565"
}
7. location : represent information about the place where tweet is created.
"location"
{
  "objectType":   ,
"displayName":   ,
"name":   ,
"country_code":   ,
"twitter_country_code":   ,
"link":   ,
"geo":   ,
"twitter_place_type":
},
8. geo :   points to location of tweet generated
"geo":
{
  "type" : "Points",
"coordinates":
[
    ----------------,
    ----------------,
]
}
9. twitter_entities :   this contains list of urls, hashtags
"twitter_entities":
{
"hashtags":[

```
{
}
{
}
"urls":[
{
}
"user_mentions":[
{
}
"media":[
{
}
```

10. twitter_extended_entities : this object refers to multiple images and their attributes associated with the tweets.

11. Body: this object carries actual tweet text.

"body": "hello , I am testing tweeter."

12. objectType: for first time tweet it will contain "note" object and for retweet, it will contain "activity"

13. object: defines tween being posted or shared.

14. postedTime – defines the time tweet was posted

The MapReduce programming framework is employed to process the twitter data. The core of Hadoop framework is the MapReduce programming paradigm. Originally, MapReduce was developed by Google to enhance the parallel processing. Through the MapReduce framework a huge amounts of data can be processed in parallel. Data is processed individually through large Hadoop clusters, and finally aggregated to give the final result. The data can be both Structured as well as Unstructured. The Hadoop framework also consists of the Hadoop file system, which popularly known as HDFS. The HDFS is a distributed portable file system. Its cluster consists of a Namenode and a Datanode. The Namenode manages the file system metadata, whereas the Datanode stores the actual data. The advantage of the HDFS file system is its ability to store huge amounts of data in blocks across different machines in a large cluster on cheap commodity hardware. The reliability and security of data is maintained by replicating data across multiple hosts. Typically, the MapReduce consists of two individual tasks, namely the Map phase and the Reduce phase. The MapReduce architecture consists of Master/slave architecture. Master node consists of a Job tracker and a Task tracker. Each Master node controls the multiple slave nodes, where each of them comprises of a Task tracker. In the MapReduce programming paradigm, the job splits the input data into blocks. In the map phase these chunks of data are processed individually in a parallel manner, wherein the map task is executed on each chunk of data individually. Subsequent, the outputs from the map phase sorted and fed as inputs to the reduce phase. Usually, the master node is fed with a large set of data along with the problem; it chopped the problem into smaller sub problems and doles them out to the worker nodes. In the reduce phase, the outputs gathered from the map phase are fed to the reduce tasks. The Master node takes the answers to the sub problems and combines them as defined by the Hadoop framework to eventually provide the final output which represents the answer to the original problem. Inputs and outputs to the MapReduce phase work as <Key, Value> pairs, thus the MapReduce framework views any input to the job as a set of <key, value> pairs and similarly any outputs are also constructed as a set of <key, value> pairs even they may be of different types.

The input and output types of a MapReduce job are as follows:

(Input) <k1, v1>→map→<k2, v2>→combine →<k2, v2>→reduce →<k3,v3> (output)

The MapReduce Job's function is to control the execution through two major functions as follows. First, it chops the dataset into independent blocks. Secondly, it facilitates parallel processing. All the intermediate values are grouped together based on a common output key and are passed onto the reducer class which further performs the aggregation function. The actual execution is done by the Task tracker by treating each Mapper/Reducer task as a child process of separate JVM. Both the input and output to the MapReduce paradigm is stored in the HDFS.

4.3   Implementation Steps

1. By using apache flume we first fetched the data and stored it into HDFS. Afterward, a preprocessing of the data was performed by: (i) removing all the hashtags, while keeping only the hashtags' text, (ii) remove all the non-letter symbols, punctuations, and http links, and (iii) replace the two identical letters by a single letter for example "verrrryyy" was replaced by "very", while keeping words such as "too" as they were.

2. After the pre-processing step, data analysis was performed to find out the following:

   (1) Trending tweets from the January 2017 to September 2017.The prominent themes that emerged from the data set were political and international affairs, economic and social affairs (for example ManKiBat: which is an Indian radio programme hosted by the prime minister of India, where he addresses the people of the nation), sports (for example Dalit which is a traditional Indian caste system), entertainment, technology, health and wellness, cultural and religious festivals, crime and punishment. The most significant ten words in each group from the prominent themes are depicted in Table 4.1.

   (2) Trending tweets depending upon the geolocation. For this we divide India depending upon the region that is North India, West India, South India, East India, Central India, Northeast India. Various states which were covered into these regions are depicted in Table 4.2.

Table 4.1 Words from prominent themes

Group	Significant words
Political and international affairs	Government, ministerial, party, political, diplomatic, legislative, administrative, governance, embassy, consulates, decision making, political action, security
Economic and social affairs	Demonetization, black money, population, census, hike, jobs, pensioners, power, entrepreneurs, tax, unemployed, MannKiBaat
Sports	Sports, cricket, football, wickets, athlete, hockey, tennis, athletics, motorsport, races. World T20, Dalit
Entertainment	Movie, latest release, theater, art. concert, literature, music, leisure, architecture, hotel, catering, gardens, parks
Technology	Robotics, biometrics, sensor, artificial intelligence, computer games, hardware, software, aircraft, space, aeronautical, satellite
Healthcare and wellness	Nutrition, weight loss, health, medical insurance, diet, fitness, doctors, hospital, disease, precautions, treatment, examine
Cultural and religious festivals	Religious, god, temple, worship, festive mood
Crime and punishment	IPC, arrested, crime, guilty, death, custodial, juvenile, stolen, raped, murdered, corruption

Table 4.2 Words from prominent themes

Region	States covered
North India	Haryana, Himachal Pradesh, Jammu and Kashmir, Punjab, Rajasthan Uttar Pradesh, Uttrakhand
West India	Goa, Gujarat, Maharashtra
South India	Andhra Pradesh, Karnataka, Kerala, Tamil Nadu, Telangana
East India	Bihar, Jharkhand, Orissa, West Bengal
Central India	Chhatisgarh, Madhya Pradesh

3. In map reduce, firstly we read the complete data line by line. After that, we created the objects according to our requirement.
4. Approaches to extract geo-location information from the tweets. There are multiple approaches used to extract geo-spatial location from the tweets. General approaches used are:

   1. Extraction of Geo-Spatial Meta Data associated with tweets. This approach is used only when geo-location is enabled on the device used for tweeting.
   2. Content-Based approach in which machine learning algorithm is used to analyze the tweet text and based on the content user location is estimated.
   3. Extraction of location from the profile of user location field.

From the above approaches if device of the user is not geo-spatial location enabled approach second and 3rd are used, otherwise first approach proves to be more effective and accurate.

Mapper Algorithm
#Hash tag Extraction:

```
1.   class Hashtags {
2.   private String text;
3.   private List <Integer> indices;
4.   public String getText() {
5.   return text;
6.   }
7.   public void setText(String text) {
8.   this.text = text;
9.   }
10.  public List <Integer> getIndices() {
11.  return indices;
12.  }
13.  public void setIndices(List <Integer> indices) {
14.  this.indices = indices;
15.  }
16.  }
```

Geo location Extraction:

```
1.   public class Geo {
2.   private String type;
3.   private List <Float> coordinates;
4.   public String getType() {
5.   return type;
6.   }
7.   public void setType(String type) {
8.   this.type = type;
9.   }
10.  public List <Float> getCoordinates() {
11.  return coordinates;
12.  }
13.  public void setCoordinates(List <Float> coordinates) {
14.  this.coordinates = coordinates;
15.  }
16.  }
```

Mapper and Reducer Algorithm

1. Determine geolocation in terms of latitude and longitude by using My GeoPosition and Compose search string: geocode: latitude, longitude, radius, searchterm
2. Assume N is the number of tweets

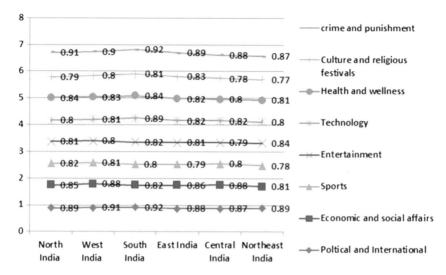

Fig. 4.2 Percentage of tweets in each month

3.   String a[8][], where a[i][] array of strings representing group i
4.   c[8] represents the number of tweets belonging to group i = c[i]
5.   p[8] represents the tweets belonging to group i = p[i]
6.   for i=1 to N
7.   for j=1 to 8
8.   if(tweet[i] has any word in a[j][]
9.   c[j]++
10. End for
11. End for

Reducer Algorithm:

1.   For i=1 to 8
2.   Calculate the percentage of tweet belongs to category i
3.   End for

In Figs. 4.2 and 4.3 x axis represents the months and the regions while y axis represents percentage of the tweets belongs to each category. From the Fig. 4.3 it can be interpreted that political and international affairs was the most discussed topic in the month of August while least in February. Economic and social affairs were the trending topic in the month of March while least in the month of January.

Similarly from the Fig. 4.3. it can be interpreted that North Indians discuss crime and punishment the most while culture and religious affairs the least. While South Indians largely discuss about technology, political and international affairs while least interested in sports.

However, some limitations of the proposed approach are addressed as follows, which can be considered in the future:

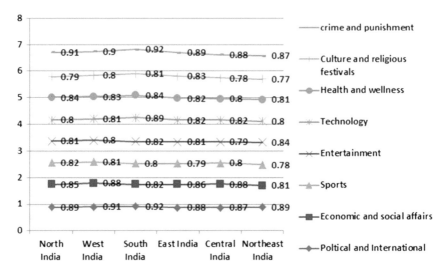

Fig. 4.3 Percentage of tweets regionally

- The used Pseudo-Distributed hadoop cluster mode is hadoop daemons run on the local machine.
- Sentiment analysis is another popular tool used to infernetizens opinions about events, policies, product offerings and other entities. Social media portal users react to events and product launches expressing their personal opinion about them. Twitter allows only a 140-character long Tweet. Thus, the messages are short, crisp and to the point. Opinion mining techniques can be applied to data set.
- Querying twitter based on geocoded data is not the perfect method because each tweet specific location can be trapped only if twitter user has location enabled for tweets; this parameter is by default set to disabled.

  For getting geolocation of the tweet user has to set location enabled for tweets, if it is disabled the next thing done by twitter is to fetch the "from" data from the profile of the user. If location is enabled on the mobile device and user moves from one place to another while tweeting its GPS coordinates are trapped, but if location is not enabled and from data from the profile of the user may not be accurate information. The user can be citizen of one country and at the time of posting tweet he/she may be in some another country, this is a noise in the data. Although this prevents privacy of user but at the same time induce gaps in the available data also many people do not have location enabled phone, their tweets appear via any publicly accessible twitter location search method.
- Many people across the world do not have access to digital technology or they may not be interested in taking part on any discussion on twitter, therefore they are not the part of data. These portions of population are excluded from the available data. Even the population having access to digital technology and geo location enabled

devices, there are few users who take active part where as some are only interested in reading tweets.

4.4 Conclusions

In this chapter we have found the trending tweets from January 2017 to September 2017 depending upon the eight prominent themes that emerged from the data set and trending tweets depending upon the geolocation. For this we divide India depending upon the region that is North India, West India, South India, East India, Central India, Northeast India. The generated data from these social sources is real time and includes information about author's daily activities, feelings and emotions. The messages often include images, geo-locations and many other annotations. This vast data repository provides researchers with opportunities to study the individuals' behavior/emotions that subject to different conditions.

Acknowledgements We would like to thank Ambedkar Institute of Advanced Communication Technologies and Research for providing us the infrastructure for carrying out the research work efficiently.

References

1. Al-Jarrah, O. Y., Yoo, P. D., Muhaidat, S., Karagiannidis, G. K., & Taha, K. (2015). Efficient machine learning for Big data: A review. *Big Data Research, 2*(3), 87–93.
2. Aye, K. N., & Thein, T. (2015). A platform for big data analytics on distributed scale-out storage system. *International Journal of Big Data, Intelligence, 2*(2), 127–141.
3. Barker, K. J., Amato, J., & Sheridon, J. (2008). Credit card fraud: Awareness and prevention. *Journal of Financial Crime, 15*(4), 398–410.
4. Bhanu, S. K., & Tripathy, B. K. (2016). Rough set based similarity measures for data analytics in spatial epidemiology. *International Journal of Rough Seta and Data Analysis, 3*(1), 114–123.
5. Carr, C. T., & Hayes, R. A. (2015). Social media: defining, developing, and divining. *Atlantic Journal of Communication, 23*(1), 46–65.
6. Chandra, S., Khan, L., Muhaya, F. B. (2011). Estimating twitter user location using social interactions–a content based approach. In *2011 IEEE Third International Conference on Privacy, Security, Risk and Trust (PASSAT), and 2011 IEEE Third International Conference on Social Computing (SOCIALCOM)* (pp. 838–843). IEEE.
7. Chen, M., Mao, S., & Liu, Y. (2009). Big Data: A survey. *Springer-Mobile Networks and Applications, 19*(2), 171–209.
8. Chen, H., Chiang, R., & Storey, V. (2012). Busines intelligence and analytics: From Big Data to big impact. *MIS Quaterly, 36*(4), 1–10.
9. Chen, X., Vorvoreanu, M., & Madhavan, K. (2014). Mining social media data for understanding student's learning experience. *IEEE Transaction on Learning Technologies, 7*(3), 246–259.
10. Cheng, Z., Caverlee, J., & Lee, K. (2010). You are where you tweet: a content-based approach to geo-locating twitter users. In *Proceedings of the 19th ACM International Conference on Information and Knowledge Management* (pp. 759–768). ACM.
11. Davis Jr, C. A., Pappa, G. L., de Oliveira, D. R. R., & de L Arcanjo, F. (2011). Inferring the location of twitter messages based on user relationships. *Transactions in GIS, 15*(6), 735–751.

12. Deepak, D., & John, S. J. (2016). Information systems on hesitant fuzzy sets. *International Journal of Rough Seta and Data Analysis, 3*(1), 55–70.
13. Fedoryszak, M.,Tkaczyk, D. and Bolikowski,L. (2013). Large scale citation matching using Apache Hadoop. Springer-Research and Advanced Technology for Digital Libraries Lecture Notes in Computer Science (Vol. 8092, pp. 362–365).
14. Gelernter, J., & Mushegian, N. (2011). Geo-parsing messages from microtext. *Transactions in GIS, 15*(6), 753–773.
15. González-Vélez, H., & Kontagora, M. (2011). Performance evaluation of MapReduce using full virtualisation on a departmental cloud. *International Journal of Applied Mathematics and Computer Science, 21*(2), 275–284.
16. Hashem, I. A. T., Yaqoob, I., Anuar, N. B., Mokhtar, S., Gani, A., & Khan, S. U. (2015). The rise of "big data" on cloud computing: Review and open research issues. *Information System, 47,* 98–115.
17. Hassanien, A. E., Azar, A. T., Snasel, V., Kacprzyk, J., & Abawajy, J. H. (2015). *Big Data in complex systems: Challenges and opportunities.* Studies in Big Data (Vol. 9). Berlin/Heidelberg: Verlag GmbH, Springer.
18. Hays, R., & Daker-White, G. (2015). The care.data consensus? A qualitative analysis of opinions expressed on Twitter. *BMC Public Health, 15*(1), 1.
19. Hecht, B., Hong, L., Suh, B., & Chi, E. H. (2011). Tweets from justin bieber's heart: The dynamics of the location field in user profiles. In *Proceedings of the SIGCHI Conference on Human Factors in Computing Systems* (pp. 237–246). ACM.
20. Hoffmann, A. O. I., & Birnbrich, C. (2012). The impact of fraud prevention on bank-customer relationships. *International Journal of Bank Marketing., 30*(5), 390–407.
21. Huang, T., Lan, L., Fang, X., An, P., Min, J., & Wang, F. (2015). Promises and challenges of big data computing in health science. *Big Data Research, 2*(1), 2–11.
22. Ibrahim, S., Jin, H., Lu, L., Qi, L., Wu, S., & Shi, X. (2009). Evaluating MapReduce on virtual machines: The Hadoop Case. Springer: Cloud Computing. Lecture Notes in Computer Science (Vol. 5931, pp. 519–528).
23. Jacobs, A. (2009). The pathologies of big data. *Communications of the ACM—A Blind Person's Interaction with Technology, 52*(8), 36–44.
24. Jagadish, H. V. (2015). Big Data and science: Myths and reality. *Big Data Research, 2*(2), 49–52.
25. Jin, X., Wah, B. W., Cheng, X., & Wang, Y. (2015). Significance and challenges of big data research. *Big Data Research, 2*(2), 59–64.
26. Khanwalkar, S., Seldin, M., Srivastava, A., Kumar, A., & Colbath, S. (2013, September). Content-based geo-location detection for placing tweets pertaining to trending news on map. In *The Fourth International Workshop on Mining Ubiquitous and Social Environments* (p. 37).
27. Kolomvatsos, K., Anagnostopoulos, C., & Hadjiefthymiades, S. (2015). An efficient time optimized scheme for progressive analytics in Big Data. *Big Data Research, 2*(4), 155–165.
28. Labrinidis, A., & Jagadish, H. V. (2012). Challenges and opportunities with big data.ACM-. *Proceedings of the VLDB Endowment, 5*(12), 2032–2033.
29. Lee, Y. (2013). Toward scalable internet traffic measurement and analysis with Hadoop. *ACM SIGCOMM Computer Communication, 43*(1), 5–13.
30. Mahmud, J., Nichols, J., & Drews, C. (2014). *Home location identification of twitter users.* arXiv:1403.2345.
31. Ryan, T., & Lee, Y. C. (2015). Multi-tier resource allocation for data-intensive computing. *Big Data Research, 2*(3), 110–116.
32. Samanta, S., Acharjee, S., Mukherjee, A., Das, D., & Dey, N. (2013). Ant Weight Lifting algorithm for image segmentation. In *IEEE International Conference on Computational Intelligence and Computing Research* (pp. 1–5).
33. Shabeera, T. P., & Madhu Kumar, S. D. (2015). Optimizing virtual machine allocation in MapReduce cloud for improved data locality. *International Journal of Big Data Intelligence, 2*(1), 2–8.

34. Srivastava, U., & Gopalkrishnan, S. (2015). Impact of Big Data analytics on banking sector: Learning for Indian Bank. *Big Data, Cloud and Computing Challenges, 50,* 643–652.
35. Terry, M. (2009). Twittering healthcare: Social media and medicine. *Telemedicine and e-Health, 15*(6), 507–510.
36. Tiwari, P. K., & Joshi, S. (2015). Data security for software as a service. *International Journal of Service Science, Management, Engineering, and Technology, 6*(3), 47–63.
37. Tumasjan, A., Sprenger, T. O., Sandner, P. G., & Welpe, I. M. (2010). Predicting elections with twitter: What 140 characters reveal about political sentiment. *ICWSM, 10,* 178–185.
38. Wahi, A. K., Medury, Y., & Misra, R. K. (2014). Social Media: The core of enterprise 2.0. *International Journal of Service Science, Management, Engineering, and Technology, 5*(3), 1–15.
39. Wahi, A. K., Medury, Y., & Misra, R. K. (2015). Big Data: Enabler or Challenge for Enterprise 2.0. *International Journal of Service Science, Management, Engineering, and Technology, 6*(2), 1–17.
40. Zhang, W., & Gelernter, J. (2014). Geocoding location expressions in twitter messages: A preference learning method. *Journal of Spatial Information Science, 2014*(9), 37–70.
41. Zikopoulos, P., & Eaton, C. (2011). *Understanding big data: Analytics for enterprise class hadoop and streaming data.* McGraw-Hill Osborne Media.

Part II
Social Network Application:
An Introduction

Chapter 5
A Survey on the Scalability
of Recommender Systems for Social
Networks

C. Sardianos, N. Tsirakis and I. Varlamis

Abstract It is typical among online social networks' users to share their status, activity and other information with fellow users, to interact on the information shared by others and to express their trust or interest for each other. The result is a rich information repository which can be used to improve the user experience and increase their engagement if handled properly. In order to create a personalized user experience in social networks, we need data management solutions that scale well on the huge amounts of information generated on a daily basis. The social information of an online social network can be useful both for improving content personalization but also for allowing existing algorithms to scale to huge datasets. All current real-world large-scale recommender systems have invested on scalable distributed database systems for data storage and parallel and distributed algorithms for finding recommendations. This chapter, focuses on collaborative filtering algorithms for recommender systems, briefly explains how they work and what their limitations are.

Keywords Collaborative filtering · Recommender systems · Scalability
High-performance

5.1 Introduction

A social network is a platform that facilitates individuals, connected through social relations, such as family, friends, and colleagues [1, 2] to communicate with each

C. Sardianos (✉) · I. Varlamis
Department of Informatics and Telematics, Harokopio University of Athens,
Omirou 9, Athens, Greece
e-mail: sardianos@hua.gr

I. Varlamis
e-mail: varlamis@hua.gr

N. Tsirakis
Department of Computer Engineering & Informatics, University of
Patras, Rio, Patras 26500, Greece
e-mail: tsirakis@ceid.upatras.gr

© Springer International Publishing AG, part of Springer Nature 2018   89
N. Dey et al. (eds.), *Social Networks Science: Design, Implementation,*
Security, and Challenges, https://doi.org/10.1007/978-3-319-90059-9_5

Fig. 5.1 Components of the
Recommender Systems

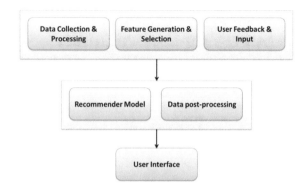

other. When social networks expand at world-scale, as it is the case with the most popular social networking sites and applications (e.g. Facebook, YouTube, Instagram, Twitter etc.), the supporting software and hardware must scale too, in order to support the millions of users. According to [3], scalable computing systems maintain consistent performance under an expanded workload. Referring to scalability in social networks, we expect no compromise on performance from a social network and also expect a standard level of latency, without significant changes, no matter how its provision changes as new users are connecting or new content is being added.

Undoubtedly, the continued and differentiated expansion of social networks has changed the way in which users communicate and interact with each other. There are now more ways to exchange ideas, share opinions and learn in collaboration. In the same time, the need for new features in social networking applications, which will allow user to follow this expansion and delve with the increasing information, has emerged. Trying to meet this need, Recommender Systems have come to provide a solution and there are many techniques that have been used for different approaches to this problem. Such systems become integral parts of most social networking applications, takes advantage of the stated or implicit preferences of users, the additional information concerning their interaction with other users and the content they access or share, and makes suggestions for new content, contacts or actions. They usually act as systems trying to predict the user's score for any potential item [4] or the user's opinion based on some item aspects.

As depicted in Fig. 5.1, the main components of a recommender system are:

- Data Collection and Processing: This is the task for the collection of data which most of the times are large.
- Feature Generation and Selection: In this task algorithms are responsible for feature generation and selection that can be performed either pre-calculate these features or dynamically generates them.
- User Feedback and Input: In this task the user is invited through the system interface to provide ratings for items in order to construct and improve his model.
- Recommender Model: This is the main part of any recommender that orchestrates the recommendation algorithm with all the previous data that it gets.

- Data post-processing: Data post-processing is used in many systems in order to optimize any measure generated by the model.
- User Interface: This is the final step of any system and is the component where the user interacts with the system.

Lately, the field of application of recommender systems has expanded in a wide area of domains such as creating movie or music recommendations, suggesting related news, finding useful scientific research papers, recommending possible social connections or potential products users could be interested in buying. But the type of domains recommender systems are used for are not limited to the above. There have been developed many domain-specific RSs such as for finding experts based on a query string and the domain characteristics [5], or potential researcher for collaborating with [6], even for supporting suggestions on loans etc. [7], or just simply suggesting pages of interest in Twitter [8]. In general, RSs aim to solve the information overload problem for the users of a social network by recommending items, which can either be content, products, services or even other users. In general, the input of the process for creating recommendations is a set of users U and a set of items I, whilst the function f that represents their relation is:

$$f : U \times I \rightarrow R \tag{5.1}$$

This means that the recommendation algorithm "rates" each user-to-item relation with a predicted score that represents the interest of user u for item i, which in terms is the rating that the system predicts the user would give to this item and is created in one of the following ways: (i) by defining a similarity between the user profile and the item, using their content information (e.g. description, stated preferences etc.), (ii) by defining a similarity between user profiles and then using only users with similar profiles to the target user to predict item ratings, (iii) by filtering out items of low interest to the target user [9]. In the latter case, information filtering methods are based on user demographic information (demographic), the content of previously rated items (content-based filtering [10]) or simply the ratings and the ratings provided by other users, also referred as collaborative filtering [11] and are able to predict unknown item-ratings for a user. Several combinations of more than one technique from the aforementioned categories have also been proposed in the literature resulting to hybrid recommender systems [12]. Based on the predicted ratings for the unseen items, recommender systems create a set of items to be recommended to user.

The success of Recommender Systems is undoubtedly over the last ten years or more, but any current real-world large-scale recommender has to consider two of the main points of concern: The quality of the produced recommendations, which is defined by the actual recommendation accuracy, and the scalability, which is limited by the computational cost to provide these recommendations [13]. Scalability is a problem associated with recommendation algorithms (more often in collaborative filtering techniques) because computation normally grows at a linear rate to users and items [14]. A recommendation technique that can be efficient for a limited number of users and items may fail to produce satisfactory recommendations when the volume of the data increases. In general, some of the most important characteristics of collaborative filtering are the ability to generate personalized recommendations based on the user's prior activity in the system, or the activity data of other users that seem to have similar tastes to the given user and the ease of incorporation depending on the selected approach. Collaborative filtering algorithms can be categorized into three major types based on its functionality (Memory-based, Model-based and Hybrid), that are fully analyzed in Sect. 5.2. While many recommender system algorithms have been developed, unless the system can reach unusually high diversity, each algorithm can face different types of problems. One of the main issues collaborative filtering algorithms face these days is scalability and data management due to the exponential growth of user data all over the web.

While product ratings can be found in many product review sites, another useful information provided by social media is the social network information, user-level interactions (likes/dislikes, comments etc.), that is a useful type of information for improving RS predictions. This is based on the idea that a user's circle of friends directly affects the user's ratings. When using this social information, we can use friendship information alone, combine it with user provided ratings, or even filter recommendations using social information. In the process of dealing with scalability and time performance issues that recommender systems usually face, using user profile information for computing user similarity and applying user clustering can be a useful approach. Other approaches build on dimensionality reduction techniques in order to reduce the problem complexity (e.g. Singular Value Decomposition-SVD). When social and other information is added to item ratings the complexity of the recommendation problem increases and scalability solutions have to be reconsidered.

This chapter focuses on collaborative filtering algorithms for recommender systems and surveys the various alternatives for processing huge and sparse rating graphs, with or without external knowledge. The section that follows briefly illustrates the steps of the recommendation process and briefly describes the most widely adopted techniques. Section 5.3 lists the open challenges for recommender systems. Section 5.4 targets on the solutions that have been proposed in the literature for handling recommendations over large data and more specifically in algorithms and implementations that scale up to millions of users and items and billions of ratings. The solutions fall into three main categories: i) those that focus on Factorization of the user-to-item ratings' Matrix and propose parallel and distributed implementation, ii) those that partition the huge set of ratings into clusters taking advantage of external knowledge from the social network (e.g. user or item content similarity, social network bonds etc.) and thus split the recommendation problem into smaller parts, iii) hybrid methods that build mainly on external knowledge trying to boost the results of the distributed Matrix Factorization methods. Finally, Sect. 5.5 summarizes the chapter and highlights the future challenges in the field of recommender systems for social networks.

Fig. 5.2 Phases of
recommendation process

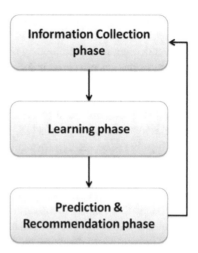

5.2 Recommendation Techniques

From a system-oriented perspective, the recommendation process takes as input a collection of users and their ratings for a collection of items and produces a per-user personalized set of recommended items. In order to achieve this, a recommender system operates in three stages, which is depicted in Fig. 5.2 and detailed in the following.

Information collection phase: In the first phase, the system collects any relevant information about the users in order to create their profile. Depending on the type of the system, this information must have a minimum size and detail so as the desired model that will be used in the recommendation phase could be prepare. There are systems with specific information collection protocols under which they use this information in order to determine the current state of knowledge and support any decision making for learning any available user profile information for all users taking part in the recommendation process. The information used as input by Recommender Systems in order to prepare a full picture of their users. Such types are either high quality explicit feedback, which includes explicit input by users regarding their interest in items or implicit feedback by inferring user preferences indirectly through observing user's behavior [15].

Learning phase: In the second phase, the system feed the collected information to a learning algorithm that filters and exploits users' features/attributes that will better serve in the recommendation phase. In other words, the system builds the model which is actually an abstraction of the relationship between the items and users.

Prediction and Recommendation phase: This last phase predicts and/or recommends what kind of items the user may prefer. This can be performed either directly, based on the dataset collected in the first phase of information collection, which results to the memory-based or model-based approaches or combined with data that refers to other user activities and preferences, which results to hybrid approaches [12], which are all explained in the following section. The user reaction to the recommended items is continuously recorded and used as a feedback that improves the recommender system performance over time.

In the case of Recommender Systems for Social Networks, the information provided within the social network serves for three main objectives: (a) improving the quality of predictions and recommendations [16, 17], (b) proposing or generating novel Recommender Systems [18, 19], and (c) elucidating the most significant relationships between social information and collaborative processes [20, 21].

There are three main kinds of recommendation techniques based on the information employed for filtering out items of low interest to the target user, predicting item ratings and producing recommendations [9, 22]: (i) Collaborative Filtering techniques that mainly focus on the user-item ratings, (ii) Content-based Filtering techniques that employ additional content for users and items and define several similarity measures and matching models to produce recommendations and (iii) Hybrid techniques that combine the merits of both worlds.

5.2.1 Content-Based Filtering

Content-based filtering is also referred to as cognitive filtering. In content-based filtering techniques, an item is recommended to a user when similarity between this item and the items user had already expressed his preference in the past is high. More specifically, the recommendation is being made by comparing the items' content description. The content of each item is represented as a set of descriptors or keywords and the user profile is represented with the same keywords and is created by examining the content of items which have been seen by the user in the past. In order to use content-based filtering, the similarities for all items are being computed, the items get ranked based on these similarities and the top-N ranked items are finally get recommended to the target user.

5.2.2 Collaborative Filtering

Collaborative filtering (CF) is considered as one of the leading approaches for creating recommendations and that is why it is used by some of the largest commercial platforms. The recognition of its usability is shown by the fact that many variations and techniques have been developed for this purpose. The basic idea behind this technique is that a user provides his preferences in the form of ratings for the available items, either implicitly or explicitly and a customer, who seemed to have similar preferences in the past, would probably still have the same preferences. A basic advantage of this kind of techniques is that there is a limited or no need for semantic information in order to produce recommendations. This is the reason behind their popularity among major social network-based applications including Amazon, Netflix, iTunes, IMDB etc.

Collaborative Filtering (CF) is based on user (or item) similarity [23] measured over the users' (or items') rating information. The aim of CF systems [22] is to predict users' interest for items they have not yet reviewed, based on the ratings they have provided for other items and the ratings of other users for all items. The items with the highest predicted ratings are recommended to the user.

Collaborative Filtering systems can be categorized in two major categories: the memory-based that search for the top-k similar users (i.e. users with similar ratings on the commonly evaluated items) or items (i.e. items that have been rated similar to the items preferred by the user) and use only this information to create their recommendations and the model-based, which use all ratings to train a model for predicting user's preferences for an unseen item.

5.2.3 Hybrid Techniques

Hybrid techniques combine more than one filtering strategies, which are implemented as sub-components of the recommender system. This kind of techniques try to integrate characteristics from collaborative filtering and content based techniques with an ultimate goal of enhancing recommendation quality and overcome the disadvantages of the single filtering techniques. Hybrid filtering is classified in six categories (i) mixed hybrid (ii) weighted hybrid (iii) switching hybrid (iv) cascaded hybrid (v) feature-combination hybrid and (vi) meta-level hybrid. One simple approach, proposed by [24] is to create two sets of ranked recommendations (one with each technique) and then combine them to produce one final list.

The success of deep learning networks in several application domains, also opened a new research field for hybrid recommender systems, which feed the deep learning networks both with rating and content information about users and items and improve the quality of recommendations [25]. Although they better solve many several know issues recommender systems face, such as the cold-start problem [26, 27] or the ratings matrix sparsity [28], they still do not handle scalability issues [29].

5.3 The Challenges of Recommender Systems

Some of the most challenging issues Recommender systems face are scalability, diversity and the long tail, sparsity and of course the cold-start problem. In addition, content-based filtering faces the problem of content analysis in the cases where the sets of items lack of a respectively sufficient set of features. This is justified by the fact that the accuracy of the content-based filtering predictions depends on the amount of information used for classifying the items. Finally, the combination of collaborative filtering and content-based filtering approaches in an efficient way still remains an open issue in many hybrid filtering cases. Some major of the already mentioned challenges are described in more details in the next subsections.

5.3.1 Cold-Start Problem

Cold-start problem is one of the major issues for techniques like collaborative filtering and content-based filtering [30]. During the learning stage of these methods, the analysis of information derived by the user's profile at the system, so in scenarios where this information is provided directly by the user, the existence of users with little to none info available is very common. Specifically in collaborative filtering, the problem occurs when the system tries to predict the score of an item while this item may not have been rated at all by any user. Of course the same issue occurs when new items (and thus never rated before) are being added into the system, which is also known as first-rater problem.

When a new user comes into the system, is very difficult for the recommender system to produce prediction, since the user preferences is yet unknown and there are no items in his history, so both collaborative and content-based filtering can hardly compute any user similarity or create any content profile information respectively. This kind of problems can be eliminated by using hybrid approaches, which are presented in the techniques section, since each technique can be more tolerant to this issue.

5.3.2 Data Sparsity

According to [11], some of the largest commercial sites use recommender systems in order to provide recommendations over very large sets of products. When input data (i.e. user-to-item ratings) are not sufficient for calculating user (or item) similarities then we face the data sparsity issue. This constitutes a critical point in the process of creating high accuracy recommendations which may consequently limit the overall applicability of such systems especially in applications with large and sparse data sources. In other words, the items that have not yet received any ratings from a sufficient number of users, in the case of newly added items for example, can not contribute to the recommendation process as they can not be recommended to any user.

This issue occurs as a result of lack of enough information. Representing the entities that participate in the recommendation process (users and items) as a matrix, it is clear that when the data face the sparsity issue, any user vector that contains the user's ratings for all of the items, will contain more zeros. That means that looking for the positions only of the rated items will produce a more compact format. This in terms leads to reduced demand for memory processing resources.

5.3.3 Synonymy

Word synonymy and polysemy are two major issues for many text mining algorithms that depend on text similarity [31]. Consequently it affects content-based recommender systems that rely on textual descriptions of items or user profiles in order to find similarities. For example, a content-based recommender system is unable to understand that the terms "scary movie" and "horror film" in the description of two items have similar meaning, and fails to associate the two items.

The ambiguity introduced by synonymous and polysemous terms in descriptions decreases the recommendation performance and must be considered. Latent semantic analysis techniques [11] and knowledge-based methods are used to overcome the synonymy problem and improve the content-based recommender systems' performance.

5.3.4 Attacks

The recommender system may be vulnerable to attacks that make it to recommend items that otherwise wouldn't be recommended. There are cases where users have the ability to give recommendations on their own. This means that they can give positive recommendations for their items or friends and also negative for competitor's items or friends. This normally shouldn't be allowed. These are called shilling attacks [32].

There are some other attacks, where users exploit the recommendation mechanism by creating fake profiles and providing false ratings to items in order to promote items of their interest. These are called push attacks. Finally, there are attacks that are called nuke attacks which try to make the recommendation algorithm nonfunctional and thus, stop the recommendation process. Due to these kinds of threats, any production level recommender system should be accompanied by some kind of security mechanism against these attacks [33].

5.3.5 Privacy

Privacy plays an important role regardless of the system type. The concern on keeping data private is to identify the limits between privacy and data access for creating personalized modern applications. Of course, defining these limits is a difficult task, as more data is needed for creating a more personalized profile. This is why these limits are easily violated or ignored in recommendation techniques [34], while profile data are gathered and processed. So privacy protection is a crucial point at the process of the data by every recommender system for personalized systems. In order to provide accurate and valuable recommendations, most techniques require using as much information as possible about the user. Of course there are approaches that try to solve this problem. Randomized transformations of the user-item rating matrix, preserve users' differential privacy [35] without significantly degrading the performance of collaborative filtering algorithms.

5.3.6   Explanation

Explanation, or interpretability of recommendations, is also a characteristic of recommender systems. An instinctive argumentation like "since you already like these movies, you will also like this one as well" gets easily understood by the users, no matter the precision of this statement [36]. Unfortunately, there are systems don't provide good explanations and sometimes are not inspiring users to trust the recommendations and increase their satisfaction. Explanations need to be considered as a must in recommendation systems in order to help the user understand how the system works and take part in the recommendations that are made by giving feedback where is needed. An easy way to provide good explanations is through A/B testing. Satisfaction can also be measured indirectly, measuring user loyalty [37].

5.3.7   Stability

The stability problem occurs when the extent of changes in the recommendation algorithm predictions grows. A stable recommender can make users trust more the system as they will get consistent predictions, whereas a recommender that provides predictions that change over time can confuse users. Stability can be measured if we compare the predictions between two periods during which new ratings have added. Several attempts discount the weight of older ratings by time, in order to reduce their influence to the final recommendation [38] but again they do so at the risk of losing information about permanent, long-term interests that are sporadically expressed.

5.3.8   Scalability

Scalability issues starts to exist when the total number of users and items in the system grows excessively, above the level that traditional Collaborative Filtering algorithms reach their limits of performance. This is the point where the computational resources needed for processing become extremely high to be practically used [11]. The problem can be solved with dimensionality reduction techniques, like SVD, that apply several matrix factorization steps in order to produce good quality recommendations with fewer resources, achieving high quality results with better scalability.

When additional information exists, such as user profile, social network information etc., data partitioning can be applied to the original user-item rating matrix and parallel and distributed algorithms can be used to allow maximum scalability. Nayebzadeh et al. proposed an improved version of Collaborative Filtering [39] to deal with the disadvantage of cold-start problem. Their approach proposes the creation of a model that combines the user preferences as expressed for example in the user profiles, the item acceptance which describes the estimation for a given item i that will be rated with value k by the users, and the friend inference which describes the relation of any given target user with his neighbors/friends based though on the commonly rated items, and based on this probabilistic model try to predict the user's' ratings for the given items. Although the results of the experiments suggest that this model can perform better or equal to the traditional CF, since the evaluation was performed over a heuristic dataset, this needs to be tested to actual datasets of real large-scale networks to verify the level of solution to the scalability problem.

More details about scalability and possible solutions are presented in the next section.

5.4   Scalability of Recommender Systems for Social Networks

The scalability of an information system is subject to the available resources, the architecture it implements and the algorithms it employs. Similarly, the scalability of a recommender system for social networks relies both on the resources that are available and the system architecture that may allow for distributed or parallel data management and processing, but also on the algorithms that are employed and whether they can adapt to the scalable architecture or to large data sizes. In the former case, parallel and distributed algorithms that must be designed, whereas in the latter case, new algorithms that can achieve comparable performance without using all the available data must be created.

Multimedia content is the second dimension input of recommendation engines over the web after the user dimension. Especially after the prevalence of smartphones that provide multiple ways of accessibility to different content, social media have taken advantage of it and are continually try to provide recommendation based on this different type of data. The challenges though are many. Multimedia data often contains a lot of high-level semantic meanings. Moreover, the scale of data is big with high growth rate, and this requires huge amount of computing resources. Finally, when we referring to multimedia then we are talking about different kinds of content like image, video, audio, text or combinations of them. The majority of techniques in this area exploit high level metadata which is extracted from low level features either in an automatic or a semi-automatic way. This data is compared with user preferences at the end.

5.4.1 Scalability and Data Management

Database Management Systems (DBMS) have a crucial role in social networking applications, where a huge amount of data, produced and consumed at multiple, geographically distinct locations, must be stored, retrieved and delivered efficiently. Centralized Relational DBMSs are designed to provide guaranteed consistency but can hardly scale-up to the requirements of worldwide social networks. These limitations are the reason that popular social networks such as Facebook, and Twitter have explored alternative Distributed and NoSQL data storage systems [40] such as Cassandra [41], Megastore, PNUTS, Dynamo, MongoDB, COPS and SCADS [42].

Although RDBMSs are "not cloud friendly" due to the relationships and dependencies among stored data, NoSQL databases can scale better even when running on commodity hardware with increased fault-tolerance when using cloud infrastructure. However, they also face several challenges that relate to data partitioning and replication [43, 44] and middleware solutions have been developed for this purpose. For example, SPAR [45], a social partitioning and replication middle-ware, which has been designed for supporting social networking applications. SPAR supports different data partition methods (both random and social graph based) and data-stores (both Key-Value store - Cassandra and a relational database -MySQL) and allows scalability, without restricting to a specific database implementation.

5.4.1.1 Data Partitioning

As addressed in [13], the problem of applying Collaborative Filtering to large product-rating graphs is still an open and challenging issue. Collaborative Filtering methods generate recommendations based on product-review information and ratings history for users and products. In the core of their functionality, they need to process a matrix, also represented as bipartite graph, which stores the user ratings for the products. In practice, however these methods strangle to scale to large bipartite graphs. In the following, we assume that both representations -matrix and bipartite graph- are equivalent.

Over the past years, there has been a bulk of research interest regarding several Collaborative Filtering techniques and data partitioning methods that allow existing algorithms to scale up to a larger scale. The technique proposed in [13] predicts the performance of Collaborative Filtering algorithms using the structural features of the bipartite graphs and a machine learning approach in order to find the best partitioning of the original graph. To this end, the authors employ graph partitioning in order to split the original bipartite product-rating graph to smaller sub-graphs and apply the Collaborative Filtering techniques in a parallel setup. With the use of Lenskit Recommender library and Apache Spark [46], they are able to scale the CF-based recommender to large-scale bipartite ratings graphs. In the partitioning step, they take advantage of the undirected social graph, which contains friendship relations between users in the social network. This graph is partitioned first and user partitions are created. Then the bipartite graph is split into sub-graphs by keeping in each bipartite partition only the ratings provided by the users of the respective user partition. In order to deliver good recommendations, the authors generate different numbers of user partitions (and rating sub-graphs respectively) and then predict CF performance in order to determine the best partitioning scheme. For CF performance prediction, they consider additional (bipartite) graph structure metrics compared to previous studies.

Many alternatives for partitioning the rating data and splitting the large CF task to smaller tasks have been proposed in the literature. The proposed methods either group users together based on their social connections [47], or cluster the items together based on the ratings they share in common [48]. Finally, several methods first merge the rating information with the user social network information and then apply factorization techniques [49] or multi-way spectral clustering, using only the top few eigenvectors and eigenvalues to partition the data [50].

5.4.1.2   Parallel and Distributed Algorithms

Since the volume of data from social networks keeps growing to huge levels and many state-of-the-art collaborative filtering algorithms struggle to keep up with, it was clear to the research community that parallel and distributed system techniques could be utilized to deal with the data processing and solve scalability issues. Based on this idea, a large number of researches have been published that describe implementations of traditional collaborative filtering algorithms on parallel and distributed setups. In this context, frameworks such as OpenMP, Pthreads and Java Threads for parallel programming have been used for collaborative filtering [51]. Two of the most popular distributed frameworks, Mahout [52] and Apache Spark [46] have been widely used for high-volume data processing.

Based on the idea of distributed processing, authors in [53] proposed a Distributed Partitioned Merge (DPM) model, which is a hybrid model for large social network graphs processing. For the creation of their model they leverage the simplicity provided by Fork-Join programing and the scalability provided by Pregel framework. As reported by the evaluation findings, DPM seems to outperform both Pregel and Fork-Join in terms of recommendation time, but with a minor penalization in network usage.

Another group of research has been focused on recommender systems in decentralized, P2P environments. The peers of such networks can share profile and history information only with peers having similar interests, thus reducing the load for the recommender system and allowing a decentralized and scalable implementation [54].

The PipeCF algorithm [55, 56], has also been designed for P2P networks. The algorithm first divides the original user database into buckets which are stored in different peers and each is assigned an identifier in order to use this as a key when needed. Then PipeCF uses the information from all users in the same bucket with the active user to compute the predictions. The algorithm increases the weights for the contributions of the most similar users (unanimous amplification) and decreases the weights for users that have rated many items (significance refinement) in a process which is similar to TF/IDF weighting of terms in a text collection.

Authors in [57] created a model for predicting user to item relevance scores proposing the use of buddy-tables, which are actually tables for storing the relevance among items in ranked order (the information about the top-N relevant items). The information of these tables "follows" each item and is available among the peers of a P2P network. The buddy tables are implicitly used to create a kind of semantic layer of information in order to cluster together similar multimedia files. Every time a user starts a transaction (e.g. downloads a file), the buddy tables are updated keeping the system up-to-date. With regard to the recommendation process, given a user profile that we would like the system to create recommendation for, the buddy tables for this user have to be downloaded and the relevance scores for every item in these tables are calculated. Based on these calculations, the items that were "classified" in the top-N suggestions return to the user in the form of recommended items. Simulation experiments conducted on user logs from the Audioscrobbler community showed promising results for this P2P recommendation technique.

Another approach on dealing with the sparsity and scalability problem of the model-based Collaborative Filtering methods is the scalable clustering-based Collaborative Filtering (ACFSC), which focuses on reducing time complexity for the neighborhood creation for dealing with scalability [58]. The minimized usage of external data such as user profile and item metadata can maximize the adaptable domain. In addition, the combination of rating and external data can help on solving at some point the cold-start problem and the formation of better clusters by relocating users and items using the newly arrived ratings can increase the model coverage. Based on these policies, their architecture consists of four steps. Initially, the cluster model is created based on the user or item feature vectors. Based on this model, the top-N selected items are recommended, depending on the user's preferences. As a third step, the users' missing preferences caused by ratings matrix sparsity have to be predicted using other users and items clusters. Finally, at the learning phase, user and item feature vectors are learned to quantify the users' and items' qualitative characteristic.

There are also some clustering based methods proposed that use similarities between users and items to create clusters of users or items. Taking this further, multi-dimensional clustering can be used to cluster metadata information like user and item profile data and as a second step, the pruning of the created clusters is used to calculate the weighted average of the neighbor scores as a prediction for the user preference [59]. Another clustering based method proposed by Bellogin and Parapar [60] who used N-cut graph clustering to produce clusters with high user similarity, improving Collaborative Filtering performance but their approach lacks of coverage. The main limitation of the clustering based approaches is the higher computational cost for the cluster creation step than that for the Collaborative Filtering itself.

5.4.2 Scalable and Incremental CF Algorithms

In a common real-life scenario, a recommender is given a $i \times j$ ratings matrix where i and j is the number of Users and Items/Users/Products etc. respectively. and the system has to predict the unknown elements of the matrix. However, when the rating matrices are sparse, collaborative filtering suffers from noise in similarity calculations and results in poor recommendation quality. Latent factor analysis methods have been proposed in this case, in order to discover underlying user and item correlation and tackle the critical issue of similarity computational cost. In model-based approaches, several techniques that use the rating matrix in order to train a prediction model have been proposed, such as Principal Component Analysis (PCA), Latent Dirichlet Analysis (LDA) and Singular Value Decomposition (SVD). As stated by [4], these matrix factorization techniques are often preferred because they offer high accuracy and scalability. Factorization of the user-item ratings matrix [61] has become a quite popular solution for recommender systems after the Netflix prize competition, which indicated the ability of matrix factorization technique to achieve higher accuracy than the neighborhood-based techniques for creating item recommendations. In addition, using matrix factorization techniques allowed the use not only of explicit but implicit information as well.

The idea behind matrix factorization is the expression of both nodes of the system (i.e. users and items) into feature vectors based on patterns (latent factors) recognized in the edge list (i.e. user-to-item ratings). For the same reason, matrix factorization has been employed in many latent factor models, where recommendations are based on similarities computed over the generated item and user factors. Their ability to model different real life data and to provide good predictions made them very popular.

In order to achieve scalability in matrix factorization and keep the quality of recommendations high, the proposed methods, use overlapping partitions or decompositions of the original matrix and external knowledge (e.g. from content or from social networks) that decreases the sparsity of the original matrix. In a different direction, incremental methods use only new ratings to (re-)train an existing model.

In [62] describe how Amazon uses topic diversification algorithms to improve its recommendation. In more detail, the system that they present, uses collaborative filtering method to overcome scalability issue by generating a table of similar items offline through the use of item-to-item matrix. The system then recommends other products which are similar online according to the users' purchase history.

The idea of combining ratings and social network information has been revisited in SoRec algorithm [63] resulting in a huge sparse matrix. This time probabilistic matrix factorization has been applied in order to reduce the sparsity of the matrix. A common shared latent factor that captures both user-item rating and users' social trust led to improved predictions.

An incremental learning approach has been introduced in [64], in order to recommend high-quality videos in real-time. The factorized matrix was updated using implicit feedback from different user actions and item similarity considered additional factors, such as video type and duration. Finally, they propose the scalable implementation of their algorithm together with some optimizations to make the recommendations more efficient and accurate, including the demographic filtering and demographic training.

The use of incremental algorithms, can also improve the scalability of model-based recommender systems, since only the newer information is used to train the model. Luo et al. [65] used Regularized Matrix Factorization to create an incremental Recommender System. The Recommender System that they proposed creates an initial model with the given parameters and allows their model to be incrementally trained, meaning that their model is incrementally updated as new ratings arrive. These kind of approaches provide real improvement of the quality of recommendations solving partially the problem of sparsity of the rating matrices but actually deteriorate the scalability issue.

In the compact latent factor model proposed in [66], the item-scoring function was trained periodically, to reduce the training overhead. Authors introduced a buffer mechanism to retrieve the data incrementally and compared to traditional learning, achieved better scalability, since their model updated only when the number of data instances in the current buffer is sufficient rather than each time a rating was added.

Finally, in [67] authors exploit the parallel computing platform and application programming interface (API), known as CUDA, which improved the performance, exploiting the graphics processing unit (GPU) capabilities in high processing and propose a CUDA based matrix factorization library called CuMF that uses the method of alternate least squares (ALS) to implement matrix factorization in large-scale datasets. This proposed method aims on increasing performance in both single and multiple GPUs. Some key features are the leverage of the GPU memory structure and hierarchy in order to provide easy access to sparse data and the minimization of the communication costs by using data and model parallelism.

5.4.3 Scalability of Deep Learning Solutions in Recommender Systems

Another way to confront, sparsity, cold-start, scalability and other issues is the use of hybrid filtering. This approach involves the combination of different techniques for creating recommendations, trying to improve the accuracy of the predictions [68, 69], while leveling out individual method weaknesses [70]. They can be classified based on their operations into weighted hybrid, mixed hybrid, switching hybrid, feature-combination hybrid, cascade hybrid, feature-augmented hybrid and meta-level hybrid [71].

The rise of deep learning techniques also affected the recommender systems. Towards this direction, Peska and Trojanova [72] used the visual descriptors of the deep neural networks for creating item-based recommendations as an evaluation scenario for creating a photo lineup assembling task. This is a great example of how broad is the utility of deep learning and recommendation processes in wide areas of research.

Many current researches on deep learning for recommendation systems address a variety of potentials open for discussion. In this context, Smirnova and Vasile [73], address the limitation of not using implicit information from the user profile, such as the timestamp of a user-item transaction or the user's inactivity time interval, by the Recurrent Neural Networks. Based on this, authors propose a class of RNN, called Contextual Recurrent Neural Networks (CRNNs), that uses the contextual information of the network both in the input and output of the CRNN and rectifies the behavior of the neural network in order to produce item predictions. Based on the experimental results, using YooChoose dataset and a proprietary dataset consisted by user browsing and purchasing activity on various e-commerces, this approach can achieve noteworthy results against sequential and nonsequential state of the art models.

Tackling the problem of boosting a recommender system's performance, Chatzis et al. [74] proposed the creation of a machine learning model that can derive hidden or implicit information from the sparse user session data. This idea is typically based on traditional RNN approaches which define the state-of-the-art in this domain. Towards the same direction, Zanotti et al. [75] collect and combine data from multiple sources such as user-item ratings, user-item reviews and item descriptive data in the effort of forming rich distributed representations and enhancing this information in the classic RNN systems. The further goal of this method is to try to boost the prediction of the user to item actual score.

Based on the experimental findings of the approaches mentioned above, all of these enhancements can help recommender systems achieve better results with the use of deep learning methods such as neural networks. Based on the survey of research on deep learning and recommender systems, the pinpoint that need attention is that even though there is plenty of research in deep learning for these kind of purposes and many approaches seem to outperform traditional techniques for providing higher results of recommendations in many cases, all these approaches mainly target on improving the actual recommendation algorithm scores rather than solving the scalability issues. In that sense, we consider that there is plenty of research interest towards this area and the need for that seems necessary.

5.5   Conclusions

Dealing with the problem of creating real-life recommendations in large-scale and sparse networks can be a challenging task both regarding scalability, data sparsity and recommendation quality of course.

The major challenges in RS are the scalability, diversity and the long tail, sparsity and the cold-start problem. In addition, content-based filtering faces the problem of content analysis in the cases where the sets of items lack of a respectively sufficient set of features. Finally another challenge is the combination of collaborative filtering and content-based filtering approaches in hybrid filtering cases. A solution about the scalability and data management problem in CF-recommenders, can be the idea of splitting the (social) graph into sub-graphs as long as the use of parallel and distributed algorithms. Matrix factorization is another solution for scalable and incremental CF-algorithms. Finally a way to confront, sparsity, cold-start, scalability and other related problems is the use of hybrid filtering techniques especially based on deep learning.

Since many state-of-the-art collaborative filtering algorithms struggle to keep up with the three main characteristics of big data, that could describe the current state in many large scale social networks, Volume, Velocity, Variety -the also known as three Vs- it was clear that parallel and distributed technologies could and would offer potential solutions to some of these issues. In this context, many research works have proposed the implementation of existing recommendations algorithms on parallel and distributed systems. Many modern recommender systems are based in partitioning or clustering methods trying to deal with the scalability, but a trend in using parallel and distributed systems is observed. Most of these approaches try to distribute the data over a cluster or parallelize the classic collaborative filtering algorithms used in traditional techniques to deal with the scalability problem.

The last few years the field of deep learning seems to gain a lot of research focusing in the use of techniques like Recurrent Neural Networks for processing data and creating very accurate recommendations. However, the main point of concern is that although these methods outperform traditional approaches in many cases, still they try to encounter the issues of sparsity and cold-start recommendations and not the problem of scalability. Based on this, there seems to be plenty of open space for research towards this direction.

References

1. Symeonidis, P., Ntempos, D., & Manolopoulos, Y. (2014). *Recommender systems for location-based social networks*. Springer Science & Business Media.
2. Nepali, R., & Wang, Y. (2014). *SocBridge: Bridging the gap between online social networks*.
3. Chakradhar, S., & Raghunathan, A. (2010). IEEE: Best-effort computing: Re-thinking parallel software and hardware. In *2010 47th ACM/IEEE on Design Automation Conference (DAC)* (pp. 865–870).
4. Ricci, F., Rokach, L., & Shapira, B. (2011). *Introduction to recommender systems handbook* (pp. 1–35). Springer.
5. Chen, H.-H., Ororbia, I., Alexander, G., & Giles, C. (2015). ExpertSeer: A Keyphrase Based Expert Recommender for Digital Libraries. arXiv:1511.02058.
6. Chen, H.-H., Gou, L., Zhang, X., & Giles, C. (2011). ACM: Collabseer: a search engine for collaboration discovery. In *Conference Proceedings of the 11th Annual International ACM/IEEE Joint Conference on Digital Libraries* (pp. 231–240).
7. Felfernig, A., Isak, K., Szabo, K., & Zachar, P. (1999). The VITA financial services sales support environment. In *Conference Proceedings of the National Conference on Artificial Intelligence* (Vol. 22, p. 1692). Menlo Park, CA; Cambridge, MA; London; AAAI Press; MIT Press.
8. Gupta, P., Goel, A., Lin, J., Sharma, A., Wang, D., & Zadeh, R. (2013). ACM: Wtf: The who to follow service at twitter. In *Conference Proceedings of the 22nd International Conference on World Wide Web* (pp. 505–514).

9. Montaner, M., López, B., & De La Rosa, J. (2003). A taxonomy of recommender agents on the internet. *Artificial Intelligence Review, 19*(4), 285–330.
10. Lops, P., De Gemmis, M., & Semeraro, G. (2011). *Content-based recommender systems: State of the art and trends* (pp. 73–105). Springer.
11. Su, X., & Khoshgoftaar, T. (2009). A survey of collaborative filtering techniques. *Advances in artificial intelligence* (Vol. 4).
12. Burke, R.: Hybrid recommender systems: Survey and experiments. *User Modeling and User-Adapted Interaction, 12*(4), 331–370.
13. Sardianos, C., Varlamis, I., & Eirinaki, M. (2017). Scaling collaborative filtering to large-scale bipartite rating graphs using lenskit and spark. In *BigDataService* (pp. 70–79).
14. Park, D., Kim, H., Choi, I., & Kim, J. (2012). A literature review and classification of recommender systems research. *Expert Systems with Applications, 39*(11), 10059–10072.
15. Oard, D., Kim, J., others, Menlo Park, CA: AAAI Press: Implicit feedback for recommender systems. In *Conference Proceedings of the AAAI workshop on recommender systems* (pp. 81–83).
16. Carrer-Neto, W., Hernández-Alcaraz, M., Valencia-García, R., & García-Sánchez, F. (2012). Social knowledge-based recommender system. Application to the movies domain. *Expert Systems with Applications, 39*(12), 10990–11000.
17. Arazy, O., Kumar, N., & Shapira, B. (2009). Improving social recommender systems. *IT professional, 11*(4).
18. Li, Y.-M., Liao, T.-F., & Lai, C.-Y. (2012). A social recommender mechanism for improving knowledge sharing in online forums. *Information Processing & Management, 48*(5), 978–994.
19. Siersdorfer, S., & Sizov, S. (2009). ACM: Social recommender systems for web 2.0 folksonomies. In *Conference Proceedings of the 20th ACM Conference on Hypertext and hypermedia* (pp. 261–270).
20. Hossain, L., & Fazio, D. (2009). The social networks of collaborative process. *The Journal of High Technology Management Research, 20*(2), 119–130.
21. Perugini, S., Gonçalves, M., & Fox, E. (2004). Recommender systems research: A connection-centric survey. *Journal of Intelligent Information Systems, 23*(2), 107–143.
22. Melville, P., & Sindhwani, V. (2011). *Recommender systems* (pp. 829–838). Springer.
23. Sarwar, B., Karypis, G., Konstan, J., & Riedl, J. (2001). ACM: Item-based collaborative filtering recommendation algorithms. In *Conference Proceedings of the 10th International Conference on World Wide Web*, pp. 285–295 (2001)
24. Cotter, P., Smyth, B.: Ptv: Intelligent personalised tv guides. In *AAAI/IAAI* (pp. 957–964).
25. Strub, F., Gaudel, R., & Mary, J. (2016). ACM: Hybrid recommender system based on autoencoders. In *Conference Proceedings of the 1st Workshop on Deep Learning for Recommender Systems* (pp. 11–16).
26. Zhao, W., Li, S., He, Y., Chang, E., Wen, J.-R., & Li, X. (2016). Connecting social media to e-commerce: Cold-start product recommendation using microblogging information. *IEEE Transactions on Knowledge and Data Engineering, 28*(5), 1147–1159.
27. Wei, J., He, J., Chen, K., Zhou, Y., & Tang, Z. (2017). Collaborative filtering and deep learning based recommendation system for cold start items. *Expert Systems with Applications, 69*, 29–39.
28. Wang, H., Wang, N., & Yeung, D.-Y. (2015). ACM: Collaborative deep learning for recommender systems. In *Conference Proceedings of the 21th ACM SIGKDD International Conference on Knowledge Discovery and Data Mining* (pp. 1235–1244).
29. Liu, J., Wu, C., Springer: Deep Learning Based Recommendation: A Survey. In *International Conference on Information Science and Applications* (pp. 451–458).
30. Schein, A., Popescul, A., Ungar, L., & Pennock, D. (2002). ACM: Methods and metrics for cold-start recommendations. In *Conference Proceedings of the 25th Annual International ACM SIGIR Conference on Research and Development in Information Retrieval* (pp. 253–260).
31. Sparck Jones, K.: A statistical interpretation of term specificity and its application in retrieval. *Journal of Documentation, 28*(1), 11–21.

32. Patel, K., Thakkar, A., Shah, C., & Makvana, K. (2016). Springer: A state of art survey on shilling attack in collaborative filtering based recommendation system. In *Conference Proceedings of First International Conference on Information and Communication Technology for Intelligent Systems* (Vol. 1, pp. 377–385).
33. Hurley, N., O'Mahony, M., & Silvestre, G. (2007). Attacking recommender systems: A cost-benefit analysis. *IEEE Intelligent Systems, 22*(3).
34. Shyong, K., Frankowski, D., & Riedl, J. (2006). others: Do you trust your recommendations? *An exploration of security and privacy issues in recommender systems* (pp. 14–29). Springer.
35. McSherry, F., & Mironov, I. (2009). ACM: Differentially private recommender systems: building privacy into the net. In *Conference Proceedings of the 15th ACM SIGKDD International Conference on Knowledge Discovery and Data Mining* (pp. 627–636).
36. Koren, Y. (2008). ACM: Tutorial on recent progress in collaborative filtering. In *Conference Proceedings of the 2008 ACM Conference on Recommender Systems* (pp. 333–334).
37. Felfernig, A., & Gula, B. (2006). IEEE: An empirical study on consumer behavior in the interaction with knowledge-based recommender applications. In *The 3rd IEEE International Conference on E-Commerce Technology, 2006. The 8th IEEE International Conference on and Enterprise Computing, E-Commerce, and E-Services* (pp. 37–37).
38. Agrawal, D., & Aggarwal, C. (2001). ACM: On the design and quantification of privacy preserving data mining algorithms. In *Conference Proceedings of the twentieth ACM SIGMOD-SIGACT-SIGART Symposium on Principles of Database Systems* (pp. 247–255).
39. Nayebzadeh, M., Moazzam, A., Saba, A., Abdolrahimpour, H., & Shahab, E. (2017). *An investigation on social network recommender systems and collaborative filtering techniques.* arXiv: 1708.00417.
40. Agrawal, D., El Abbadi, A., Das, S., & Elmore, A. (2011). Springer: Database scalability, elasticity, and autonomy in the cloud. In *International Conference on Database Systems for Advanced Applications* (pp. 2–15).
41. Lakshman, A., & Malik, P. (2010). Cassandra: a decentralized structured storage system. *ACM SIGOPS Operating Systems Review, 44*(2), 35–40.
42. Maqsood, T., Khalid, O., Irfan, R., Madani, S., & Khan, S. (2016). Scalability Issues in Online Social Networks. *ACM Computing Surveys (CSUR), 49*(2), 40.
43. Bobadilla, J., Ortega, F., Hernando, A., & Gutiérrez, A. (2013). Recommender systems survey. *Knowledge-Based Systems, 46*, 109–132.
44. Lloyd, W., Freedman, M., Kaminsky, M., & Andersen, D. (2014). Don't settle for eventual consistency. *Communications of the ACM, 57*(5), 61–68.
45. Pujol, J., Erramilli, V., Siganos, G., Yang, X., Laoutaris, N., Chhabra, P., et al. (2010). The little engine (s) that could: scaling online social networks. *ACM SIGCOMM Computer Communication Review, 40*(4), 375–386.
46. Shanahan, J., & Dai, L. (2015). ACM: Large scale distributed data science using apache spark. In *Conference Proceedings of the 21th ACM SIGKDD International Conference on Knowledge Discovery and Data Mining* (pp. 2323–2324).
47. Pham, M., Cao, Y., Klamma, R., & Jarke, M. (2011). A clustering approach for collaborative filtering recommendation using social network analysis. *Journal of UCS, 17*(4), 583–604.
48. O'Connor, M., Herlocker, J., & Berkeley, U. (1999). Clustering items for collaborative filtering. In *Conference Proceedings of the ACM SIGIR Workshop on Recommender Systems* (Vol. 128).
49. De Meo, P., Ferrara, E., Fiumara, G., & Provetti, A. (2011). IEEE: Improving recommendation quality by merging collaborative filtering and social relationships. In *2011 11th International Conference on Intelligent Systems Design and Applications (ISDA)* (pp. 587–592).
50. Symeonidis, P., Iakovidou, N., Mantas, N., Manolopoulos, Y. (2013). From biological to social networks: Link prediction based on multi-way spectral clustering. *Data & Knowledge Engineering, 87*, 226–242.
51. Eirinaki, M., Gao, J., Varlamis, I., Tserpes, K. (2017). Recommender systems for large-scale social networks: A review of challenges and solutions. *Future Generation Computer Systems, 78*, 412–417.

52. Owen, S., Anil, R., Dunning, T., & Friedman, E. (2011). *Mahout in action: Manning Shelter Island.*
53. Corbellini, A., Godoy, D., Mateos, C., Schiaffino, S., & Zunino, A. (2017). DPM: A novel distributed large-scale social graph processing framework for link prediction algorithms. *Future Generation Computer Systems.*
54. Shavitt, Y., Weinsberg, E., & Weinsberg, U. (2010). ACM: Building recommendation systems using peer-to-peer shared content. In *Conference Proceedings of the 19th ACM International Conference on Information and Knowledge Management* (pp. 1457–1460).
55. Han, P., Xie, B., Yang, F., & Shen, R. (2004). A scalable P2P recommender system based on distributed collaborative filtering. *Expert Systems with Applications, 27*(2), 203–210.
56. Han, P., Xie, B., Yang, F., Wang, J., & Shen, R. (2004). Springer: A novel distributed collaborative filtering algorithm and its implementation on p 2p overlay network. In *Pacific-Asia Conference on Knowledge Discovery and Data Mining* (pp. 106–115).
57. Wang, J., Pouwelse, J., Lagendijk, R., & Reinders, M. (2006). ACM: Distributed collaborative filtering for peer-to-peer file sharing systems. In *Conference Proceedings of the 2006 ACM Symposium on Applied Computing* (pp. 1026–1030).
58. Lee, O.-J., Hong, M.-S., Jung, J., Shin, J., & Kim, P. (2016). Adaptive collaborative filtering based on scalable clustering for big recommender systems. *Acta Polytechnica Hungarica, 13*(2), 179–194.
59. Li, X., & Murata, T. (2012). IEEE Computer Society: Using multidimensional clustering based collaborative filtering approach improving recommendation diversity. In *Conference Proceedings of the The 2012 IEEE/WIC/ACM International Joint Conferences on Web Intelligence and Intelligent Agent Technology-Volume 03* (pp. 169–174).
60. Bellogin, A., & Parapar, J. (2012). ACM: Using graph partitioning techniques for neighbour selection in user-based collaborative filtering. In *Conference Proceedings of the Sixth ACM Conference on Recommender Systems* (pp. 213–216).
61. Koren, Y., Bell, R., & Volinsky, C. (2009). Matrix factorization techniques for recommender systems. *Computer, 42*(8).
62. Ziegler, C.-N., McNee, S., Konstan, J., & Lausen, G. (2005). ACM: Improving recommendation lists through topic diversification. In *Conference Proceedings of the 14th International Conference on World Wide Web* (pp. 22–32).
63. Ma, H., Yang, H., Lyu, M., & King, I. (2008). ACM: Sorec: social recommendation using probabilistic matrix factorization. In *Conference Proceedings of the 17th ACM Conference on Information and Knowledge Management* (pp. 931–940).
64. Huang, Y., Cui, B., Jiang, J., Hong, K., Zhang, W., & Xie, Y. (2016). ACM: Real-time video recommendation exploration. In *Conference Proceedings of the 2016 International Conference on Management of Data* (pp. 35–46).
65. Luo, X., Xia, Y., & Zhu, Q. (2012). Incremental collaborative filtering recommender based on regularized matrix factorization. *Knowledge-Based Systems, 27*, 271–280.
66. Liu, C.-L., & Wu, X.-W. (2016). Large-scale recommender system with compact latent factor model. *Expert Systems with Applications, 64*, 467–475.
67. Tan, W., Cao, L., & Fong, L. (2016). ACM: Faster and cheaper: Parallelizing large-scale matrix factorization on gpus. In *Conference Proceedings of the 25th ACM International Symposium on High-Performance Parallel and Distributed Computing* (pp. 219–230).
68. Göksedef, M., & Gündüz-Ö\ugüdücü, S. (2010). Combination of Web page recommender systems. *Expert Systems with Applications, 37*(4), 2911–2922.
69. Mobasher, B. (2007). Recommender Systems. *KI, 21*(3), 41–43.
70. Al-Shamri, M., & Bharadwaj, K. (2008). Fuzzy-genetic approach to recommender systems based on a novel hybrid user model. *Expert Systems with Applications, 35*(3), 1386–1399.
71. Mican, D., & Tomai, N. (2010). Springer: Association-rules-based recommender system for personalization in adaptive web-based applications. In *International Conference on Web Engineering* (pp. 85–90).
72. Peska, L., & Trojanova, H. (2017). *Towards recommender systems for Police Photo Lineup.* arXiv:1707.01389.

73. Smirnova, E., & Vasile, F. (2017). *Contextual sequence modeling for recommendation with recurrent neural networks*. arXiv:1706.07684.

74. Chatzis, S., Christodoulou, P., & Andreou, A. (2017). *Recurrent latent variable networks for session-based recommendation*. arXiv:1706.04026.

75. Zanotti, G., Horvath, M., Barbosa, L., Immedisetty, V., & Gemmell, J. (2016). ACM: Infusing collaborative recommenders with distributed representations. In *Conference Proceedings of the 1st Workshop on Deep Learning for Recommender Systems* (pp. 35–42).

Chapter 6
Social Network Applications for Education: The Case of College Connect

A. L. Chapman, M. Lei and C. Greenhow

Abstract In this chapter, the design, implementation, benefits, and challenges of using a Facebook application, College Connect, are presented. College Connect was designed to address the persistent educational problem of college access in the United States, part of which stems from students' lack of social capital, the human and information resources available to them in their social networks that can provide needed information, such as how to apply to, enroll in, and pay for college. College Connect, a social networking application which runs on Facebook, the parent platform, was designed to help address this problem by creating a network visualization of each student's Facebook Friends network and showing the student who within the network has college information in their Facebook profile. In this chapter, we explain the theory and procedures that led to the design of the College Connect application, the process of launching the application, and the benefits and challenges of implementing it with adolescent students preparing for college.

Keywords Social media · Social network sites · College knowledge · Design

The original version of this chapter was revised: Acknowledgment section, Reference citations and foot note had been included as a belated correction. The correction to this chapter is available at https://doi.org/10.1007/978-3-319-90059-9_9

A. L. Chapman (✉) · M. Lei · C. Greenhow
Counseling, Educational Psychology, & Special Education,
Michigan State University, East Lansing, MI, USA
e-mail: chapm276@msu.edu

M. Lei
e-mail: minglei@msu.edu

C. Greenhow
e-mail: greenhow@msu.edu

6.1 Introduction

In today's rapidly-changing world, people from across the globe are increasingly using social media for real-time information and connection in their everyday lives. Nearly 2.5 billion people, one-third of the world's population, use social networks, which cross geographical, cultural, and economic borders, numbers which are expected to rise as the usage of both mobile devices and social media grow worldwide [1]. In the United States, a full 78% of the population has a profile on at least one social networking site [1]. These social networking sites, including Facebook, Twitter, Instagram, Snapchat, YouTube, and Pinterest, find broad engagement in personal, professional, political, and entertainment domains. Facebook is the world's most popular social network site, though Twitter has experienced a drastic growth of users, which rose from 30 million active monthly users at the beginning of 2010 to 328 million active monthly users at the beginning of 2017 [1].

In this ever-increasing and diversifying social media space, individuals and communities involved in education—students, parents, teachers, administrators, policymakers, and other stakeholders—must better understand the affordances and constraints of this space in order to use it to an educational advantage. Social media, through online communities, communication tools, and a variety of modes and methods of communication, presents many possibilities for education. Social media can facilitate low-cost resource and information sharing, which may increase educational opportunities regardless of geography, socioeconomic context, or other barriers to educational resources.

Though the educational uses and potential of social media are considerable, educational applications that build on Facebook's features and affordances are rare. This chapter is concerned with the design, implementation, benefits, and challenges of one such Facebook application, College Connect, which was created to facilitate adolescents' college knowledge and help-seeking. Teenagers' development of college knowledge and help-seeking is important to advancing their college access, or whether students are able to and intend to attend college. Historically, in the United States, college access has varied among groups. In 1992, 42% of Whites, 35% of African Americans, and 26% of Latinos attended a 4-year college or university [2]. The disparity in college enrollment has existed between White students and students of color since the 1970s and has persisted into the new millennium [3]. Differences in college access have been attributed to socioeconomic status, but others have argued that income alone does not account for this gap [4]. Parents and students who play the "game of education," behaving in ways that are considered desirable and legitimate, have an advantage over those who do not [5, 6]. Therefore, a critical element of accessing college is possessing and activating the knowledge of college in the way that is determined by the dominant cultural group.

College knowledge includes, among other things, the process of applying to, selecting, and enrolling in a college; of understanding and choosing how to pay for college; and of understanding the academic and cultural differences between high school and college [7]. In choosing a college and preparing to attend college, most students examine financial aid, standardized test and GPA requirements for admission, a college's graduation rate, and a college's reputation [8]. However, this information, and college knowledge more generally, is not always readily available to all high school students who are interested in attending college, and students' choices for schools may be based on incomplete information about their eligibility [9]. Students who have fewer resources in their immediate physical networks often are at a disadvantage in the college application and selection process [10]. Alternatively, social network sites have the potential to be effective information-seeking channels due to their technical and social affordances, such as the ability to broadcast content and aggregate one's contacts.

Recent scholarship suggests that social networks can provide the space and tools which help users more easily access resources that are not immediately apparent, particularly in the area of college access [11–13]. Although some research has examined how youth seek information through social media use, little is known about students' use of social media to develop college knowledge [14]. As adolescents are inclined to seek out others to meet their need for information, investigating their social media use regarding outreach to others in the college application process is an important extension to the literature [15].

In the case presented in this chapter, we examine the design and implementation of the College Connect application, which runs on the social media platform Facebook, built for the purpose of addressing the aforementioned gap in access to college knowledge among American high school students. The purpose of College Connect was to allow users to visualize their Facebook network and to identify who in their network has college knowledge. The application also has features through which users can ask Friends in their network questions about college generally or about a particular college more specifically. A design-based research approach guided this project's design and implementation efforts [16–18]. Design-based research helps bridge the research-to-practice gap by drawing on established research methods with the goal of informing not just the knowledge base but also improving educational practices [18]. Reeves advocates four steps in the design-based research process: (1) analyze the practical problem; (2) develop solutions; (3) implement the solution in situ, building in evaluation and refinement in successive iterations; and (4) reflect on findings to produce theoretical and practical insights [17]. In alignment with steps 1–3 of this model, this chapter describes the process undertaken to assess the problem by reviewing selected, previous research on college knowledge, help-seeking, social capital and social network sites, especially research which addresses the experiences of high school students, our target users. Moreover, the designed solution, in the form of an educational application built on Facebook is presented. From our testing and evaluation of College Connect, we draw insights on its benefits and challenges to inform future efforts.

In the following sections, we first seek to situate our work in the current landscape of relevant educational theory and research. Second, we present the design and implementation of the College Connect application, including why it was designed and the challenges of implementing that design as intended. Third, we conclude by offering practical guidance and recommendations intended to inspire designers and researchers who seek to design similar applications, especially those targeting adolescents and academic contexts.

6.2   Social Network Sites

The College Connect application was designed to run on the social network site Facebook. Social network sites (SNS) are a form of social media, which differ from other types of social media and virtual communities by relying on user-created content and the links that users make with each other. Specifically, there are three hallmarks of social network sites. First, social network sites have profiles unique to each user which consist of user-supplied content, information provided by other users, and/or data which is supplied by the system. Secondly, social network sites have public connections which can be viewed and navigated by others. Thirdly, participants on social network sites can consume, produce, and interact with user-created content contributed by other users [19]. Interactions between users on social network sites have been shown to increase and diversify the connections that users make, as well as helping those users to create and sustain social ties [20, 21].

6.3   The Use of Social Network Sites in Education

Given the widespread and increasing use of social network sites, researchers have begun to explore and evaluate their educational uses. Kert and Kert, for instance, researched the use of social network sites by high school students and asked them about their perceptions of whether social network sites could be useful for education and learning [22]. This research showed that high school students often use social network sites to keep in touch with other similar-age peers, and that students who were surveyed felt it would be good to use these sites for educational reasons. Another study by Ekici and Kiyici showed that students who used social network site applications for specific educational purposes were more academically successful than students who did not have access to these social media applications and were educated without that technology [23].

In thinking about the educational uses of Facebook, Lin, Hou, Wang, and Chang argued that Facebook shows great potential for use in education because of its structure for creating applications, communication tools, and interactive interface [24]. Another important aspect of Facebook is how common and frequently it is used by high school students. A study by Cakir and Serkan Tan found that students spent on average 15 hours per week on Facebook [25]. These authors concluded that the educational use of applications built on social network sites was inevitable, as high school students are familiar with these sites and frequent users of them. However, recent work by Cakir and Tan, published in 2017, noted that of the first 10 applications with the most active users on Facebook, 7 are games primarily for entertainment (e.g., Candy Crush Saga, Farmville, Angry Birds) and not for instruction. While the educational potential for applications built on Facebook is substantial, the creation, use, and evaluation of these applications has been rare in both educational research and practice [25].

6.4   Theoretical Perspectives

In the case of the College Connect application, we drew upon social capital research and theory from the field of sociology and the help-seeking literature from the field of psychology to guide the design and study of the application. Critical to the help-seeking literature is the identification of two types of help-seeking [26]. There is *executive help-seeking*, when the seeker is looking for another person to solve a problem. Alternatively, there is *instrumental help-seeking* when the seeker is asking for help which would allow the seeker to solve the problem [26]. Help-seeking can and should be seen as a sign of independence, but obstacles can preclude people from seeking the help that they need. These barriers include fear of a loss of credit when something goes well; the perception of a lack of competence; and a desire not to appear helpless. Adolescents' help-seeking processes are important to observe and evaluate because the processes can influence major life choices and affect identity development and later life experiences [27–29].

Social capital has been defined as the sum of resources available in one's network of relationships with other people [30]. Social capital can be generated by mutualistic relationships involving reciprocity and mutually-adopted norms [31]. According to Portes, some of the benefits of increased social capital are access to privileged information and increased access to economic resources. Social capital has been described as being distributed unequally among groups, particularly members of minority groups [32]. For example, individuals from a lower social class who have few connections would continue to propagate that lack of connections to future generations and be unable to acquire information for economic opportunities. This will be addressed in more detail in this section.

Social capital for any given individual comes directly from relationships with other people, and the nature of those relationships makes others a resource to the individual [31]. One example provided by Portes is the norm of "repaying one's debts." The knowledge one has of another's adherence to that norm becomes a resource which can be used to lend money with the peace of mind that the borrower will repay the loan. Moreover, social capital may also be seen as the sum of favors or obligations owed, which may be settled at some undetermined time and in an undecided form, also known as reciprocity exchanges [31]. Similar to the expectation of reciprocation, enforceable trust can be a source of social capital, where behaviors are community-enforced. For example, students may participate in class because of their fear of social disapproval for being quiet; therefore, a teacher may use this resource to ask more questions and build in more student-centered activities in the class. Moreover, people in the same situation tend to be supportive of others in the same situation, which makes "bounded solidarity" another source of social capital [31].

Aside from the direct economic implications of social capital for students and young adults (e.g., improved opportunities for job-seeking), social capital can affect their college-going experiences. One part of many college applications, teacher recommendation letters, are produced through accessing social capital through reciprocity exchanges. In high school, students are supposed to be active learners in class, involved by asking questions, taking on challenges, and generally displaying interest for the subject matter. Accordingly, teachers are supposed to recognize these students and be prepared to reciprocate in response to the students' efforts by providing a well-written endorsement for the acceptance of that student into their college of choice. Students who are not aware of this dynamic would be significantly disadvantaged, as they would have fewer individuals, specifically teachers, who they could call upon to provide a recommendation letter. Similarly, bounded solidarity appears in schools as students provide support to their peers in the same situation. For example, students who are applying to the same competitive college may be more inclined to put forth their greatest effort on a group project in class, since both their chances of acceptance are dependent on their grades in the class. Furthermore, students who all identify as being first-generation college students may band together and form an organization to support each other and others in the same situation.

Bounded solidarity is one source of social capital that tools like College Connect may afford to students. By helping prospective students find current students or alumni from their school of choice, we are tapping into those individuals' inherent willingness to help students they feel are similar to themselves (e.g., I remember what it was like applying to that college, I think they should know about…"). Additionally, expanding a student's pool of social connections also increases access to sources of social capital. For example, while a student may not have any set of reciprocity exchanges for applying to college, a connection may have such a source of capital, which he or she could use to help the student.

Portes outlined three main types of effects due to social capital [31]. Social capital may serve as a way of controlling socially desirable behaviors, providing family-based support, and gaining support from contacts outside of the family. These effects can be influenced by multiple social factors, such as family structure (e.g., number of parents) and can be disrupted by life circumstances, such as relocation. When a family moves from one community to another, potential extra-familial supports may be lost, diminishing the family's social capital, which may explain the decreased probability of attending college among students from more mobile families [33]. Similarly, the number of years students have lived in their home has a positive effect on staying in school [34]. Within the family, the parents may or may not be able to help their children with the college-going process, based on their own experiences and resources. For example, parents who did not attend college were less likely to talk to their children about the college application process and were less likely to engage in activities related to applying to college, such as attending college visits and learning about financial aid [35].

The ways in which social capital benefits students is affected by the nature of the relationship, and may originate from the family, the school, and the community [36]. However, for students, the quantity and quality of relationships at home, in school, and in the community may vary greatly. Fortunately, for many students, their connections with others go beyond those people in their immediate microsystems, or people they interact with directly in their homes, school, or community [37]. Instead, with online social networks, students may cultivate weak ties, or relationships outside of one's immediate social circle, who may help one gain social mobility, such as employment prospects [38]. Therefore, the potential affordance of social media in the context of college access is its ability to help students access social capital from their extended social networks to help with the college-going process.

Furthermore, the help-seeking process in relation to college knowledge and the process of college-going is particularly important for high school juniors and seniors. College knowledge, what students need to know in order to successfully apply, select, and matriculate to college, includes obtaining practical information (such as application procedures and deadlines or financial aid), social information (such as the general community of a particular college) and the development of an identity related to college-going (such as learning to navigate college campuses and understanding the structures of college) [39]. In examining human resources who have college knowledge, it has been found that not all students have equal access to people with college knowledge [40]. Tornatzky, Culter, and Lee found that parents who had low socioeconomic status were the least likely (of low, middle, and high socioeconomic status parents) to have college knowledge [40]. This was also found to be true of parents who were first generation immigrants (compared to second and third generation immigrants) [40]. Both the low SES parents and the first generation immigrant parents had a far more difficult time in accessing college information; they were also far more likely to lack college knowledge themselves. However, this study also found that the use of interactive media was able to break many of the access problems that were experienced by low SES and first-generation immigrant parents [40].

When students look to online sources for college knowledge, one of the primary sources of information is a college's website [41]. However, college websites are limited in their applicability as sources of college knowledge. One such limitation is that websites do not often offer two-way communication. Prospective students independently locate blogs and message boards where they can interactively find information about a specific college, but most college websites do not help prospective students to find these sources of information [42]. The use of online sources of information for college knowledge seeking was the focus of a study by Brown, Wohn, and Ellison, who examined the role that online sources of help played in the college knowledge seeking process of students from low-income communities [43]. This study looked at how and where students accessed information about college online, how the students evaluated the information that they found, what human resources were available to these students in their college knowledge seeking process, and how online sources of information were used by the students [43]. The authors found that students used websites to get information about the cost, ranking, and programs of different colleges, but they used social media to connect with current college students to gain insight into college culture [43]. The study also found that the students they surveyed posted on social media about college, but they did not use social media to ask questions or crowd-source information [43].

Seeking to advance this literature, the College Connect application was designed to examine whether using popular social network sites (in this case, Facebook) and specialized applications within those sites could facilitate students' process of acquiring college knowledge. First generation high school students especially may have fewer informational resources in their household regarding the college application process and other aspects of getting to college. Wohn, Ellison, Khan, Fewins-Bliss and Gray found that for first generation students, the extent to which students felt they could access information via Facebook played a large role in their efficacy regarding college-going [13]. In other words, the more students felt they could access information about college via their Facebook network, the more confident they felt about their knowledge of the college application processes (e.g., being Friends with someone on Facebook who graduated from or currently attends college contributed to students' perception of how successful they would be in attending and completing college). However, the same finding was not true for students who had parents that attended college.

In addition, high school students are often unaware of who knows what in their network. In their interviews with high school students, Wohn and colleagues learned that many students did not know who in their network attended college or what college they attended [13]. Some students did not know whether their parents had attended college. The College Connect Facebook application addresses two components of social capital: helping to identify sources of useful information and providing access to those sources (or connections). As Ellison, Steinfield, and Lampe suggested, Facebook can lower barriers for communication because it offers private and public messaging features and provides access to identity information via users' profiles [44]. These affordances allow students to determine who would be useful to talk to about a particular question, and also help them to find common ground.

6.5   Design of the College Connect Facebook Application

College Connect was a web-based Facebook application designed in 2013 with funding from the Gates Foundation's College Knowledge Challenge Grant competition. The application was created to help students identify useful people in their Facebook Friends' network and ask these people questions about college. The development of the College Connect application was a collaboration between researchers and software developers at Oxford University (Dr. Bernie Hogan and his team) and researcher-evaluators at Michigan State University (Dr. Christine Greenhow) and the University of Michigan (Dr. Nicole Ellison)[1]. After reviewing the academic literature on college access, social media, and social capital, these scholars decided to

---

[1]Jeon et al. [45]

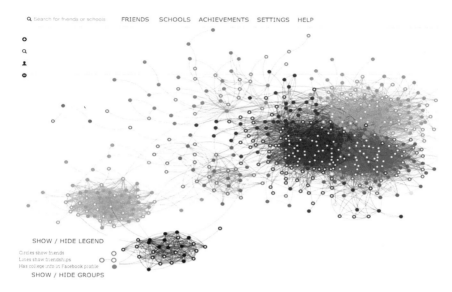

Fig. 6.1 Example of the College Connect network visualization

run College Connect on Facebook, because relationship and profile data available within Facebook could be harnessed to surface relevant social resources for teens as they envision their future and engage in the college application process [46]. The College Connect app draws upon data from Facebook and works most effectively when users reach out to other Facebook Friends. More specifically, College Connect visualizes a user's Facebook network, or the set of their Facebook Friends as well as the friendships between these Friends (See Fig. 6.1).

The designers used conventions from social network analysis to represent this network. A user is a 'node' signified by a circle. A Friend is an 'edge' signified as a line between two nodes. The arrangement of the nodes is automatically determined by a network layout algorithm. The coloring of the nodes is automatically determined by a community detection algorithm, such that likely members of a specific cluster have like-colored nodes. If the Friend has a college or university listed in his or her profile, the dot is colored-in; Friends who do not have a college or university listed in his or her profile are indicated by a dot that is not colored-in (See Fig. 6.2). College Connect users can explore their network visualization (e.g., by zooming in or clicking on specific nodes) for Friends that have college information in their profile, and they can search for specific Friends or colleges/universities in which they are interested (See Fig. 6.2).

Furthermore, the College Connect Facebook application was designed to include a list of suggested questions, that address common college-related information needs, which students could ask their Friends network (See Fig. 6.3). The app allows users to send inquiries to people in their network via Facebook's private messaging (See Fig. 6.4).

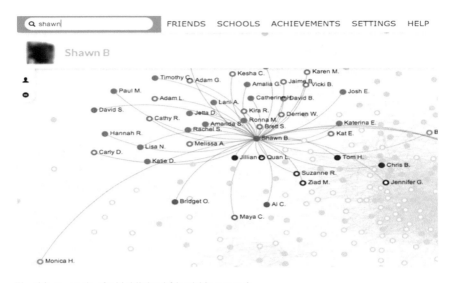

Fig. 6.2 Example of a highlighted friendship network

Ask a question

Choosing a college	I am interested in applying to your school. Could I ask you a few questions about it?
Applying to College	
Success in College	I'm interested in a specific school. Could you introduce me to someone who attended it?
Paying for college	How did you choose which college or university to attend?
Academic Support	If you could give a high school junior or senior one piece of advice about applying to college, what would it be?
Preparing for a Career	
College Life	Was your college or university a good fit for you?
Other	What is the most important factor to consider when deciding which college or university to attend?

Fig. 6.3 Example of a list of suggested questions

The College Connect application connects to the Facebook Graph API (version 1.0) to access a user's Friends and the connections between these Friends. To use the API, the College Connect application must be granted explicit permission by the user to view Friends and Friend data. The ability for third parties to access this data was no longer available as of Facebook Graph API (version 2.0). Nevertheless, this work demonstrates what can be done with social network data, not exclusively with Facebook data in their current state.

The design of the College Connect Facebook application was fueled by research which found that Facebook use increases social capital when users are active and engaged [20, 47]. College Connect was designed to accelerate this process for a key demographic (i.e., high school students) at a critical time in their adolescent and

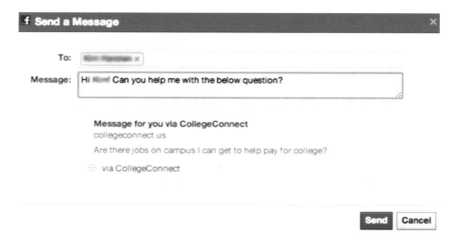

Fig. 6.4 Example of sending a question

educational development (i.e., transition between high school and college). Robelia, Greenhow, and Burton, in studying another Facebook app (HotDish), found that 16–24 year olds were more likely to adopt Facebook apps than use other online resources for educational purposes because: (1) they are easily integrated into their existing daily Facebooking routines, (2) Facebook provided an informal context with which they were already familiar and compelled to participate, and (3) they perceived people on Facebook as 'like-minded' and so felt comfortable interacting [48].

The findings of this prior research were taken into account during the development of the College Connect app, and thus the design of the app was unique; at the time it was developed, there were no other apps that did exactly what College Connect was designed to do. Although there were free, online apps that produced visualizations of users' Facebook networks (e.g., Touchgraph, Friendwheel), there were no applications that offered young people a compelling, easy-to-navigate visualization of their network which was tailored specifically to address information-based college access issues. The College Connect app was designed to provide students with a fun, engaging way to see who is connected to whom within their network and to surface relevant college-related information from these contacts.

The foundation and catalyst for the College Connect application was a Facebook application called NameGenWeb, developed by Hogan and his colleagues at the Oxford Internet Institute. This more generic Facebook application was the culmination of years of work trying to optimize the algorithms for interfacing with social network information on Facebook in a way that respects privacy policies, leverages API standards at Facebook, and keeps abreast of visualization technologies[2]. Using NameGenWeb, the average user could authorize the application, download their own network, visualize it, and begin exploring friendship relationships among their Face-

---

[2]Hogan [49]

book Friends. The application visualized network relationships in an enlightening way, inviting users to explore their network and the web of relationships that constitute it.

Moreover, to guide the development of College Connect, Ellison and Greenhow interviewed 45 high school students in rural Michigan. Students were shown a version of their own Facebook network visualized by a modified version of NameGenWeb, developed by Hogan, and were interviewed about it. These preliminary data informed the design of the College Connect app. Following these interviews, NameGenWeb was modified for the purpose of enabling high school students to visualize their Facebook network and important personal characteristics of their connections in relation to college-going.

Thus, the new application, College Connect, was a social network visualization and exploration tool that downloaded, processed, and represented Facebook personal networks. Most importantly, compared to NameGenWeb, College Connect was designed to have a stronger emphasis on deployment and usefulness for addressing the user's need for college knowledge as identified in preliminary interviews with high school students and in the educational research literature. Where NameGen-Web showed an individual's network with contemporary layouts and clustering, pan and zoom, and click-to-filter functionality, College Connect extended these tools in two significant ways to make it an app for prompting trust-based conversations about issues that are relevant to high school students' college-going. First, the app highlighted individuals in the student's network who either had college experience or "liked" a particular college. This capability was supposed to make the challenge of locating college-related resources in one's network easier, faster, and friendlier. Secondly, College Connect allowed users to easily reach out to Friends who may have college knowledge. This process of reaching out was facilitated through both technical and social affordances embedded in the College Connect app and in Facebook itself. With one click, students were able to send a message pre-populated with questions derived from the academic literature on barriers to college access. They could also type their own queries if desired. By embedding this conversation in the Facebook system, the project team hoped that users would be able to capitalize on shared common ground (as indicated in profile fields) and the shared connections between them. Our data from the interviews with high school students suggests students are more comfortable inquiring of a Facebook Friend or a "Friend of a Friend" than a complete stranger.

6.6 The Benefits and Challenges of the Implementation of College Connect

Upon launching College Connect in late 2013, we encountered several implementation benefits and challenges. First, we were pleased that the application provided key functions as intended. These included a network visualization of the students'

Friends network; an indication of who in-network had college information in his or her profile; the capacity to search the network for a college or university name, by geography, or by person; and the ability to message people a question related to college through Facebook's direct messaging. In beta-testing with a small group of high school juniors and seniors, we found that students generally understood the application's features and could see the utility of having a Facebook application devoted to messaging potential contacts about college-going issues.

However, we also encountered a number of implementation challenges that limited College Connect's utility and broad deployment. First, we found that students experienced long wait times for their network visualizations to be generated during beta-testing and follow-up implementation. This was the result of Facebook's design and API. For College Connect to function properly, it needed access to information from its users' profiles and social networks, for which users had to grant explicit permission. The process of collecting and representing this information was affected by the size of social networks. In cases when users had an excess of 700 connections, the process as long as 15 min. Given that the research has suggested the average size of adolescents' Facebook networks were around 500 Friends, this posed a significant hurdle to College Connect's utility [21].

A second implementation challenge we faced was that we did not have sufficient server space to accommodate more than a small number of College Connect users at any given time. While the metrics for the College Connect application (i.e., number of daily, weekly, and monthly users via Facebook insights) revealed an average of approximately 10 users per day in November 2013, resolving these issues was paramount if the app was to scale.

To that end, we requested supplemental funding, from the College Knowledge Grant program sponsored by the Gates Foundation, to help kick start the success of the College Connect (CC) application and increase its impact on students. In early 2014 funds were requested for additional development efforts to optimize the app's performance through a re-designed workflow. Specifically, while the generation and presentation of the College Connect network visualization was very slow and time intensive, much of the querying of the user's friends and the friends' schools was not. Thus, a re-designed work flow, we hoped, would expose search and browse by school and by friend while students were waiting for the network to load. As College Connect was originally designed, it did not provide a way for the user to do much of the querying by school and messaging without going through the network download step. Additional development efforts that focused on redesigning the workflow so that students could see and browse by school and message first and then see the network when it was ready would have been a significant improvement. This supplemental request was ultimately unfunded. Thus, a third implementation challenge we faced was in generating the additional resources (i.e., paid developers' time, improved server capacity, continued beta-testing and bug fixing, marketing to attract and grow a user base), beyond the initial pilot investment (i.e., $100,000). These resources were needed to improve the immediate feedback and engagement that student-users expected, while continuing to refine, grow and market the application.

6.7   College Connect as a Proof-of-Concept Pilot Study

In order to understand whether and how high school students perceived the application as helpful for their college going process, we conducted a small-scale pilot study with two groups of high school students in 2014. We recruited 12th grade students (n = 22) from two schools: a Minnesota high school, where they were involved in an afterschool program which aimed to help low-income students apply for and gain admission to a four-year college; and a Michigan public magnet school, which focused on college preparation. All students were high school seniors, had used Facebook for at least one year, and were actively using Facebook at least twice a week.

In trying out the College Connect app with this group of students, we were particularly interested in students' conceptions of *help* related to college information-seeking and the types of information, such as that related to the college knowledge literature, that students identified using College Connect. Participants completed an online survey prior to using the College Connect app; this survey asked them about their help-seeking practices regarding their searches for information related to the college-going process. As part of the survey, participants were asked to identify people from whom they could seek help regarding college information.

Following the online survey, participants completed one-on-one, semi-structured interviews about their help-seeking processes as they pertained to college knowledge. Within the interview, subjects participated in a think-aloud activity with a researcher while using the College Connect application. Participants were invited to navigate their individual Facebook networks using the College Connect app as the researcher asked open-ended questions about what they were seeing, how they were understanding the app, and whether and how it was useful. While results from this research have been published elsewhere, we point out here that although students did not view Facebook as a platform they would use for help with college-going, they did see value in a designed Facebook application for this purpose [50]. We are currently working on a more detailed analysis from this pilot data to report on the nature of their help-seeking with College Connect compared to their perceived use of Facebook generally and other online resources.

6.8   Conclusions and Recommendations

The College Connect Facebook application, from conception through design to implementation, was intended to be unique, helpful to high school students' college-going process, and piggyback on their existing Facebooking routines. Developing and implementing the app, however, presented several challenges, as described above. As a result of both the benefits and challenges to the design and implementation of the College Connect app, the authors seek to provide practical guidance and recommendations for designers of future social network site applications.

Creating a visualization of one's social network, and making it attractive, is not an idea unique to the College Connect app. However, to our knowledge, there have been few efforts to leverage people's initial interest and engagement in their visualized social network into long-term, strategic social interactions toward actionable goals (e.g., building a college-going peer group) that address pressing social problems (e.g., improving college access and college-going). By adding features such as messaging with identified 'experts,' or more knowledgeable peers in the network, we believe we have moved network visualizations beyond 'cool' to make them useful for students in addressing the college knowledge challenge. (Note that by using the term "experts," we do not mean those with privileged or rare information or skills, but rather someone who knows something that the user wishes to know more about.) This could be a particular school (e.g., Michigan State University), a particular major (Nursing), or a particular experience (e.g., being a Latina in a mostly White college). Our application is a novel consolidation of rapidly maturing visual technologies and access to Facebook's rich source of personally-meaningful data. Many applications can already display networks. Many applications can provide simple summaries of users' networks. However, the focused unification of these two aspects in a way that makes networks both visually appealing and actionable is a distinct novel experience.

Furthermore, one of the most significant challenges to the successful roll out of the app was the length of time required by the app to download user's Facebook data. This wait time negatively impacted user experience and the overall utility of the College Connect app. Going forward, future social network site apps should take into account not only user experience broadly but also specifics (as in our case, the need to download significant amounts of data) which can and likely will greatly impact user experience. We recommend that throughout the design process that researchers, developers, and educators work more closely with the Facebook developer community to ensure that the structures (including, but not limited to, hardware and financial considerations) which support the application being built can fully support that application.

We hope design teams might build on the insights we have generated in this small scale, exploratory project to engage with Facebook's development community over a longer time horizon to design similar, novel applications aimed at addressing persistent educational problems. Facebook is a global platform, and it continues to be the single largest social media platform adopted by today's young people, connecting billions of youth all over the world. Yet, educators and educational technology designers have not only under-examined Facebook's potential for K-12 students' learning and teachers' pedagogy, the Facebook parent platform remains largely un-leveraged by learning technology designers [51–53].

We offer this rich description of the process of developing and implementing the College Connect app as a case study for future researchers, designers, and educators, as well as the many people who are interested in the varied and interesting ways in which social media, and social network sites specifically, can be used in the field of education. In spite of the challenges that we faced in our initial implementation of the College Connect application, the applicability of social network sites in the field of education remains viable and substantial. Our focus on usability, a visually appealing interface, and an academic interest in effective outcomes provides a template for future social network site applications to strive to be even more seamless, creative and usable as College Connect.

Acknowledgements This research was conducted with support from the Bill & Melinda Gates Foundation and the King Center Charter School.

References

1. Social Media Statistics and Facts. (August 2017). Retrieved August 30, 2017, from https://www.statista.com/topics/1164/social-networks/.
2. Perna, L. W. (2000) Differences in the decision to attend college among African Americans, Hispanics, and Whites. *The Journal of Higher Education, 71*(2), 117.
3. Lucia, K. E., & Baumann, R. W. (2009). Differences in the college enrollment decision across race. *American Economist, 53*(1), 60–74.
4. Peng, S. S. (1977). Trends in the entry to higher education: 1961–1972. *Educational Researcher, 6*(1).
5. Lamont, M., & Lareau, A. (1988). Cultural capital: Allusions, gaps and glissandos in recent theoretical developments. *Sociological Theory, 6*(2).
6. Lareau, A., & Horvat, E. M. (1999). Moments of social inclusion and exclusion: Race, class, and cultural capital in family-school relationships. *Sociology of Education, 72*(1), 37–53.
7. Hooker, S., & Brand, B. (2010). College knowledge: A critical component of college and career readiness. *New Directions for Youth Development, 127*.
8. Hoxby, C. M., & Turner, S. (2015). What high-achieving low-income students know about college. *American Economic Review, 105*(5), 514–517.
9. Orfield, G. (1992). Money, equity, and college access. *Harvard Educational Review, 62*(3), 337–372.
10. Ellison, N. B., Wohn, D. Y., & Brown, M. G. (2014). Social media and college access. *Interactions 21*(4), 62–65.
11. DeAndrea, D. C., Ellison, N. B., LaRose, R., Steinfield, C., & Fiore, A. (2012). Serious social media: On the use of social media for improving students' adjustment to college. *The Internet and Higher Education, 15*(1), 15–23.
12. Gray, R., Vitak, J., Easton, E. W., & Ellison, N. B. (2013) Examining social adjustment to college in the age of social media: Factors influencing successful transitions and persistence. *Computers & Education, 67*, 193–207.
13. Wohn, D. Y., Ellison, N. B., Khan, M. L., Fewins-Bliss, R., & Gray, R. (2013). The role of social media in shaping first-generation high school students' college aspirations: A social capital lens. *Computers & Education, 63*, 424–436.
14. Forte, A., Dickard, M., Magee, R., & Agosto, D. E. (2014). What do teens ask their online social networks?: Social search practices among high school students. In *Proceedings of the 17th ACM Conference on Computer Supported Cooperative Work & Social Computing (CSCW '14)* (pp. 28–37).
15. Meyers, E. M., Fisher, K. E., & Marcoux, E. (2009). Making sense of an information world: The everyday-life information behavior of preteens. *The Library Quarterly, 79*(3), 301–341.
16. Barab, S. (2006). Design-based research: A methodological toolkit for the learning scientist. In R.K. Sawyer (Ed.), *Cambridge handbook of the learning sciences* (pp. 153–170). Cambridge: Cambridge University Press.
17. Reeves, T. C. (2006). Design research from a technology perspective. In J. V. den Akker, K. Gravemeijer, S. McKenney, & N. Nieveen (Eds.), *Education design research* (pp. 52–66). London: Routledge.

18. Vanderhoven, E., Schellens, T., Vanderlinde, R., & Valcke, M. (2016). Developing educational materials and risks on social network sites: A design-based research approach. *Educational Technology Research and Development, 64*(3), 459–480.
19. Ellison, N. B., & Boyd, D. M. (2013). Sociality through social network sites. In W. H. Dutton (Ed.), The Oxford handbook of internet studies (pp. 151–172). Oxford: Oxford University Press.
20. Ellison, N. B., Steinfield, C., & Lampe, C. (2007). The benefits of Facebook "Friends": Social capital and college students' use of online social network sites. *Journal of Computer Mediated Communication, 12*(4), article 1.
21. Greenhow, C., & Burton, L. (2011). Help from my "friends": Social capital in the social network sites of low-income students. *Journal of Educational Computing Research, 45*(2), 223–245.
22. Kert, S. B., & Kert, A. (2010). The usage potential of social network sites for educational purposes. *International Online Journal of Educational Sciences, 2*(2), 486–507.
23. Ekici, M., & Kiyici, M. (2012). Using social networks in educational context. *Usak Universitesi Sosyal Bilimler Dergisi, 5/2*, 156–167.
24. Lin, P. C., Hou, H. T., Wang, S. M., & Chang, K. E. (2013). Analyzing knowledge dimensions and cognitive process of a project-based online discussion instructional activity using Facebook in an adult and continuing education course. *Computers & Education, 60*(1), 110–121.
25. Cakir, R., & Serkan Tan, S. (2017). Development of educational applications on the social network of Facebook and its effects on students' academic achievement. *Educational Sciences: Theory & Practice, 17*(5).
26. Nelson-Le Gall, S. (1981). Help-seeking: An understudied problem-solving skill in children. *Developmental Review, 1*(3), 224–246.
27. Nurmi, J. E. (1991). How do adolescents see their future? A review of the development of future orientation and planning. *Developmental Review, 11*(1), 1–59.
28. Clausen, J. (1991). Adolescent Competence and the shaping of the life course. *American Journal of Sociology, 96*(4), 805–842.
29. Sirin, S. R., Diemer, M. A., Jackson, L. R., Gonsalves, L., & Howell, A. (2004) Future aspirations of urban adolescents: a person-in-context model. *International Journal of Qualitative Studies in Education, 17*(3), 437–456.
30. Bourdieu, P. (1985). The forms of capital. In J. G. Richardson (Ed.), *Handbook of theory and research for the sociology of education* (pp. 241–258). New York: Greenwood.
31. Portes, A. (1998). Social capital: Its origins and applications in modern sociology. *Annual Review of Sociology, 24*(1), 1–24.
32. Loury, G. (1977). A dynamic theory of racial income differences. *Women, Minorities, and Employment Discrimination, 153*, 86–153.
33. Kim, D. H., & Schneider, B. (2005). Social capital in action: Alignment of parental support in adolescents' transition to postsecondary education. *Social Forces, 84*(2), 1181–1206.
34. Israel, G., & Beaulieu, L. J. (2004). Investing in communities: Social capital's role in keeping youth in school. *Journal of the Community Development Society, 34*(2), 34–57.
35. Choy, S. P., Horn, L. J., Nuñez, A. M., & Chen, X. (2000). Transition to college: What helps at-risk students and students whose parents did not attend college. *New Directions for Institutional Research, 2000*(107), 45–63.
36. Nelson, I. A. (2016). Rural students' social capital in the college search and application process: Rural students' social capital. *Rural Sociology, 81*(2), 249–281.
37. Bronfenbrenner, U. (1977). Toward an experimental ecology of human development. *American Psychologist, 32*(7), 513.
38. Granovetter, M. S. (1974). *Getting a job: A study of contacts and careers.* Cambridge, MA: Harvard University Press.
39. Hooker, S., Brand, B. (2010). College knowledge: A critical component of college and career readiness. *New Directions for Youth Development, 127.*
40. The Tomás Rivera Policy Institute. (2002). *College knowledge: What Latino parents need to know and why they don't know it.* Claremont, CA: Tornatzky LG, Cutler R, & Lee J.

41. Stoner, M. (2004). How the web can speak to prospective students. *The Chronicle of Higher Education, 50*(34), B10–B11.
42. Tucciarone, K. M. (2009). Speaking the same language: Information college seekers look for on a college web site. *College and University, 84*(4), 22.
43. Brown, M. G., Wohn, D. Y., & Ellison, N. B. (2016). Without a map: College access and the online practices of youth from low-income communities. *Computers & Education, 92,* 104–116.
44. Ellison, N. B., Steinfield, C., & Lampe, C. (2011). Connection strategies: Social capital implications of Facebook-enabled communication practices. *New Media & Society, 13*(6), 873–892.
45. Jeon, G. Y., Ellison, N. B., Hogan, B., & Greenhow, C. (2016). First-Generation Students and College: The Role of Facebook Networks as Information Sources. In *Proceedings of the 2016 ACM Conference on Computer-Supported Cooperative Work and Social Computing [CSCW'16]*. San Francisco, CA.
46. Ellison, N. B., Wohn, D. Y., Khan, M. L., & Fewins-Bliss, R. (2012). Reshaping access: An overview of research on access to higher education, social media and social capital [White paper].
47. Greenhow, C., &Burton, L. (2011). Help from my "friends": Social capital in the social network sites of low-income students. *Journal of Educational Computing Research, 45*(2), 223–245.
48. Robelia, B. A., Greenhow, C., & Burton, L. (2011). Environmental learning in online social networks: Adopting environmentally responsible behaviors. *Environmental Education Research, 17*(4), 553–575.
49. Hogan, B. (2015). From Invisible Algorithms to Interactive Affordances: Data After the Ideology of Machine Learning. In *Roles, Trust, and Reputation in Social Media Knowledge Markets* (pp.103–117). Springer.
50. Greenhow, C., Chapman, A., & Lei, M. (2017). Help from friends: Facebook's pPotential for adolescents' academic help-seeking. In P. Resta & S. Smith (Eds.), *Proceedings of Society for Information Technology & Teacher Education International Conference 2017* (pp. 852–855). Chesapeake, VA: Association for the Advancement of Computing in Education (AACE).
51. Greenhow, C., & Askari, E. (2017). Learning and teaching with social network sites: A decade of research in K-12 related education. *Education and Information Technologies*, 1–23.
52. Manca, S., & Ranieri, M. (2013). Is it a tool suitable for learning? A critical review of the literature on Facebook as a technology-enhanced learning environment. *Journal of Computer Assisted Learning, 29*(6), 487–504.
53. Manca, S., & Ranieri, M. (2016). Is Facebook still a suitable technology-enhanced learning environment? An updated critical review of the literature from 2012 to 2015. *Journal of Computer Assisted Learning, 32*(6), 503–528.

Part III
Social Network Security and Challenges

Chapter 7
Massively Multi-user Online Social Virtual Reality Systems: Ethical Issues and Risks for Long-Term Use

Jolanda Tromp, Chung Le, Bao Le and Dac-Nhuong Le

Abstract This chapter covers the convergence of Social Media Networks and Virtual Reality Systems, labeled as Social Virtual Reality. It reviews the evolution of the World Wide Web from a single user, static experience into the futuristic 3D multi user interactive experience. This is followed by a review of bulk data collection in Virtual Reality, and the ethical risks and threats to privacy that this could create for Social Virtual Reality users. The chapter ends with recommendations to mitigate the ethical risks and threats to privacy for adult VR users, parents of VR users, psychologists, VR software and hardware manufacturers, governments and other regulatory institutions and VR researchers.

Keywords Social VR · Web VR · MMOGs · Metaverse · Web 5.0

7.1 Introduction

The year 2017 will go down in history as the year Social Media Networks (SMNs) and Virtual Reality (VR) converged, although not everyone will be aware of the significance of this convergence. Facebook opened their Virtual Reality world called

J. Tromp (✉) · C. Le · B. Le
Center for Visualization and Simulation, Duy Tan University, Da Nang, Vietnam
e-mail: jolanda.tromp@duytan.edu.vn

C. Le
e-mail: levanchung@duytan.edu.vn

B. Le
e-mail: baole@duytan.edu.vn

D.-N. Le
Faculty of Information Technology, Haiphong University, Haiphong, Vietnam
e-mail: nhuongld@dhhp.edu.vn

© Springer International Publishing AG, part of Springer Nature 2018
N. Dey et al. (eds.), *Social Networks Science: Design, Implementation, Security, and Challenges*, https://doi.org/10.1007/978-3-319-90059-9_7

"Spaces" (April 18, public launch of the Beta version).[1] Within a few months, Microsoft bought the Social VR application called *"AltspaceVR"* (October 3),[2] after it had to briefly shut down due to lack of funding (July 28 August 16).[3,4,5,6] Alongside this, Microsoft has launched a major update for Windows 10 (October, 17, 2017),[7] which includes full support for Windows Mixed Reality (named after the continuum of shared functionalities between Reality, Augmented Reality (AR) and VR,[8] that runs on headsets from Acer, Dell, HP, Lenovo, new Samsung VR headset, with competitive features and price.

Users of Social Media Networks (SMNs) share information about their lives and their interests, and the number of users and the frequency with which they share information is on the increase. They share this information with others as a means to communicate with those they identify as friends, family and like-minded others, such as members of their online special interests groups. Online user conversations, user searches and literally everything users do and look at on the Internet and on an SMN are automatically stored and can then be analyzed for purposes such as mass-surveillance and marketing. This is current standard practice, which culminates in massive databases of personal information or Bulk Personal Datasets (BPDs), which are collected, traded, and sold by all kinds of parties with different kinds of intentions from personalized targeted marketing to fighting serious crime.

Multi-user Virtual Reality (*also known as Social VR*) systems provide huge potential to give users similar social networking opportunities, because multi-user VR systems allow users to see a virtual representation of other users, talk to each other, and collaborate on something together, such as a game or building something together - all within a shared 3D computer generated virtual environment. These types of VR systems can be divided into applications for serious long-distance work: Collaborative Virtual Environments (CVEs) and fun games: Massively Multiplayer Online Games (*MMOGs or MMO for short*), depending on the purpose for which the VR system was developed. CVEs can be used for long-distance meetings, replacing or adding to the existing video-conferencing and audio-conferencing applications. At minimum a CVE will have a blackboard or presentation-screen, and other types of meeting tools that facilitate long-distance collaboration, see Fig. 7.1 for an impression of a CVE and the different levels of design: architectural layout of the shared spaces, semantic layout of the functional objects for collaboration, social layout of the users in the virtual-world, which continuously change configuration based on

---

[1]https://newsroom.fb.com/news/2017/04/facebook-spaces/.

[2]https://altvr.com/joining-microsoft/.

[3]https://altvr.com/good-bye/.

[4]https://vrscout.com/news/altspacevr-is-closing-down/.

[5]https://www.theverge.com/2017/7/28/16055222/altspacevr-virtual-reality-social-network-shutdown-funding.

[6]https://www.theverge.com/2017/8/16/16156806/altspacevr-vr-social-network-not-shutting-down.

[7]https://developer.microsoft.com/en-us/windows/mixed-reality.

[8]https://en.wikipedia.org/wiki/Reality%E2%80%93virtuality_continuum.

Fig. 7.1 Collaborative
Virtual Environment with
functional layers:
architectural, semantic and
social

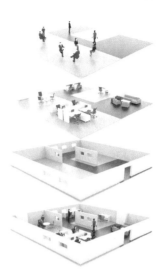

interactions of users with objects and other users within the virtual, thus changing the virtual world over time, adding a 4th functional level, the space-time continuum [15, 16]. MMOs are online games which can be used by large numbers of players (*ranging from hundreds to thousands*) who are simultaneously in the same virtual world, consisting of one persistent space or of multiple connected spaces, depending on the purpose and design of the game. However, Social VR systems can also simply be just that: a space to meet and talk, or collaborate on a building or viewing shared virtual 3D objects in the virtual world. Users can access these virtual worlds via their Desktop PC, Smartphone, Tablet and Head-Mounted Display. These types of Head-Mounted Displays range from affordable low-end to high-end devices, such as Google Cardboard (~$5) to the Oculus Rift (~$500) and the HTC Vive (~$600). In fact, both Oculus and HTC dropped the price of their VR headsets with $200 during summer 2017, in a bid to obtain a larger share of the market. Facebook, who owns Oculus, ran an ad during the summer of 2017, calling the price drop part of the "*Summer of VR*". Facebook has announced (October, 2017) new additional social tools for Spaces, to enhance social creative collaboration, such as live-video streaming in Spaces and a stylized drawing tool called Quill.[9]

The convergence of Social Networks and VR is taking place, and due to the size and magnitude of the user-base of Facebook and Microsoft, the number of users for these new 3D Computer Graphics based Social Networks can increase at a rapid rate, which brings with it an exponential increase of ethical and privacy risks. The ethical issues are not necessarily all new. They are similar to the risks in Social Networks, but the potential anticipated increase in the number of users of VR for non-gaming

---

[9]https://www.theverge.com/2017/10/11/16460080/facebook-spaces-live-360-degree-video-3d-posts.

purposes, means that these ethical concerns are more all-pervasive. It can be predicted that there will be an exponential growth in the number of Social VR users, based on the popularity and number of users of Facebook and Microsoft software. This increase in the number of users of Social VR would mean that the ethical problems and risks potentially also become more widespread and all-encompassing. In this chapter we analyze the historic growth of Social Media usage and bulk surveillance, the World Wide Web and the evolution it is going through, illustrating how these systems converge and grow into a World Wide 3D social VR-based browsing experience. Next the ethical problems and risks are reviewed and discussed. The chapter ends with concrete suggestions on how to manage these risks for:

- VR users,
- VR software and hardware companies,
- the government,
- psychologists and
- researchers.

7.1.1 Historical Growth of Social Media Networks

According to the Pew Research Center in 2005 only 5% of American adults used at least one SMN and by end of 2016 this had risen to 69%. By July 2016, 86% of the youngest adult age group 18–29 was reported to use at least one SMN, and for the older groups 30–49 80%, 50–64 64% and 65+ 34%. See Fig. 7.2 [10] for an illustration of the growth curve of Social Media users and Table 7.1 [11] for an overview of the number of users per Social Media Network (SMN), based on data from September, 2017.

Reference [6] studied Social Media user perceptions of their own frequency of use, usefulness, and enjoyment of Facebook, Twitter and Pinterest, analyzed against their actual use of the different features of these SMNs. The study found that for males and females, most often used features were contact with friends, posting information about themselves and finding information about others and these were highly correlated with the users' perceived usefulness for all three Social Media Networks. Some correlations were also found for perceived usefulness of these SMNs for finding information about products and stores. What is remarkable is that low ease-of-use had little impact on perceived usefulness, which suggests that even when SMNs are perceived as not easy to use, persist in using it because of the inherent value they reported getting from it.

---

[10] http://www.statisticbrain.com/social-networking-statistics.

[11] http://www.statisticbrain.com/social-networking-statistics/.

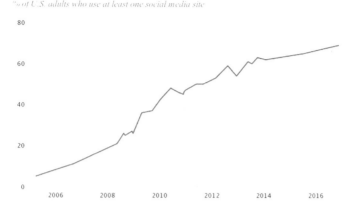

% of U.S. adults who use at least one social media site

Fig. 7.2 Growth curve of social media users. http://www.statisticbrain.com/social-networking-statistics.

7.1.2 Historical Developments of Social Virtual Reality

Earlier multi-user VR applications that received world-wide active user groups are ActiveWorlds (*June 28, 1995, called AlphaWorld in the early days*),[12] blaxxun Interactive (August 1995),[13] notable because it was one of the first companies to use VRML (Virtual Reality Markup Language (now called X3D[14, 15]) an extension of HTML, the language that is used to construct webpages for the WWW). Amongst a list of other ones, some mostly focused on some form of gaming, rather than socializing,[16] the Social VR's which captured some form of world-wide attention are "*SecondLife*" (June 23, 2003),[17] and their next versions "*High Fidelity*" (April, 2013) and Sansar (public launch of the Beta version, June 23, 2017).[18, 19] Interestingly, Google also opened a Social VR world called "*Google Lively*", but closed it again very quickly (July 8 December 31, 2008).[20]

A distinction is often made between Massively Multiplayer Online Games (MMOGs or MMOs) and Social VR applications that are part of a much bigger future vision for the Internet, called "*the Metaverse*"[21] [8], a term coined by Cyber-

---

[12]https://en.wikipedia.org/wiki/Active_Worlds.

[13]https://en.wikipedia.org/wiki/Blaxxun.

[14]https://en.wikipedia.org/wiki/X3D.

[15]https://en.wikipedia.org/wiki/Web3D.

[16]https://en.wikipedia.org/wiki/Metaverse#Timeline_of_virtual_environments_inspired_by_the_concept.

[17]https://en.wikipedia.org/wiki/Second_Life.

[18]https://www.sansar.com/.

[19]https://singularityhub.com/2017/06/23/new-virtual-world-sansar-is-ready-to-pick-up-where-second-life-left-off/.

[20]https://en.wikipedia.org/wiki/Google_Lively.

[21]https://web.archive.org/web/20140608135859/.

Table 7.1 Number of users per Social Media Network. http://www.statisticbrain.com/social-networking-statistics/.

Percent of people who use social networks	Percent yes
Do you ever use / have a profile on	
Any social network	58%
Facebook	56%
LinkedIn	14%
Twitter	11%
Google+	9%
Largest socials networks in the world	Number of users
Facebook	1,374,000,000
QZone	635,000,000
Google+	347,000,000
LinkedIn	336,000,000
Instagram	302,000,000
Twitter	289,000,000
Tumblr	237,000,000
Sina weibo	162,000,000
Snapchat	113,000,000
Pinterest	73,500,000
Top reasons for using social networking sites	Percent yes
Percent who said the following was a MAJOR reason for using social networking sites	
Staying in touch with current friends	67%
Staying in touch with family members	64%
Connecting with old friends you've lost touch with	50%
Connecting with others with shared hobbies or interests	14%
Making new friends	9%
Reading comments by celebrities, athletes or politicians	5%
Finding potential romantic or dating partners	3%

punk writer Neal Stephenson in his novel "*Snowcrash*" (1992).[22] The Metaverse is envisioned by Stephenson as a collective virtual shared space, created by the convergence of virtually enhanced physical reality and physically persistent virtual space [8], including the sum of all virtual worlds, augmented reality, and the internet, it is used to describe the concept of a future iteration of the internet, made up of persistent, shared, 3D virtual spaces linked into a computer generated virtual universe.[23]

---

[22]https://en.wikipedia.org/wiki/Snow_Crash.

[23]https://en.wikipedia.org/wiki/Metaverse.

7.1.3 Historical Developments of the Three-Dimensional World Wide Web

The first version of the WWW (*publicly available January 1991*), was a "*Read-Only*" collection of interconnected websites and webpages, that the user could browse by clicking on "*hyperlinks*", but creating one's own website was generally something only experts in the HTML code with access to a server were capable of. This led to the dot.com boom, which turned into a "*bubble that burst*" (1999–2001) due to over-inflated expectations, and perpetuated by the far-reaching repercussions of the financial crisis. It was the beginning of the Web-browser development efforts, and the e-commerce and e-marketing efforts. The next version (beginning of 2002[24]), now referred to as Web 2.0, was a "*Read-Write*" version, that allowed non-programming users to create their own websites and Social Media sites like MySpace, Facebook, Twitter and Flickr started and quickly gained popularity, especially amongst the younger Internet users [3]. Web 2.0 allowed many new service-oriented startups to boom, including Ebay, Amazon, YouTube and Google Search engine. Web 3.0 was intended as a Read-Write-Executable and to this end HTML was extended with semantic-markup. It was intended to bridge the communication gap between human web users and computerized applications. The "*execute*" part of the Web 3.0 functionality refers to formatting data in such a way that it can be understood by automated "*software agents*". By combining a semantic markup and web services, Web 3.0 applications can communicate with each other directly, and this allowed "*automatic contextual search*"; i.e. broader searches for information through simpler interfaces. In order for the search function to understand the context of the user, the system has to collect user search behaviour and user interests through monitoring and collecting "*cookies*" (*small data files, saved within the web browser on the user's computer or other device, as they view a website*) and the clicks the user makes and it is possible to analyze where and how long a user spends reading or looking on a page. This led to the development of Google Analytics and the debate about privacy.[25,26]

The numbering of the next versions of the Web become less clear cut and some predicted developments took longer than expected (*for instance the semantic web and the symbiotic web*) while others progressed faster than expected (*for instance social networking via the smartphone*) and yet other developments are taking place that were not really expected at all (*for instance Augmented Reality applications for the smartphone*). The general consensus seems that Web 4.0 was about the transition to mobile devices, allowing all devices to be connected at all times, creating an Internet of Things (IoT) and people, connecting the real world and the digital domain or "*virtual world*" anywhere and everywhere. The Internet of Things is the network of all physical devices, vehicles, and other items that have built-in electronics, software, sensors, actuators, and network connectivity which enable these objects to collect

---

[24]https://en.wikipedia.org/wiki/History_of_the_World_Wide_Web.

[25]http://freespeechdebate.com/cookies/.

[26]https://searchengineland.com/its-not-about-cookies-privacy-debate-happening-at-wrong-level-77980.

Fig. 7.3 Overview of the evolution of Web 1.0 to Web 5.0 (by TrendOne, 2008)

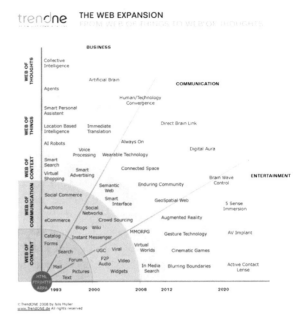

and exchange data.[27] Each device has a unique identifier and devices are capable of communicating with each other. The IoT is predicted to consist of 30 billion objects by 2020. For instance, with the GPS tracker built into smartphones, user's mobile location, orientation, speed and altitude can be tracked in realtime, allowing the collection of this data on web servers, for analysis and viewing of location worldwide, historical trails, battery life, signal strength, etc. This led to the rise of location based services and apps, such as Google maps, Uber, Foursquare, Tripadvisor, Instagram, Pokemon Go, etc., allowing users to find relevant information near them, such as a restaurant or individuals, where location, time, personal interests and keywords from searches can be used as triggers to push information at a smartphone user.

Web 5.0, a Read-Write-Execution-Concurrency web (2009), was aiming to be a sensory emotive web; a linked web which communicates with users like they communicate with each other (*akin a personal assistant*), also known as the Symbiotic web and the Ubiquitous web. This has led to the rise of personal voice assistants like Google's Echo, Amazon's Alexa, Echo, Echo Dot, and the portable device Amazon Tap.[28] Many large companies, for instance Ford,Whirlpool and Lenovo announced they are going to build Amazon's voice-activated personal assistant into their devices and research firm Gartner[29] predicts that by 2019, 20 % of all smartphone interactions will take place through personal assistants, and by 2020 most gadgets will be designed to work with "zero or minimal touch. In order for these devices to work,

---

[27]https://en.wikipedia.org/wiki/Internet_of_things.

[28]http://time.com/4624067/amazon-echo-alexa-ces-2017/.

[29]https://www.gartner.com/newsroom/id/3551217.

they have to continuously record what is being said in their surroundings so that they can respond adequately to requests from the user. Consumers are raising questions about privacy and security,[30] for instance: What are Google or Amazon doing with the information and how secure is this information from third parties? The magnitude of information that will be gathered through these devices is currently beyond prediction.

Further predictions for Web 5.0, are that it will be a 3D Virtual web, rather than the current 2.5D webpages. This is now quite feasible in principle with the release of WebVR,[31] an open application that makes it possible to experience VR from the web browser and supports VR hardware, such as the Oculus Rift, HTC Vive and Google cardboard. Other predictions are that this 3D Virtual web will be viewed through Active Contact Lenses rather than the large cumbersome VR headsets. Additionally, predictions are that all this will be integrated with Artificial Intelligence (*IBM Watson*[32] *is a forerunner for this*) providing intelligent self-learning virtual assistants, and a Brain-Human-Machine interface, making the use of keyboard and mouse redundant. See Fig. 7.3 for an overview of these different versions of the WWW.

7.2   Digital Footprint Collections from Internet, Social Media and Virtual Reality

A study (2016)[32] for the United Nations by special rapporteur on counter-terrorism and human rights lawyer Emmerson, concluded that while the internet is composed of many layers of private as well as social and public realms, bulk access technologies are indiscriminately corrosive of online privacy and pose a direct and ongoing challenge to established norms of international privacy laws. However, at the same time rules governing privacy and the use of these bulk personal datasets, are currently legislated very differently in different countries.[33]

One of the most common forms of mass surveillance is carried out by commercial organizations. For instance, when a person joins a shop's loyalty card program, they essentially agree to share their personal data and shopping data in exchange for small discounts on the purchases made in that shop. The aggregated data from all customers shopping behaviours can provide valuable insights for the shop owners to help in planning which and how many products will be needed and to anticipate customer needs and trends. This kind of market-analysis can be performed for online shops, without a loyalty-card system, because customers of online shops need to make an

---

[30]http://komonews.com/news/consumer/personal-assistant-devices-are-always-listening-at-what-cost.

[31]https://en.wikipedia.org/wiki/WebVR.

[32]https://www.theguardian.com/world/2014/oct/15/internet-surveillance-report-edward-snowden-leaks.

[33]https://en.wikipedia.org/wiki/Mass_surveillance.

Fig. 7.4 Example
"heatmap" visualization of
where the user looked and
for how long

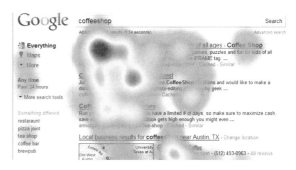

account in order to have their purchases delivered to their address. This allows the
shopping platform to collect data about their buying behaviours.

In addition to online shopping behaviours, many web sites are collecting user
information about the sites users visited, how long they stayed on the site and each
page, and where they looked on the page, who they chat with and the words they
used, see Fig. 7.4[34] for an example of this type of "heatmap" data visualisation.
This information can all be collected via the web browser. This data is valuable for
authorities, marketeers and anyone interested in profiling user behaviours, trends and
the performance analysis of the effectiveness of a website in converting a curious
visitor into a buying and returning customer. As the number of users they collect data
from increases, their "reach" increases and the aggregated data becomes increasingly
more all-inclusive, which makes it more valuable.

Google, Facebook, Microsoft, etc., are increasingly more critically questioned by
users about this data collection process. This is illustrated with a recent article[35] by
Facebook that made the global news, in which they attempt to defuse a rumour that the
Facebook app collects audio data from users. Facebook declared that businesses are
able to push relevant ads to users, based on the analysis of user interests, demographic
data and location information, but that they were not doing this through the collection
of audio data from the Facebook app.

With mobile computing devices, geolocation - where users are physically located
- can be tracked and data about users' physical movements can be collected without
any need for user involvement. This data can be used for location-based advertising,
which can benefit the user, because it allows them to do searches like: *"restaurants
near me"* with high quality and quantity results. Organizations like the Electronic
Frontier Foundation (EFF) are constantly informing users on the importance of privacy, and considerations about technologies like geolocation, etc.[36]

---

[34]http://line6.ca/wp-content/uploads/2017/03/heat-map.jpg.

[35]http://newsroom.fb.com/news/h/facebook-does-not-use-your-phones-microphone-for-ads-or-
news-feed-stories/.

[36]https://en.wikipedia.org/wiki/Electronic_Frontier_Foundation.

Fig. 7.5 Facial expression
analysis markers

More detailed personal information collection is also taking place via advances
in other new technologies, such as face-recognition, for instance Windows Hello,
Google Vision, Blink!, AMD Face Login, and facial expression analysis software,
such as for instance FaceReader and Affectiva, which can combine demographic data,
with emotion recognition and eye-tracking, see Fig. 7.5.[37] To illustrate the power
of these combined new technologies, consider the following example: researchers
reported being able to automatically recognize sheep facial expressions, based on
techniques for human face recognition. "Our multi-level approach starts with detection of sheep faces, localisation of facial landmarks, normalisation and then extraction
of facial features." They reported that their computer system was able to classify 9
different sheep faces and consequently estimate their pain levels with an overall
accuracy was 67%.[38]

Emotion recognition and gaze direction is also being built into Virtual Reality
headsets, for instance Tobii EyeCore. The advantages of this are multitude.[39,40] It
allows for the representation of computer generated realistic reproduction of nonverbal communication cues in the virtual world, based on data collected from eye-
contact between users and virtual agents. It can also make following moving objects
and aiming at objects easier, because the computer system can help improve the aim.
Additionally it can add new interface functionality, by making gaze directed selec-

---

[37] http://cdn.windowsreport.com/wp-content/uploads/2017/08/Blink-face-logon.jpg.

[38] https://www.engadget.com/2017/06/02/facial-recognition-software-sheep-pain/.

[39] https://www.tobii.com/siteassets/tobii-tech/vr/tobii-vr-infografic.pdf/?v=1.

[40] https://www.tobii.com/siteassets/tobii-tech/vr/tobii-whitepaper-eye-tracking-next-natural-
step-for-vr.pdf/?v=1.

tions from menus possible. Finally, it can help computational constraints of visual fidelity to be lower, by only rendering in full detail what is in the direct gaze of the user in an instant. In order for facial, emotional and gaze direction recognition to work, the system has to record and analyse this data. A user watching something on a screen, will show changing facial expressions, their pupils will react, and their bodily systems will respond to the stimuli in numerous, unconscious ways and it is possible to show the relation of these physical reactions to the exact online stimuli. This means that data can be gathered about a person such as the length of time they look at something and more importantly their physical reaction to it. This kind of tracking and recording of personal emotions, movements and social interactions creates data collections that were never possible before and are as detailed and predictive as any forensic scientist could wish for [2].

This digital footprint then, provides a wealth of information about individuals, their preferences and that of their network of work-colleagues, acquaintances, as well as their friends and family. The information becomes a valuable commodity in both commercial, social and political sense, as it is used by companies to target advertisements and analyze trends and behaviours. Recently the first VR, in-world advertisement was made feasible via the Unity ads platform.[41] Companies that own the data collected via these new technologies, especially those that collect data from combinations and convergences of social network and virtual reality systems, have enormously influential positions, because they can collect data from all users and analyze their behaviours. This makes them the gatekeepers to key elements of individual and social life e.g. fulfilment of informational needs, social environments, and entertainment [5]. Already, questions and concerns are raised about advertising in VR.[42] Both Facebook and Microsoft already have large user-groups. Add to this the "*killer-app*" functionality of VR to connect geographically distributed users, which makes meeting on a regular basis so much easier, an exponential growth of the number of users and the use of VR can be expected in the near future. This means that, potentially ever more detailed information about each individual can potentially be aggregated and available, certainly more than ever before.

7.3 Ethical and Psychological Risks of Personal Data Collection with Social VR

The awareness that the Internet and Social Media can have a strong effect on a user's self-perception and social self-esteem, is becoming more mainstream. This effect, known as the Proteus Effect, has also been studied in relation to VR use [17]. The long-term consequences of how this influences and shapes user's psychological makeup are not that well known yet. If the trend of Social Networks converging with

---

[41]https://blogs.unity3d.com/2017/10/20/vr-advertising-experience-lionsgates-jigsaw-in-vr-with-a-virtual-room-ad/.

[42]https://venturebeat.com/2017/10/25/the-vr-industry-must-avoid-intrusive-ads-for-as-long-as-possible/amp/.

Virtual Reality technology continues, in the not too distant future large parts of the human population will be immersed in virtual environments, while we actually do not fully know what the psychological impact of long-term immersion will be. It is clear that this is particularly important to understand better, when we consider that the majority of VR headsets are being purchased by younger Internet users, whose minds and brains are not fully matured.

Users of VR systems are represented in the virtual world, by a personal virtual embodiment, also known as "Avatar", and they can interact with other users' Avatars, in real-time, either via audio, text or a combination of both and to a certain degree they can move and virtually touch other avatar's with their own avatar. An avatar is a computer generated representation of a user, and in many VR systems users can chose from a number of different types of embodiments, in terms of shape, colours and outfits, depending on what is available in the system. There is an ongoing trend in terms of the realism of avatars, both in terms of movement and appearance. A high degree of realism can be achieved by using 3D 360° photo's of the physique of a real user, made with 360 camera. The avatar is controlled via the user interface to the virtual world and the avatar, which means that control of the avatar is always mediated by technology. While the user interacts with the virtual environments via the avatar, they build up a representation of the virtual self and the virtual world, that temporarily replaces the awareness of their, real self and their real body and the real world around them. They enter a state of absorbed attention and identification with the VB in the VE, which has been compared to mystical experiences and can take first-time VR users by pleasant surprise, making them seek out further VR experiences [14], see Fig. 7.6 for a diagram that depicts this effect. This is not to say that the user loses touch with their real self, but in order to concentrate on the avatar their awareness is focused on this immersive experience at the expense of their ability to pay attention to the real world around them.

The psychological effects of immersion in a VR world have been researched by quite a few researchers in one form or another since the early days of VR. A recent

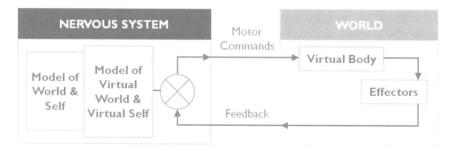

Fig. 7.6 Interaction in a virtual world through a virtual body representation temporarily replaces awareness of one's usual self [14]

review of the research results has been reported by the VERE Project [4]. The authors see a number of risks involved with long-term immersion in VR:

1. *Additiction*: it is not unheard of that users get addicted to being their avatar and prefer this over being themselves, finding it hard to deal with the real world and stuggle to take breaks from the VR world. This can lead to neglect of their real body and their immediate real family, friends, work colleagues and job in the real world.
2. *Manipulation of agency*: users control their avatar via the interface to the VR world. This means that their avatar can be manipulated in subtle ways outside of their immediate awareness and the user might think they are in control, but actually their avatar is directed in certain ways and exposed to manipulated imagery and experiences, rather than the users picking and choosing these. This is related to a concept called "*nudging*" in which for instance marketing agencies present information in a certain way or in a limited way, so that citizens' thinking, behaviour and expectations spontaniously follow a desired direction.
3. *Unnoticed psychological change*: it is not unusual for new users and long-term users to feel a certain euphoria when being immersed in the virtual world, because it is vivid and attractive. They might feel a sense of power and control over their virtual world and virtual self that they lack in the real world, thus giving them a false sense of their own abilities when the power and control does not translate to the real world, the so called Proteus Effect. This can be more difficult to understand and handle for some users than for others, and could lead to Depersonalization or other types of mental illness for some users [1].
4. *Privacy*: as described in previous sections, VR of the future can record user's physical and psychological responses, which can be analyzed automatically and use for targeted advertising, a new method called "*neuromarketing*". This could be argued to be a breach of someones privacy and autonomy. These two concepts are further explored below.

According to [5] there are two central ethical concerns, that are broken down into three subcategories each, which in turn are further broken down into actual threaths to end-users: Privacy (subcategories: *Informational Privacy, Physical Privacy and Associational Privacy)* and Autonomy (subcategories: *Freedom, Knowledge, and Authenticity*). Consider what would happen if a large part of the Internet users is using VR for business and daily social interactions, this might erode societal norms to a status-quo in which privacy and autonomy are deminished in undesirable ways.

People develop themselves and explore their ideas, by making mistakes, experimenting, and exploring different aspects of themselves. They require a certain degree of privacy in which to feel free to do this. Life in a world of diminished privacy will affect the development of individuals' moral characters. Without privacy, the ability of governments *and companies* to influence individual and group behaviour will be extensive. Three types of privacy and their associated threats are distinguished (O'Brolchain, et al, ibid; [11]): Informational privacy, Physical Privacy, Associational Privacy. These concepts are further explained below.

- *Informational Privacy*: protection against third party access to all kinds of information about an individual including an individual's thoughts, utterances, correspondence, and financial, medical and educational records. Threats to Informational Privacy are increased vulnerability of data; misuse of data from virtual meetings with supervisors, doctors, accountants, partners etc. In VR that means information about work performance, health, financial status and sexual preferences is captured and no longer private, and people might face discrimination as a result of what is known about them.
- *Physical Privacy*: shelter against third party sensory access to an individual's body and actions. Thus it concerns modesty, separateness, bodily integrity and the like. Threats to Physical Privacy are recordings of people's faces, emotional states, bodily movements. Three types are distinguished: losing control over being observed in our physical environment; unintended revelation of physical information; loss of anonymity.
- *Associational Privacy*: an individual's control over excluding and including third parties in certain specific experiences. It thus guarantees the intimacy of certain social situations that an individual wishes to be intimate. Threats to Associational Privacy refer to the ability to include or exclude people from certain events and has two aspects: Online socialising, which means that it will be harder to control who attends a virtual event, and more difficult to control who knows about it, and the Global Village problem, which refers to the fact that when we socialize online with realistic avatars, many of our real-time reactions and conversations about trivial and important matters are recorded and potentially available to third parties.
- *Autonomy defines an important quality of human beings*: the ability to independently make plans and form goals. It is intertwined with privacy because we need a certain amount of privacy to think through our options in order to be able to come to our indepdent decisions. Autonomy requires three components (O'Brolchain, ibid): Knowledge, Freedom and Authenticity. These concepts are briefly described below. Knowledge: people need access to relevant information in order to make choices. Threats to Knowledge come from filter bubbles, cyberbalkanization, and from gatekeepers. If VR users primarily access news and information about the world based on what the Virtual Environment shows them or recommends, then they are at risk of the *"Filter Bubble"* [9]. This refers to information being filtered based on the preferences of the user as analyzed from their searches and time spend looking at information, The analysis means that they can then be provided with targeted information based on their appearent interests, giving them a personalised online experience. This could be intensified by the social aspect of VR, where the VR system could help them find only information that confirms their views (*also called Cyberbalkanization or Gatekeeping*) and virtually meet only like minded other's, thus creating their own filter bubble. Virtual worlds might become ever more appealing to users if their beliefs and perspectives are prevalent in the VR bubble they inhabit. And finally, a company could use artificial intelligence (AI) or a chatbot in a virtual world, that presents information in a certain way, with the aim of influencing public opinion, effectively making the AI chatbots the new gatekeepers. Freedom: people need a certain lack of constraints

so that their autonomy is not hollow. Threats to Freedom are based on addiction, manipulation, the Big Brother scenario, and self-censorship. Authenticity or being one's own person: people need to be able to choose for themselves according to their own ideas and values. Threats to Authenticity are based on being exposed to a virtual environment that creates a false sense of autonomic agency, where in fact the user is presented with information that is selected for them outside of their awareness.

7.4 Recommendation to Mitigate Ethical and Psychological Risks of Social VR

People will increasingly more use VR for their daily tasks and activities, leaving an increasingly more detailed digital record of their likes and dislikes and their daily needs and routines. For instance, in the near future VR users might not just meet their friends or family in a virtual environment, but they might also virtually meet their supervisor, their doctor, their accountant, their teachers via VR, rather than physically travelling to meet them. It has been found that people are likely to reveal more intimate and personal information in online scenarios, placing them at an even higher risk than ordinary Social Media users. A virtual environment can give the illusion of greater anonimity and privacy, and a VR user may temporarily forget that their actions can be recorded and replayed, both within and outside of the VR system, because the recording devices may be not be so obvious, embedded in the virtual spaces they visit or the VR hardware or software they are using. There are a number of recommendations for mitigating the possible and currently unknown risks of large-scale (*many users*) and or long-term (*many hours*) in social VR. Separate recommendations are made for Psychologists, adult VR users and parents of VR users, Regulatory Agencies, VR Software and Hardware developer companies and VR researchers.

7.4.1 Recommendations for Psychologists, Adult VR Users and Parents of VR Users

Similar to Internet Use Disorder and Gaming Addiction and this may now have to include addiction to VR. Psychologists need to establish diagnostic criteria for addiction to VR and how these differ from the criteria for Internet Use Disorder and Gaming Addiction. The neurophysiological underpinnings of VR addiction may differ from that of internet use disorder due to the prolonged illusion of embodiment created by VR technology, and because it implies causal interaction with the low-level mechanisms constituting the UI [4]. Psychologist also need to establish if the treatments for Internet Use Disorder and Gaming Addiction will help VR addiction sufferers. Adult VR users and parents of young VR users need to be aware that Psychologists are not fully versed in how to treat VR addition yet.

7.4.2 Recommendations for VR Software and Hardware Companies

The fact that there may be risks associated with long-term use, and that those risks are not known yet, needs to be directly and clearly communicated to users, preferably at the beginning and as part of the VR experience itself. Additionally, any devices that record user behaviours should clearly state this and make it very obvious how to switch this feature off.

7.4.3 Recommendation for Regulatory Institutions

Citizens need to be made aware that long-term VR exposure may have lasting psychological effects and that there is no clear information about the effects of long-term use of VR and that not much is known about the long-term effects so far. Citizens also need to be made aware that their freedom and autonomy in choosing what information they are exposed to in a VR world is manipulated in the same way as via Internet, TV and radio advertizing. Furthermore citizens need to be made aware that their behaviours and responses in VR may be recorded and analyzed to a much finer degree than is already happening via Internet user behaviour monitoring.

7.4.4 Recommendations for Researchers

In order to better understand the risks of the psychological and physical effects of long-term immersion, longitudinal studies of actual users are necessary, conducted according to the principles of informed consent, non-maleficence, and beneficence, for which the VERE Project develop a Code of Ethics ("*The Research Ethics of VR.*"), to help raise awareness and provide guidance to achieve this (Madary and Metzinger, ibid).

7.5 Conclusions

The goal of this chapter was to focus on the risks and challenges of Social VR and how these impact our society. However, there are also many potential advantages for mainstream daily use of Social VR. Firstly, having a system that is capable of analyzing whether we are bored or inspired will have tremendous potential for education. To have a virtual AI driven teacher in a virtual classroom that can be attended by anyone regardless of their physical location and abilities, will allow education to be customized to suit each individual's needs [7]. Secondly, Social VR is a green technology, because it makes the need to physically travel to meetings less frequently necessary, and this will save on fuel, time and financial resources. VR makes the world subjectively smaller as more groups connect individuals with each other. Thirdly, Social VR has an added value over other teleconferening technologies, because it allows multiple users to look at and collaboratively interact with 3D objects in the shared virtual space, even co-designing in real-time. This means that Social VR is very suitable as a tool to make the new Digital Silk Road feasible, because discussions about a design and checking dimensions of a design in relation to other objects, or the space in which they need to be utilized, can be pre-assessed by the team in the Social VR world, thus potentially saving time and manufacturing resources. Numerous theorists have argued that these new technology changes mean that we live in a cognitive, or informational, or immaterial, or knowledge economy, where collective cooperation and knowledge become a source of value [10].

VR has been put forward as game-changer in every human domain, including but not limited to love, war, worship, and learning [2]. It has been hypothesized that Social VR will impact all social institutions, bringing people together in new ways, changing the nature of activities and institutions. Recent Nobel prize winner in economics, Professor Thaler, systematically describes how human beings all succumb to biases in their thinking and make decisions that deviate from the standards of rationality. He is a proponent of the "*nudge for good*" concept, where positive social norms are reinforced through selective presentation of personalized information towards a certain societally desirable point of view, making a distinction between the nanny-state concept and libertarian paternalism [13]. Social VR provides the means to show citizens what the world would look like from all kinds of different perspectives, making it in a manner of speaking an empathy machine.

References

1. Ahn, S. J., Bailenson, J., & Park, D. (2014). Short- and long-term effects of embodied experiences in immersive virtual environments on environmental locus of control and behavior. *Computers in Human Behavior*, *39*, 235–245. https://doi.org/10.1016/j.chb.2014.07.025.
2. Blascovich, J., & Bailenson, J. (2011). *Infinite reality, the hidden blueprint of our virtual lives*. USA: HarperCollins.
3. Choudhury, N. (2014). World wide web and its journey from web 1.0 to. web 4.0. *International Journal of Computer Science and Information Technologies (IJCSIT)*, *5*(6), 8096–8100.
4. Madary, M., & Metzinger, T. K. (2016). Real virtuality: A code of ethical conduct recommendations for good scientific practice and the consumers of VR-technology. *Journal Frontiers in Robotics and AI*, *3*, 00. https://doi.org/10.3389/frobt.2016.00003. ISSN 2296-9144.
5. O'Brolchain, F., Jacquemard, T., Monaghan, D., et al. (2016). The convergence of virtual reality and social networks: Threats to privacy and autonomy. *Science and Engineering Ethics*, *22*(1), 00. https://doi.org/10.1007/s11948-014-9621-1.

6. Sago, & Brad, (2015). A comparison of user perceptions and frequency of use of social media to use of social media. *International Journal of Management and Marketing Research, 8*(1), 15–29. SSRN: https://ssrn.com/abstract=2655859.
7. Scoble, R., & Israel, S. (2017). *The fourth transformation: How augmented reality and artificial intelligence change everything.* USA: Patrick Brewster Press.
8. Smart, J.M., Cascio, J., & Paffendorf, J. (2007). Metaverse Roadmap Overview, 2007. Accelerated Studies Foundation. http://metaverseroadmap.org/resources.html#inputs
9. Spagnolli, A., Conti, M., Guerra, G., Freeman, J., Kirsh, D., & van Wynsberghe, A. (2017). Adapting the system to users based on implicit data: Ethical risks and possible solutions. In L. Gamberini, A. Spagnolli, G. Jacucci, B. Blankertz, & J. Freeman (Eds.), *Symbiotic Interaction. Symbiotic 2016. Lecture Notes in Computer Science* (vol. 9961). Cham: Springer.
10. Srnicek, N. (2017). *Platform capitalism.* UK: Polity Press.
11. Steinicke, F. (2016). *Being really virtual : Immersive natives and the future of virtual reality.* Switzerland: Springer.
12. Stephenson, N. (1992). *Snowcrash.* Bantam Books.
13. Thaler, R., & Sunstein, (2009). *Nudge: Improving decisions about health, wealth, and happiness.* USA: Penguin Group.
14. Tromp, J. G. (1995). Presence, telepresence and immersion: The cognitive factors of embodiment and interaction in virtual environments. *Proceedings of FIVE'95 Conference, Frameworks for Immersive Virtual Environments* (pp. 18–19). UK.
15. Tromp, J. G. (2001). Systematic usability design for collaborative virtual environments, Ph.D. thesis, University of, UK: Nottingham.
16. Tromp, J. G., Steed, A., & Wilson, J. (2003). Systematic usability evaluation and design issues for collaborative virtual environments. *Presence Teleoperators and Virtual Environments, 12*(3), 241–267. https://doi.org/10.1162/105474603765879512.
17. Yee, N., & Bailenson, J. (2007). The proteus effect: the effect of transformed self-representation on behavior. *Human Communication Research, 33*, 271–290. https://doi.org/10.1111/j.1468-2958.2007.00299.x.

Chapter 8
Challenges in Social Media Use Among Deaf and Hard of Hearing People

I. Kožuh and M. Debevc

Abstract The use of social media has grown considerably in recent years, spreading to diverse areas of life, such as education. It attracted researchers to examine users with hearing loss due to their challenges in use. Even though the literature is recent and provides valuable recommendations towards overcoming these challenges, due to the rapid development of social media, they may change regularly. Consequently, stakeholders may not be aware of the appropriate interpretation of these recommendations. Thus, the chapter provides a comprehensive insight into the use of social media among the deaf and hard of hearing, along with the benefits and challenges in use. Existing recommendations towards overcoming the challenges are reviewed, and approaches for design of social media and its efficient use are proposed. The findings may serve social media developers, educators, social inclusion advisors and policy makers on how to apply social media as an inclusive tool for participation in society.

Keywords Social media · Social networking sites · Hearing loss · Deaf
Hard of hearing · Communication · Challenges

8.1 Introduction

The aim of this chapter is to provide an insight into the use of social media among people with hearing loss. The motives are twofold: Social media has been changing rapidly over the years, and users with hearing loss are an important social group faced primarily with communication challenges.

Although the beginnings of social media date back to 1997 when the first social networking site Sixdegrees.com was developed and users could make profiles and

I. Kožuh (✉) · M. Debevc
Faculty of Electrical Engineering and Computer Science,
University of Maribor, Koroška Cesta 46, 2000 Maribor, Slovenia
e-mail: ines.kozuh@um.si

M. Debevc
e-mail: matjaz.debevc@um.si

© Springer International Publishing AG, part of Springer Nature 2018
N. Dey et al. (eds.), *Social Networks Science: Design, Implementation,
Security, and Challenges*, https://doi.org/10.1007/978-3-319-90059-9_8

add friends [1], not more than 15 years have passed since researchers have been publishing intensively in this domain. Due to the booming popularity of social media, researchers [2–5], have focused either on social media use and behaviour of deaf and hard of hearing users, their communication, or effects of the use on their participation in society. Researchers have thus recognised in their studies a wide range of challenges that users with hearing loss face, such as missing captions in video material published in social media. Accordingly, they provided recommendations for social media developers, educators, social inclusion advisors and policy makers to overcome these challenges.

However, in these years, social media have changed significantly, which may lead stakeholders to feel uncertain about the relevancy of recommendations, especially when they do not know the background on which these recommendations are based. For this reason, it is necessary that they are conscious of the characteristics of social media use and their antecedents, which may remain more or less stable over time. Moreover, social media has recently spread to many domains, such as users' private lives and schooling, which may indicate an increasing need of educators and other relevant stakeholders to have access to efficient recommendations for overcoming challenges in social media use.

In this vein, this chapter provides an overview of the characteristics of social media use among users with hearing loss. Moreover, it helps us understand these characteristics in the context of antecedents which trigger specific use, as well as benefits and challenges of the use. As recommendations for overcoming these challenges have already been suggested in the literature, this paper provides a critical outlook and defines guidelines for efficient use of these recommendations. In addition, approaches are proposed for design of social media and its efficient use. It may help developers of social media and other stakeholders to become conscious of the issues that are to be followed when social media users with hearing loss are considered.

8.2 Deaf and Hard of Hearing People

Hearing loss has been examined through various perspectives, such as medical (pathological) and cultural perspectives [6–9]. From the medical perspective, hearing loss is treated as a disability and hearing loss is assessed by Audiologists using a method for listening to audio signals at different frequencies from 200 Hz till 8,000 Hz with increased loudness.

There are six standardised types of hearing loss (GBD, 2013), such as mild (20–34 dB), moderate (35–49 dB), moderately severe (50–64 dB), severe (65–79 dB), profound (80–94 dB) and complete loss (95 or more dB). In this vein, a recent study shows that approximately half a billion people had disabling hearing, representing 6–8% of the world's population [10]. It is still growing, since the number of elderly, who often have elderly dependent hearing loss, is also increasing [11].

On the contrary, the cultural perspective does not predict hearing loss to be decisive for someone to become a member of the Deaf community. Rather than hearing loss itself, persons' beliefs and perceptions of hearing loss define whether deaf persons are regarded as Deaf with a capital letter D, or deaf with a lowercase d. Accordingly, the Deaf share with members of the Deaf community their language, values, experiences, as well as common ways of interacting with members and non-members [12]. The deaf, on the contrary, perceive their hearing loss more as an audiological experience than as an identity which would lead to membership in the Deaf community.

Deaf and some hard of hearing persons use sign language as (the main) mode of communication [13]. Those who were born deaf, and those who have deaf parents, may even consider sign language as a mother tongue. Written or spoken language may thus be their second language, which often results in lower reading proficiency. Sign language is fundamentally different from written language. It has its own and unique grammar, syntax and structure. Thus, the deaf and hard of hearing often have difficulties accessing and learning their native language syntactical and morphological structure, and often prefer to communicate with hearing people via a sign language interpreter [14].

Compared to hearing people, the deaf may lag in reading even for three years to progress to the same level in reading as their hearing counterparts do [15]. However, many studies show that the deaf can become skilful readers as well [15]. For instance, a previous study showed that 32% of students can achieve average levels of writing, and an additional 17% is achieved above average [16].

8.3 Social Media

Social media combine online communication channels for the purpose of the interaction of people or organisations to share the multimedia based contents, and to collaborate between internal and external parties [4, 17, 18]. Similarly, social media can also be understood as web-based technologies, or collections of software applications, that enable users to connect and communicate [19, 20].

In literature, different classifications of social media types are in use. For instance, Kaplan and Haenlein [17], define six social media types: (1) Collaborative projects (Wikipedia), (2) Blogs and microblogs (WordPress, Twitter), (3) Content communities (YouTube), (4) Social network services (Facebook), (5) Virtual game worlds (World of Warcraft), and (6) Virtual social worlds (Second Life). Other researchers talked about slightly different types of social media: Wikis, blogs, microblogging, social networks, podcasts and social games [21, 22].

Lovejoy and Saxton [23] classify applications comprising social media further within the frame of three main categories: Information, Community and Action, which are connected into a triangle. Accordingly, applications are used for relationship building, content dissemination/distribution, rating/tagging, and entertainment. Within relationship building applications, supporting activities have been classified, such as microblogging, social networking and discussion. As such, Facebook, LinkedIn, Friendster, Mypace, etc., are also defined as social networking sites, whereas Twitter, Foursquare, Friendfeed, etc., are defined as microblogs.

Social media has changed significantly over the years due to recent advancements in technology. It has also affected which social media types have become more suitable for users with hearing loss. From the standpoint of technology, at the beginning, social media offered a variety of functions, such as creating profiles, adding friends, posting text messages, creating pages and groups, as well as uploading photos and, later, also videos. Users were quite reserved from showing their face, they preferred hiding behind their keywords. Over the years, the use of social media moved to mobile devices, and users were allowed to follow and create the content in social media everywhere. First, it was simple content formats and, with the evolution of mobile data transmission, users started creating more complex content formats. They released the fear and started uploading videos, escalating even to live streaming. According to Cisco [24], traffic from online videos will constitute 82% of all consumer internet traffic by 2021, while live internet video will account for 13% of internet video traffic. In 2017, social networking sites as a social media type have even conducted a step further by allowing users to socialise in virtual reality, as if they were together in real life. Accordingly, users can communicate as 3D figures in a virtual environment and share 360 live videos from inside [25].

These technology advancements have changed users' habits concerning information seeking, sharing and communicating dramatically. For instance, while YouTube has initiated the power of video possibilities in 2005, in 2015 social networking sites have started changing users' experiences emergingly by the booming use of video and, lately, the introduction of virtual reality.

As social networking sites provide users with hearing loss with a wide range of possibilities for communication and creation of content, they are considered to be the most suitable social media type for this social group. The reasons are twofold. Firstly, compared to other social media types, social networking sites allow users to communicate either synchronously or asynchronously, in verbal and nonverbal mode of communication, as well as in written and sign language. These functions are allowed by various features of social networking sites, such as posting text and video messages, live streaming and, lately, even virtual reality technology. Concurrently, users are allowed to have a profile and a list of friends with whom they can share created content. In this vein, other types of social media are limited. Secondly, while other types of social media, such as Twitter as a microblog, are more professional, information-based and allow asymmetrical relations between users, social networking sites, e.g. Facebook, could be more private, communication-based and allow symmetrical relations between users. These two reasons may place social networking sites in an advantageous position compared to other social media types when users with hearing loss are considered. Similar evidence can be found in the literature, where Facebook was defined as one of the most accessible social media types [26].

Usually, the most widely used social media types among users with hearing loss are those utilised not only specifically among users with hearing loss, but also by hearing users as well. For instance, Facebook was reported to be the most frequently used among Americans and Germans with hearing loss [3, 27]. However, the most common platforms dedicated specifically to users with hearing loss are hearZONE and Deaf YouVideo. For instance, hearZONE was launched in 2013 as a community platform, providing profiles, events, groups and media. It is also the largest portal for users with hearing loss in German speaking countries, as it reaches 10,000 visits per month and has 3,000 monthly users [28]. Moreover, Deaf YouVideo has been established to allow the deaf and hard of hearing in English speaking countries who use sign language to socialise in video blogging, social media and the online community. Sign language users are empowered to produce articles and videos in a blog that allows creating discussions through video/text comments keeping this social group together.

8.3.1 Social Networking Sites

Boyd and Ellison [1] defined social networking sites as services on the web which allow individuals to create their personal profiles, alter the list of friends they connect to, and search within the list of their friends. The definition includes users' creation of their profiles within the site, which consists of a name, personal picture, e-mail address, and other data. Users with profiles connect with other members on social networking sites who are acquaintances from the real world, or who they meet online [25].

The concept of social networking sites also refers to virtual communities, whereusers interact with each other due to a common interest, or just to "hang out" together [29]. Members can communicate via various means of communication, such as chat, video chat, etc., which provide a way for members to contact other members. In existing research, social networking sites are addressed differently. Bonds-Raacke and Raacke [30] have classified recent studies on social network sites into four main topics. These topics comprise investigating content of user profiles [31], knowledge of the characteristics of users and nonusers [32, 33], investigating association of utilising social media with psychological well-being [34, 35], and educational applications [36].

Social networking sites include websites such as Facebook [37]. Currently, these sites provide users with a wide range of features such as:

- Profiles,
- Lists of connections,
- Features supporting communication,
- Spaces for media sharing, and
- The ability to create groups.

Profiles. These are primarily static personal profiles which are created and maintained explicitly through text and other multimedia elements by the owner [38]. Over time, because of the friends list and the activity of commenting, these profiles came to be shaped by other users as well, e.g. by tagging photos.

Table 8.1 A set of keywords for literature review

A group of keywords related to	Keywords
Hearing loss	Deaf, hard of hearing, hearing loss, deafness, hearing aid, deaf students, hearing impairment
Social media	Social media, social media use, social networking sites, social networking services, social networks, Facebook, cyberspace
Communication	Communication, communication barriers, sign language, written language
Unclassified	Social support, accessibility; people with disabilities, patient, digital disability

List of connections. Users can differentiate between a public contact and a friend [38]. At the beginning, users created private lists of contacts [38], while, lately, social networking sites have focused on the practice of creating publicly visible, personally curated lists of contacts" [38, pp. 155].

Features supporting communication. Social networking sites support multiple modes of communication: One-to-many and one-to one, synchronous and asynchronous, textual and media-based, and these features can be public or private [38].

Spaces for media sharing. Spaces for media sharing are nearly universal on social networking sites, where text, video and photos can be shared [38]. Thus, shared content can be a starting point for other online activities, not being limited to viewing profiles only [38].

Ability to create groups. Users can establish groups where they can share common interests or affiliations and hold discussions. Discussion boards for discussions within groups are held as well.

8.4   Methods

The aim of the study presented in this chapter was to provide a literature review of the social media use among persons with hearing loss. The search strategy adapted by Chomutare et al. [39] was utilised. Accordingly, we focused on original research papers, conference papers and review articles "indexed by Medline, ScienceDirect, ACM (Association for Computing Machinery) Digital Library, IEEE (Institute of Electrical and Electronics Engineers) Xplore Digital Library, Google Scholar, and DBLP (Digital Bibliography & Library Project) Computer Science Bibliography" [39]. Moreover, we used the Google Scholar related articles tool.

Afterwards, a set of keywords was established, according to which we created a search string comprising both the conjunction "AND" and the disjunction "OR" logical operators. The combination of keywords was interchangeable. A set of keywords is shown in Table 8.1.

All online searches were conducted in July and August, 2017. We specified clear inclusion criteria for selection of studies: (1) Studies peer-reviewed, (2) Studies in English, (3) Primary focus on social media use, (4) Including also deaf and hard of hearing users, as one of the more mentioned groups of disabled people or as hearing aid or cochlear implant users. We also defined exclusion criteria: (1) Studies not in English, (2) Studies only on Internet use, and (3) Studies not including the deaf and hard of hearing.

The search output was 18 studies. In the following sections, we present thoroughly the relevant findings of the analysis, where the interpretative approach is followed rather than quantification of the findings [40]. The analysis of selected studies started with a review of key findings of the studies. Afterwards, we analysed antecedents for specifics of social media use among the deaf and hard of hearing, as well as the characteristics, benefits and challenges of the use. Based on that, we analysed existing recommendations towards overcoming these challenges. Given that social media has changed significantly over years (see Sect. 1.3), we provide guidelines for efficient use of these recommendations.

8.5 Results

8.5.1 Overview of Social Media Use Among the Deaf and Hard of Hearing

In general, existing studies on social media use among people with hearing loss could be classified into three main groups, while types of social media are not distinguished specifically due to ease of understanding:

1. **Social media use and behaviour of deaf and hard of hearing users** [2, 3, 26, 27, 41–48, 59],
2. **Communication between people with and without hearing loss, as well as people with other types of disabilities** [2, 4, 49], and
3. **Effects of social media use on deaf and hard of hearing users' participation in society** [5, 50].

First, the use of social media among the deaf and hard of hearing has been examined extensively from various aspects. While most studies focused on the intensity of using social media, purposes for its use and users' activities in social media [3, 5, 26, 27, 42, 44, 47, 48], Morris et al. [47] additionally examined the influence of income on intensity of social media use, as well as the use of social media during emergency events. Besides that, accessibility issues in social media were examined as well [26, 42]. For instance, deaf and hard of hearing users' frequent activity in social media was found to be associated positively with the perceived accessibility of social media.

Moreover, a fair amount of studies examined thoroughly behaviour of social media users with hearing loss. For instance, particular attention was paid to users' needs and preferences in social media use [43, 44], users' emotional involvement [48], development of their identity [2, 43] and even cyberbullying [46].

Furthermore, both deaf and hard of hearing users' activities and behaviour were examined in the context of participation in social media communities and virtual communities [2, 41, 45], where different types of users' behaviour were identified, as well as activities, and the content was presented in deaf and hard of hearing online communities and cochlear implant social media communities.

Secondly, social media provide new communication opportunities between people with and without hearing loss, as well as people with other types of disabilities. According to Chang [4], social media allow communication based on text-based and multimedia messaging advantageously, which is mostly accessible for users with hearing loss. The same was substantiated in another study [42], where those having milder hearing loss communicated more frequently with hearing persons than those who have a higher degree of hearing loss. Moreover, El-Gayyar et al. [49] substantiated that social networks, where users combine mobile devices and cloud resources, represent a venue for seamless communication between the blind and deaf people. Furthermore, Kožuh et al. [2] substantiated the positive effects of frequency of written communication on users' tendency to build online communities.

Thirdly, in the literature, there is a debate about the role of social media in overcoming restrictions for social participation. In particular, social media could serve users with hearing loss as a tool for inclusion, where they could participate more fully in the society [5, 50]. Additionally, Wong et al. [48] examined linking and bridging social capital in online and offline settings.

8.5.2 Antecedents for Specifics of Social Media Use Among the Deaf and Hard of Hearing

In the selected studies, a wide range of antecedents have been exposed, which may cause specific social media use among persons with hearing loss. In general, four main antecedents could be identified:

- Personality factors,
- Inadequate literacy,
- Inadequate social skills,
- Mainstream perception of hearing loss as a disability in society.

With regard to personality factors, deaf persons show poorer mental health in terms of a higher degree of loneliness, lack of emotional control, a higher risk of psychosocial problems, and lower level of well-being and self-esteem [51–53 cited in 46]. Likewise, deaf children were found to be more impulsive than hearing peers, which may result in different self-monitoring and judgement compared to hearing peers [54 cited in 46].

Regarding inadequate literacy, deaf and hard of hearing students reported to have difficulties with writing and spelling conventions in formal English [55 cited in 46, 48]. However, Kožuh et al. [2] did not find empirical evidence confirming that deaf and hard of hearing social media users' writing skills would affect frequency of written communication in social media, even though persons with hearing loss were found to have lower scores in literacy competence compared to hearing peers [56 cited in 2].

Inadequate social skills often reflect the social situation of persons with hearing loss. Deaf children, growing up in a mostly hearing family, differentiate from hearing counterparts in a lack of experiences of incidental learning of social information. While hearing children overhear conversations of people in their surroundings, or interpret intonation or innuendo in spoken language, deaf children are deprived of that [53 cited in 46]. When growing up, adolescents with hearing loss have fewer friends, and friendships with a lower quality compared to their hearing peers [57 cited in 3].

In society, there may prevail mainstream pathological perception of hearing loss as a disability. From the viewpoint of the hearing community, communication is viewed as the main problem of deaf and hard of hearing people, causing a communication gap between both communities [4]. This is especially evident when hearing people do not understand how members in the Deaf/Hard of Hearing community communicate [58].

8.5.3   Characteristics of Social Media Use Among the Deaf and Hard of Hearing

The above-mentioned antecedents may lead to specific patterns of social media use among people with hearing loss. From the selected studies, diverse key uses of social media are recognised and can be classified further according to the following six parameters:

• Frequency of use and activities in social media,
• Motives and reasons for use,
• Purpose of use,
• Perceived accessibility and user experience,
• Effects of use on formation of online identity and online community,
• Effects of use on social participation in the offline world.

A review of selected studies revealed that Facebook is a website which deaf and hard of hearing Americans visit the most frequently [3]. Also, it is the most frequently used social networking site among Germans with hearing loss [27]. Similarly, Facebook was found to be the predominant social media platform for the cochlear implant community as well [45]. Within the hearing aid community, the strongest activity was seen on Facebook and Twitter, while YouTube and blogs were used less frequently

[59]. The Canadian students with hearing loss and also other types of disabilities indicated that they use YouTube most frequently, while Facebook and, finally, Twitter followed [26].

Frequency of using social media depends on a wide range of factors, such as the level of hearing loss, gender etc. Recent empirical evidence shows that the deaf use social media more frequently than hard of hearing people [47]. The literature on differences between hearing people and those with hearing loss is inconsistent. On the one hand, the deaf and hard of hearing were reported not to conduct any social media activities more or less frequently than hearing people [3]. On the other hand, Kožuh et al. [42] examined German social media users, and found that those with milder hearing loss communicate more often with users who have no hearing loss in the written language than those who have heavier hearing loss. Similarly, those who have milder hearing loss, posted videos on social media more frequently than users with higher degrees of hearing loss.

When researchers [46] examined risky behaviour in social media, e.g. being in an online fight, changing one's social media profile and sharing passwords with friends, they found no significant differences between users with hearing loss and hearing users. Regarding the effects of gender, male users with hearing loss were found to be more prone to perform various activities in social media frequently, while female users tend to conduct these activities less frequently [27].

Among the most frequent motives for utilising social media are maintaining offline friendships and meeting new people, while less frequent motives are information seeking and splitting, and entertainment [5]. Likewise, Kožuh et al. [27], listed the most frequent social media activities performed by deaf and hard of hearing users. They found that pressing the "like" button is the most frequent, while posting comments, sharing the content, posting photos, updating profile, and posting videos follow.

The purposes for using social media rely largely on users' individual preferences. The literature suggests that, not only students with hearing loss, but also other types of disabilities, use social media both for personal and educational purposes [26]. The findings of the Canadian study [26] revealed that the number of hours dedicated to personal use was 12 h per week, while only 6 h were spent for educational purposes. Similarly, Kožuh et al. [27] argue that users with hearing loss reported a higher mean score for utilising social media for entertainment and a lower score for school and work.

Perceived accessibility and a flawless user experience seem to be decisive factors in social media use. In the Canadian study [26], disabled students evaluated accessibility of various types of social media. Although only 12% of 723 surveyed students had a hearing loss, they indicated that the most accessible forms of social media were: MSN/Windows Live Messenger, Facebook and YouTube. On the contrary, the least accessible social media were Conversely, InternSHARE.com and Second Life.

In the Lithuanian study, where 300 people with hearing, visual and motor disability participated, users with hearing loss evaluated usefulness of social activity better than users with visual disability and worse than users with motor disability [5]. Ease of use was the subject of research also in another previous study [27], where the reasons for using social media were examined. While helpfulness was the most important reason, ease of use followed, along with adaptability of the platform to users' needs and enjoyment in use. The least important was learnability of the social media.

Utilising social media may have effects on creating online identity and community. Kožuh et al. [2] developed a model for understanding how building online communities in social media is affected by various factors. The findings revealed that, if users identify with hearing people in social media, it affects their writing skills, their frequency of communication in written language in social media and how they tend to build online communities positively. Moreover, frequent written communication in social media is positively associated with building communities online. When identifying with the Deaf online, a positive impact was found on how frequently users communicate in written form in social media.

Concerning the principles and development of online communities, a fair amount of studies [41, 45, 59] examined behaviour and activity patterns in hearing aid communities, cochlear implant communities and other social media communities for people with hearing loss. For instance, Saxena et al. [45] substantiated that, in cochlear implant communities, the most popular functional category was personal stories. Cochlear implant users shared personal stories through publishing blogs (92%), while Twitter and YouTube posts followed. Conversely, users in hearing aid communities in social media do not share personal stories to such an extent. According to Choudhury et al. [59], in only 17% of shared posts on Twitter, 18% of YouTube and 10% of blog entries hearing aid users share their personal experiences. Rather, in hearing aid communities, 52% of Twitter posts are dominated by service providers, while on YouTube, Facebook pages and in Facebook groups, the majority of posts are related to providing and receiving advice and support.

Considering the effects of social media use on social participation in the offline world, no significant relationships were found between types of activities in social media, e.g. content production, directed communication and passive communication—and participation in the society [5].

8.5.4 Benefits of Social Media Use Among the Deaf and Hard of Hearing

In the selected studies, the benefits of utilising social media meld frequently with the benefits of the Internet use, as similar principles may apply to both. Thus, the following section highlights the benefits of the online social participation which apply to social media use, but may be the case for utilising the Internet as well. Four overarching benefits of social media use among people with hearing loss were identified:

- Psychological benefits,
- Communication benefits,
- Social benefits,

- Technical benefits.

The reviewed studies pointed out a wide range of psychological benefits which had been recognised, either based on their empirical evidence or prior research studies. For instance, Bauman and Pero [46] emphasised how previous research [51] substantiated that deaf and hard of hearing users who use Internet, report lower levels of loneliness and higher levels of self-esteem compared to those who use the Internet less frequently.

As far as communication benefits are concerned, Bauman and Pero [46] highlighted how researchers [55] had recognised technological advances of online written communication, e.g. text messaging, where a flexible writing style is used. It may lead to more comfortable communication for deaf and hard of hearing users. Moreover, these users do not even think that skills in writing are important when they communicate in social media. Kožuh et al. [2] even argue that the quality of these users' writing skills is not associated with how frequently they communicate in written language in social media. In addition, communication benefits of social media also encompass instantaneous real-time connection between users. In contrast to traditional e-mail or one-to-one phone communication, social media provide an individual an opportunity to communicate with groups of people [45].

Social benefits of utilising social media comprise increasing social capital in terms of enhancement of people's networks of relationships they have in the offline world, especially due to communication possibilities in these online environments [48]. When they communicate and access important and useful information, e.g. health issues, the interaction of deaf users with society increases [60]. In this vein, the Internet and social media allow users with hearing loss to participate advantageously in society, even without their hearing loss being known [3, 51 cited in 46].

Finally, one of the most important technical benefits are captions and subtitles when available in video and audio clips appearing in social media [26]. It may have a wide range of other types of benefits as well, such as social benefits, where subtitles and captions may allow active participation in online communities and wider society.

8.5.5 Challenges in Social Media Use Among the Deaf and Hard of Hearing

Based on review of the selected studies, we defined three main issues which challenge the deaf and hard of hearing when utilising social media. These challenges include:

- Technical issues,
- Psychological issues,
- Social issues.

Social media users with hearing loss challenge with technical issues as well. Generally, they complain about disorganised layouts, confusing navigation, missing features, privacy and security related concerns, and problems with accessibility [26,

44, 49]. Disorganised layouts refer to various types of disabilities, where colour problems and difficulties with font enlargement limit flawless user experience. Besides that, users often do not know how to use social media and where to find particular information. When the message is not delivered to the end user due to insufficient functionalities of social media, the situation is even worse. For instance, deaf and hard of hearing users miss captions/subtitles in audio and video content in social media [44, 49], or simply expect particular features for deaf people which would attract them to their community, or would help them cope with regular activities in everyday life (e.g. searching jobs) [49].

The abovementioned technical challenges may lead to psychological issues raised in deaf and hard of hearing users. For instance, when users encounter privacy problems, and even share their passwords with other peers, they engage in risky online behaviour which may lead to involvement in cyberbullying, where they become a bully or victim [46].

Challenges related to social issues could be recognised from the previous study [5] conducted on a Lithuanian sample of people with disabilities, where the author exposed not very frequent use of social media which may decrease users' opportunities to compensate restrictions appearing in their offline participation. This phenomenon may lead to neglecting their social networks and diminishing their social capital.

8.5.6 Recommendations Towards Overcoming Challenges in Social Media Use Among the Deaf and Hard of Hearing

In light of challenges recognised in social media use among the deaf and hard of hearing, it was reviewed how researchers provided recommendations towards overcoming these challenges. Since the continuous recent advances in development of social media may affect the relevance of these commendations, we provide a critical outlook on recommendations, and introduce guidelines which may help stakeholders to become aware of how to deal with these recommendations. In what follows, we present existing recommendations towards overcoming challenges in social media use which appear in the literature. These recommendations are explained according to the groups of stakeholders they serve. Based on that, we present the abovementioned guidelines. Recommendations found in the selected studies are designed for the following stakeholders:

- Social media developers and producers,
- Education, health and business sectors,
- Policy makers and other stakeholders.

Social media developers and producers were asked primarily to respect communication specificities of users with hearing loss. For instance, in a previous study [42], it was found that profoundly deaf users communicate in social media the least frequently compared to users with all other levels of hearing loss. Likewise, the least frequent activity among users with all levels of hearing loss was posting videos. Accordingly, it was suggested that the attention of social media developers should be paid to these users. Namely, communication support should improve in order to encourage users to communicate actively in both sign and written language [42].

Likewise, in the previous study [26], conducted on 723 students with various types of disabilities, the authors provided suggestions for developers and producers of social media in order to ensure a more accessible user experience. Students indicated as the most important suggestions, a need for a simpler layout, improved privacy, security and accessibility, enlarging features on the web page, and a need for captions or subtitles [26].

Education, health and business sectors were asked to be aware about the requirements of the deaf community when courses and web sites are designed [44]. Accordingly, images and text should be balanced in such courses, and it should be respected that most deaf and hard of hearing users do not have access to the bandwidth Internet connection at home.

The education sector may also benefit from the recommendations of another study [3], where it was noted that both users with and without hearing loss should be encouraged to have combined online and offline friendships. The reason is that having an online friend was found neither to have a negative effect on well-being, nor being related to higher levels of loneliness. Apart from the friendships, recommendations were provided to educators regarding teaching writing as well. It was found that written language skills seem not to be very important to users with hearing loss, since deficiencies in written language skills do not keep them away from utilising social media [2]. Thus, the educators should decide whether to support the users towards becoming skilful readers and writers, or only to encourage them towards adequate use of social media when using written language.

Moreover, Kožuh et al. [42], pointed out the relevance of using social media in education through online collaborative learning. They viewed social media as a communication tool which could be implemented into online personal learning environments, while the authors recommend that these tools should be more accustomed for users with hearing loss. For instance, with these tools, learners would be able to communicate with other users while learning within the personal learning environment. When communicating, learners would not have to leave the learning environment due to the possibility to contact their counterparts currently present on social media, but not in the personal learning environment. Furthermore, Saxena et al. [45], highlighted the issue about the biomedical ethics in social media. Due to various stakeholders, providing and receiving information, and even medical advice, within the cochlear implant communities, it was substantiated that clinicians should be aware of the establishment of paramedical communities in social media, where patients may not receive detailed medical advice. Likewise, another study [59] appealed to clinicians to be more active in utilising social media, since many hearing aid users utilise social media for obtaining information about their devices.

On a policy level, Maiorana-Basas and Pagliaro [44], highlighted the necessity to include captioning in all videos uploaded to the Internet. Even some important policy documents, e.g. the Americans with Disabilities Act, do not address online video and audio content specifically, and the entertainment industry has failed to provide full access to such content. The authors have recommended that developers and creators of online content should get information from users with disabilities to ensure compliance with laws and consequently fair access. In addition, Morris et al. [47], appealed to those creating emergency communication strategies. They highlighted that a large percentage of disabled people, and those without disabilities, use social media for everyday communication, which calls for a need to include social media in these strategies in order to be able to publish official alert information, as well as to be able to monitor traffic originating in the community.

Finally, Kožuh et al. [2], provided recommendations towards overcoming challenges related to social inclusion of the deaf and hard of hearing. Accordingly, traditional deaf clubs were suggested to strengthen their online presence in social media, which may mitigate the decline of these institutions and even improve their position in society. As a result, it may influence the way deaf clubs design their activities towards active participation of people with hearing loss in society.

Although the literature provides a comprehensive list of recommendations for various stakeholders, some of these recommendations should be considered cautiously. Accordingly, we provide a set of guidelines that are proposed to be respected when considering recommendations which appear in the literature regarding social media users with hearing loss.

Firstly, due to the recent and rapid advances in social media, it is necessary to verify how much time has passed from conduction of the study in order to make recommendations relevant. According to recent technology forecasts [24], we suggest that not more than five years pass. Secondly, it is suggested to consider the sample which was included in the study, as well as the region where the study provided recommendations in order to assess adequacy of recommendations. Thirdly, stakeholders are proposed to consider recommendations according to legal documents being currently in use. These documents include the Convention on the Rights of Persons with Disabilities, Declaration on the Rights of Disabled Persons and UNESCO: Education for All. On the international and national levels, the documents vary across regions, which should be respected.

8.6 Proposed Approach for Design of Social Media and Its Efficient Use

Based on the presented findings, an approach is proposed for social media developers about how to design social networking sites. In addition, an approach is suggested to help users with hearing loss while communicating.

When designing social media, developers are advised to follow Web Content Accessibility Guidelines (WCAG) 2.1 [61], which provide several recommendations for accessible web content. Accordingly, for developers, it is important to consider that deaf users need acess to publishing and watching multimedia content due to their listening barriers, and the right to use sign language for communication. As a result, when uploading and publishing audio and video content, deaf users should have the possibility to set their own quality of the recording, add captions/subtitles and set their display, as well as add a sign language interpreter video to regular audio or video content. As live streaming is on the rise, these features should be available in live recording and real time uploading as well. When watching audio and video content in social media, deaf users should have the possibility to use the same features as when uploading and publishing the multimedia content. Primarily, it is important that users are allowed to turn on and off captions/subtitles in video players, and that captions are synchronised with the audio and video.

When deaf people communicate with each other through social media, a certain approach may help them in efficient use of social media. From the technical point of view, users should access social media through a device with a camera, and should, concurrently, have an adequate internet connection, so that video communication and publishing videos are allowed. To use modern features, such as hanging out with friends in interactive virtual environments through virtual reality, additional equipment is required, e.g. a virtual reality headset.

8.7   Discussion and Conclusion

The aim of our study was to review the literature on social media use among persons with hearing loss. This study generated a novel perspective on social media use among persons with hearing loss. While several studies examined the use, a lack of studies reviewing the existing knowledge was evident. Accordingly, we have identified antecedents causing specific social media use: Personality factors, literacy, social skills and mainstream perception of hearing loss. Key characteristics and benefits of social media use were defined based on these antecedents. Moreover, we also highlighted technical, psychological and social challenges that can occur while utilising social media. We also discussed recommendations found in existing studies, and provided guidelines that are to be followed when considering the relevancy of these recommendations. Finally, approaches were proposed for design of social media and its efficient use.

Generally, poor mental health, low literacy level and insufficient experiences of incidental learning of social information, causing inadequate social skills were defined as the main antecedents causing specifics of utilising social media. Concerning the use of social media, Facebook was found to be a predominant social media type, where users reported the strongest activity compared to other types. Users with hearing loss do not behave in social media more riskily than hearing users do, and are motivated for the use as they want to maintain offline friendships or meet new people. Perceived accessibiltiy of the platform was also found to be decisive. When using social media, the deaf and hard of hearing may benefit importantly from recent technological communication advances, e.g. video live stream, while technical issues, such as disorganised layouts, still challenge users. To overcome these challenges, it was suggested to follow as many recent recommendations from the literature as possible. In addition, it was proposed to check the context of the study based on which recommendations were defined, as well as consider the legal documents which are in use in the country where these recommendations are to be respected. When designing and implementing social media, developers are suggested to respect WCAG 2.1, while special importance should be given to utilising video.

Several lessons may be gleaned from our review. First, some studies have found the increased quality of life of social media users with hearing loss, demonstrating lower levels of loneliness and increased self-esteem. Social media can help them overcome the obstacles of interpersonal communication and enhance their social networks. With frequent social media communication, their written language skills may also improve. Secondly, social media users with hearing loss create virtual communities that give them new communication opportunities for interacting with other deaf and hard of hearing peers, hearing people and people with other types of disabilities. Accordingly, social media has become a tool for inclusion and full participation of disabled people in society without their disability being seen. Conversely, rare use of social media can have opposite effects, such as diminishing of social capital. Thirdly, the main motives for using social media among people with hearing loss comprise maintaining offline friendships and meeting new people, while they use them less for education and entertainment. In cochlear implant communities, social media posts are mainly personal, but in hearing aid communities, most posts are made by service providers and related to advice and support. Finally, perceived accessibility and user experience were found to be key factors, along with the adaptability of social media according to users' needs.

In many respects, the finding of this chapter can help social media developers to become conscious about how to create platforms suitable for users with hearing loss, so that they would be encouraged to communicate in sign and written language. Moreover, educators and clinicians may benefit from these findings as well. While educators may benefit in terms of appropriate teaching of written language skills and online collaborative learning, clinicians may become aware of the importance of social media communities, which frequently work as paramedical communities.

This study has three limitations. Firstly, in the reviewed studies, the benefits and limitations of social media or Internet use were not differentiated clearly. As the authors often apply the principles of Internet use to social media use, these findings were presented in this chapter in line with that as well. The second limitation stems from not discussing the theories applied to the selected studies. Accordingly, the chapter does not provide an insight into the communication, psychological or sociological theories that were followed in these studies. Thirdly, due to the particular search string, not all relevant studies may have been included in the review, so there might be a bias present in the presentation of the findings.

In the future, it would be intriguing to examine behaviour of social media users with hearing loss, since these platforms are in constant development, while new platforms may appear as well. As of now, these platforms technically limit these users in many respects. Thus, we recommend analysis of good practices followed by particular social media, so that developers may benefit significantly. Moreover, we also recommend research on perception of hearing loss as a disability among users and nonusers of social media. As it was found that social media users with hearing loss have an increased life quality and participation in virtual communities has brought them closer to each other, it might change their view of disability compared to nonusers of social media.

References

1. Boyd, D. M., & Ellison, N. B. (2007). Social network sites: Definition, history, and scholarship. *Journal of Computer-Mediated Communication, 13*(1).
2. Kožuh, I., Hintermair, M., & Debevc, M. (2016). Community building among deaf and hard of hearing people by using written language on social networking sites. *Computers in Human Behaviour, 65,* 295–307. https://doi.org/10.1016/j.chb.2016.08.035.
3. Blom, H., Marschark, M., Vervloed, M. P., & Knoors, H. (2014). Finding friends online: Online activities by deaf students and their well-being. *PLoS ONE, 9*(2), e88351.
4. Chang, C. M. (2014). New media, new technologies and new communication opportunities for deaf/hard of hearing people. In *International Conference on Communication, Media, Technology and Design* (pp. 24–26).
5. Viluckiene, J. (2015). The relationship between online social networking and offline social participation among people with disability in Lithuania. *Procedia-Social and Behavioral Sciences, 185,* 453–459.
6. Jacobson, J. T. (1995). Nosology of deafness. *Journal of the American Academy of Audiology, 6,* 15–27.
7. Torres, M. T. (1995). *A postmodern perspective on the issue of deafness as culture versus Pathology: Journal of the American Deafness and Rehabilitation Association, 29,* 1–7.
8. Hoffmeister, R. J. (1996). Cross-cultural misinformation: what does special education say about deaf people? *Disability and Society, 11,* 171–189.
9. Ladd, P. (2003). *Understanding deaf culture: In search of deafhood.* Clevedon, England: Multilingual Matters Ltd.
10. Wilson, B. S., Tucci, D. L., Merson, M. H., & O'Donoghue, G. M. (2017). Global hearing health care: New findings and perspectives. *The Lancet.* https://doi.org/10.1016/S0140-6736(17)31073-5.
11. OECD Indicators, Health at a Glance. (2015). Retrieved from http://www.oecd.org/health/health-systems/health-at-a-glance-19991312.htm.
12. Baker, C., & Padden, C. (1978). *American Sign Language: A look at its history, structure, and community.* Silver Spring, MD: T.J. Publishers Inc.
13. Stokoe, W. C. Jr (2005). Sign language structure: An outline of the visual communication systems of the American deaf. *Journal of Deaf Studies and Deaf Education, 10*(1). https://doi.org/10.1093/deafed/eni001.
14. Marschark, M., & Spencer, P. E. (2010). *The Oxford handbook of deaf studies, language, and education* (Vol. 2).
15. Schirmer, B. R. (2001). *Psychological, social, and educational dimensions of deafness.* Allyn & Bacon.
16. Antia, S. D., Reed, S., & Kreimeyer, K. H. (2005). Written language of deaf and hard-of-hearing students in public schools. *Journal of Deaf Studies and Deaf Education, 10*(3), 244–255. https://doi.org/10.1093/deafed/eni026.
17. Kaplan, A. M., & Haenlein, M. (2010). Users of the world, unite! The challenges and opportunities of Social Media. *Business Horizon, 53,* 59–68.
18. Obar, J. A., & Wildman, S. S. (2015). Social media definition and the governance challenge: An introduction to the special issue.

19. Correa, T., Hinsley, A. W., & de Zuniga, H. G. (2010). Who interacts on the web? The intersection of users' personality and social media use. *Computers in Human Behavior, 26*(2), 247–253. https://doi.org/10.1016/j.chb.2009.09.003.
20. Kim, W., Ok-Ran, J., & Lee, S. (2010). On social web sites. *Information Systems, 35*(2), 215–236. https://doi.org/10.1016/j.is.2009.08.003.
21. Causer, C. (2011). The art of war. *IEEE Potentials, 30*(5), 9–14.
22. Ramdani, B., & Rajwani, T. (2010). Enterprise 2.0: the case of British Telecom. Journal of Strategic Management. *Education, 6*(2), 135–148.
23. Lovejoy, K., & Saxton, G. D. (2012). Information, community, and action: How nonprofit organizations use social media. *Journal of Computer-Mediated Communication, 17*(3), 337–353.
24. Cisco Visual networking Index: Forecast and methodology, 2017–2021, white paper, San Jose, CA, USA, Jun. 2017.
25. Wade, J. (2017). Facebooks VR updates and LinkedIn geofilters. Retrieved Octover 12, 2017, from http://www.smartinsights.com/social-media-marketing/facebooks-vr-updates-linkedin-geofilters/.
26. Asuncion, J. V., Budd, J., Fichten, C. S., Nguyen, M. N., Barile, M., & Amsel, R. (2012). Social media use by students with disabilities. *Academic Exchange Quarterly, 16*(1), 30–35.
27. Kožuh, I., Hintermair, M., Hauptman, S., & Debevc, M. (2015). What predicts the frequencies of activities on social networking sites among the d/deaf and hard of hearing?. in C. A. Velasco (Ed.), *Proceedings of the 7th International Conference on Software Development and Technologies for Enhancing Accessibility and Fighting Info-exclusion*: [June 10–12, 2015, Sankt Augustin, Germany] (Vol. 67, str. pp. 185–192). (Procedia Computer Science, ISSN 1877-0509. Oxford: Elsevier. https://doi.org/10.1016/j.procs.2015.09.262.
28. hearNEWS. (2014) Retrieved August 17, 2017, from http://www.hearnews.info/.
29. Murray, K. E., & Waller, R. (2007). Social networking goes abroad. *International Educator, 16*(3), 56–59.
30. Bonds-Raacke, J., & Raacke, J. (2010). Myspace and Facebook: Identifying dimensions of uses and gratifications for friend networking sites. *Individual Differences Research, 8*(1), 27–33.
31. Walther, J., Van Der Heide, B., Kim, S., Westerman, D., & Tong, S. (2008). The role of friends' appearance and behavior on evaluations of individuals on Fa-cebook: Are we known by the company we keep? *Human Communication Research, 34*(1), 28–49. https://doi.org/10.1111/j.1468-2958.2007.00312.x.
32. Hargittai, E. (2007). Whose space? Differences among users and non-users of social network sites. *Journal of Computer-Mediated Communication, 13*(1), 276–297.
33. Raacke, J., & Bonds-Raacke, J. (2008). MySpace and Facebook: Applying the uses and gratifications theory to exploring friend-networking sites. *Cyberpsychology & behavior, 11*(2), 169–174.
34. Ellison, N. B., Steinfield, C., & Lampe, C. (2007). The benefits of Facebook 'friends: "Social capital and college students' use of online social network sites. *Journal of Computer-Mediated Communication, 12*(4), 1.
35. Valkenburg, P. M., Peter, J., & Schouten, A. P. (2006). Friend networking sites and their relationship to adolescents' well-being and social self-esteem. *CyberPsychology & Behavior, 9*(5), 584–590.
36. Mazer, J., Murphy, R., & Simonds, C. (2007). I'll see you on "Facebook": The effects of computer-mediated teacher self-disclosure on student motivation, affective learning, and classroom climate. *Communication Education, 56*(1), 1–17.
37. Davis III, C. H. F., Deil-Amen, R., Rios-Aguilar, C., & González Canché, M. S. (2012). Social media and higher education: A literature review and research directions. Report printed by the University of Arizona and Claremont Graduate University.
38. Ellison, N., & Boyd, D. (2013). Sociality through Social Network Sites. In W. H. Dutton (Eds.), *The Oxford handbook of internet studies* (pp. 151–172). Oxford University Press: Oxford.
39. Chomutare, T., Fernandez-Luque, L., Årsand, E., & Hartvigsen, G. (2011). Features of mobile diabetes applications: Review of the literature and analysis of current applications compared against evidence-based guidelines. In G. Eysenbach (Ed.), *Journal of Medical Internet Research, 13*(3). https://doi.org/10.2196/jmir.1874.

40. Grajales, F. J., III, Sheps, S., Ho, K., Novak-Lauscher, H., & Eysenbach, G. (2014). Social media: A review and tutorial of applications in medicine and health care. *Journal of Medical Internet Research, 16*(2), e13. https://doi.org/10.2196/jmir.2912.
41. Kožuh, I., Poznič, A., & Debevc, M. (2016). A content analysis of online communities for the deaf and hard of hearing. In *Proceedings of the 7th International Conference on Software Development and Technologies for Enhancing Accessibility and Fighting Info-exclusion* (pp. 370–377). https://doi.org/10.1145/3019943.3019996.
42. Kožuh, I., Hintermair, M., & Debevc, M. (2014). Examining the characteristics of deaf and hard of hearing users of social networking sites. In: Miesenberger K (Ed.), *Computers helping people with special needs: Proceedings: part ii.* Lecture Notes in Computer Science (vol. 8548, pp. 498–505). Heidelberg: Springer.
43. Kožuh, I., Hintermair, M., Holzinger, A., Volčič, Z., & Debevc, M. (2015). Enhancing universal access: Deaf and hard of hearing people on social networking sites. *Universal Access in the Information Society, 14,* 537–545. https://doi.org/10.1007/s10209-014-0354-3.
44. Maiorana-Basas, M., & Pagliaro, C. M. (2014). Technology use among adults who are deaf and hard of hearing: A national survey. *Journal of Deaf Studies and Deaf Education, 19*(3), 400–410.
45. Saxena, R. C., Lehmann, A. E., Hight, A., Darrow, K., Remenschneider, A., Kozin, E. D., et al. (2015). Social media utilization in the cochlear implant community. *Journal of the American Academy of Audiology, 26*(2), 197–204.
46. Bauman, S., & Pero, H. (2011). Bullying and cyberbullying among deaf students and their hearing peers: An exploratory study. *J Deaf Stud Deaf Educ, 162,* 236–253.
47. Morris, J. T., Mueller, J. L., & Jones, M. L. (2014). Use of social media during public emergencies by people with disabilities. *Western Journal of Emergency Medicine, 15*(5), 567.
48. Wong, C. L., Ching, T. Y., Whitfield, J., & Duncan, J. (2016). Online social participation, social capital and literacy of adolescents with hearing loss: A pilot study. *Deafness & Education International, 18*(2), 103–116.
49. El-Gayyar, M., Elyamany, H. F., Gaber, T., & Hassanien, A. E. (2013). Social network framework for deaf and blind people based on cloud computing. Comput Sci Inf Syst (FedCSIS), pp. 1313–1319.
50. Taylor, A. (2011). Social media as a tool for inclusion. Retrieved from Homelessness Resource Center website: http://homeless.samhsa.gov/Resource/View.aspx.
51. Barak, A., & Sadovsky, Y. (2008). Internet use and personal empowerment of hearing impaired adolescents. *Comput Human Behav, 24,* 1802–1815.
52. Moeller, M. P. (2007). Current state of knowledge: Psychosocial development in children with hearing impairment. *Ear and Hearing, 28,* 729–739.
53. Kusche, C. A., Garfield, T. S., & Greenberg, M. T. (1983). The understanding of emotional and social attributions in Deaf adolescents. *Journal of Clinical Child Psychology, 12,* 153–160.
54. Greenberg, M. T., Kusche, C. A., & Speltz, M. (1991). Emotional regulation, self-control, and psychopathology: The role of relationships in early childhood. In D. Cicchetti (Eds.), *Internalizing and Externalizing Expression of Dysfunction* (pp. 21–56). Hillsdale, NJ: Erlbaum.
55. Akamatsu, C. T., Mayer, C., & Farrelly, S. (2006). An investigation of two-way text messaging use with deaf students at the secondary level. *Journal of Deaf Studies and Deaf Education, 11,* 120–131.
56. Traxler, C. B. (2000) Measuring up to performance standards in reading and mathematics: Achievement of selected deaf and hard-of-hearing students in the national norming of the 9th Edition Stanford Achievement Test. *Journal of Deaf Studies and Deaf Education, 5*(4), 337–348.
57. Kouwenberg, M. (2013). *Social-emotional factors underlying internalizing problems, peer relations in deaf or hard of hearing youth.* Leiden, the Netherlands: Leiden University.
58. Bouvet, D. (1990). *The path to language: Bilingual education for deaf children.* Clevedon: Multilingual Matters.
59. Choudhury, M., Dinger, Z., & Fichera, E. (2017). The utilization of social media in the hearing aid community. *American Journal of Audiology, 26*(1), 1–9.

60. Schefer R. P., Zaina L. A. M. (2016). *A Communicability Evaluation of Facebook in Mobile Devices: A Case Study from the Perspective of Deaf Audience in Brazil.* In: Proceedings of the 34th ACM International Conference on the De-sign of Communication xx:23.
61. W3C (2017) Web Content Accessibility Guidelines 2.1. Retrieved October 16, 2017, from https://www.w3.org/TR/WCAG21/.

Correction to: Social Network Applications for Education: The Case of College Connect

A. L. Chapman, M. Lei and C. Greenhow

Correction to:
Chapter 6 in: N. Dey et al. (eds.), *Social Networks Science: Design, Implementation, Security, and Challenges*, https://doi.org/10.1007/978-3-319-90059-9_6

In the original version of the book, acknowledgment section, reference citations and foot note had been included as a belated correction in Chapter 6. The erratum chapter and the book have been updated with the changes.

The updated online version of this chapter can be found at
https://doi.org/10.1007/978-3-319-90059-9_6

© Springer International Publishing AG, part of Springer Nature 2018
N. Dey et al. (eds.), *Social Networks Science: Design, Implementation, Security, and Challenges*, https://doi.org/10.1007/978-3-319-90059-9_9

Printed in the United States
By Bookmasters